Living the Dream

Ian William Halliwell

Living the Dream
published on behalf of the author
in the UK in 2012
by
BRIDGE BOOKS
61 Park Avenue
Wrexham
Ll12 7AW

CIP Data for this book is available
from the British Library

ISBN 978-1-84494-082-0

Printed and bound by
CTPS
China

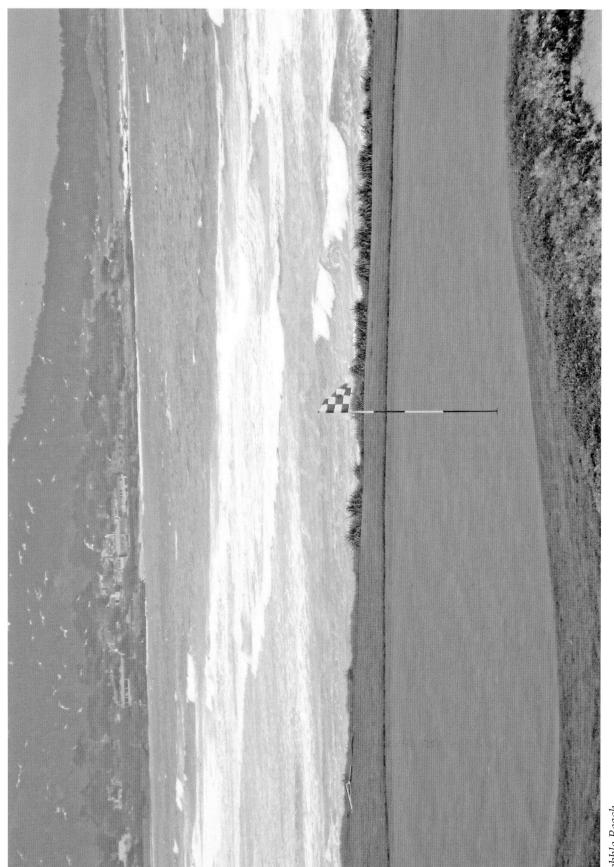

Pebble Beach.

Contents

Preface

Living the Dream is the continuing story of stroke survivor and avid golfer, Ian Halliwell. This second book takes us through his relentless pursuit to justify old British pro and legend, Bernard Hunt's description of him as 'the best damned social golfer on the planet'. Ian continues to traverse the globe, playing golf and raising stroke awareness issues, as well as continuing to raise charitable funds for the Stroke Association and supporting the cause of golfers with disabilities. Again, this is much more than a golf book as, with the original, it is a useful travel guide and a humorous and compelling tale of a social golfer who still harbours dreams of a successful golf career.

To date, Ian has raised over £30,000 from the original book sales, charitable golf days and after-dinner speeches. He hopes to double this with the publication of this book. He is a regular contributor to the Stroke Network and supports the Stroke Association by holding motivational talks and seminars for other stroke victims and their carers.

If you were to ask Ian what he makes of this success late in life, he would say, 'I am simply living the dream …'

At the British Par Three in 2008, Ian sponsored a stall for the Stroke Association offering free blood pressure tests and advice to all competitors and spectators.

The Social Golfer tees off at the prestigious Pebble Beach.

Introduction

When I had my stroke in 2006, my first instinct was simply to survive, to quite literally get back on my feet and return my life to some sort of normality. Part of that normality would have to be golf, the sport I love so much, and travel, my second love. In my first book, I chronicled my desire to play on every continent and at the same time become involved in competitive golf as well as supporting stroke awareness issues. In 2008, when the *Social Golfer* was published, my wife and family in particular, perhaps perceived that I had satisfied these desires. Not at all, it simply whetted my appetite to take all three things to an even higher level. I planned a round the world trip, to be some kind of modern day Phileas Fogg with Karen as my Passepartout. My outings to the British Par Three, Wrest Point Masters in Tasmania, the Barney Barnato in South Africa and the Edwin Watts Tour in Florida had started an increased competitive urge that needed satisfying. I wanted to use the social golfer concept as a focal point to enhance opportunities for disadvantaged or disabled golfers and to continue to set an example of what can still be achieved no matter how serious or life-threatening an illness can be. This book will take you through this continued journey.

Above: Satisfying that competitive urge, Ian tees off at The British Par Three Championship in 2010.

Right: Not all golf as Ian and Karen enjoy their stay at the luxurious Palace Hotel in Sun City, South Africa.

Lost City course, Sun City.

Acknowledgement

My darling wife Karen for her unstinting support during the past four years.

My children – Paul, Emma, Shelley and Tanya for continuing to make me proud and never having to worry on my travels.

To Mum, whose courage and strength shown through repeated illnesses, is the inspiration I draw on when I am down.

Neil Darby at Travelbag, the flight specialists, who ensures my trips all proceed smoothly.

Rick, John and all at the BP3 … the best amateur event in the world.

Tom Mirus and all at the Edwin Watts Tour – cheers for making me so welcome on tour.

All my fellow social golfers I have met on my trips, each and every one of you has made an impact on my life.

My mucker, Charles M. Brugh … read on and you will see just what a special guy this fella is.

Northlands Golf Club, Vancouver.

The Emirates Golf Club, Dubai.

1. The Competitive Edge

Golf is possibly the sports world's paradox. It lures us in as we play, set in the most beautiful, often tranquil, peaceful settings. It entices us with fresh air, sweet smells and offers the occasional thrill of a great shot. But, after spending four hours in the outdoors, the game can begin to play Twister with our insides and can gnaw on our minds like a squirrel on an acorn. It can be played as a solitary sport, the player simply playing against the course design and nature. Indeed, I have enjoyed many of my best days simply playing this way and relishing my own solitude, at one with God's great design. However, even the most social of golfers, and I consider myself to be one, has that in-built human urge to play with, and hopefully beat, his fellow competitors. The game of golf can promise great fun and joy, but, in the end, often leads to frustration and heartbreak. However, the exhilaration of winning any golf event where you have triumphed, not only against your peers but also the course and the elements, is a feeling which is quite unique in sporting circles.

Golf is similar to tennis in its very singular, individual competitive nature. With its lack of team competitions, the winning exultations are totally different for individual triumphs as opposed to those where you are part of a team. I have always been competitive, that's why I would not let the kids beat me at anything when they were growing up and any sporting match, be it bowls, pool, darts, squash or chess, between me and my son, Paul, are still bitterly contested even though I am old enough to know better and at twenty-six, you would have thought he would be used to losing by now. If he does look like beating me, then I can always revert to good old-fashioned psychology or plain cheating to maintain this feeling of invincibility. So, after my stroke and despite the obvious restrictions to my golfing ability, it was inevitable I would still want to satisfy that competitive urge and my cravings for golfing success. In the past two years, I have been fortunate enough to have achieved this to some degree.

The unique scoring of golf, i.e. Stableford and Handicaps, and differing style of competitions such as Scrambles, effectively means players of limited abilities can still enjoy the thrill of competition. My main quibble with Premiership Football in England is that around sixteen out of twenty teams are in a competition they cannot win or aspire to win. It simply does not make sense. In golf, you can always find competitions in which you have an opportunity of success. It is this which makes our pastime so unique. Also, as famous writer A. A. Milne famously said, 'Golf is so popular as it is simply the best game in the world in which to be bad'. Failure and disappointment will inevitably still have moments of joy. Over the past two years, I have enjoyed a modicum of success, a bucket load of failure but a plethora of joy and great memories.

In my golfing career, pre-stroke, my undeniable, my only credible achievements had both been at the Kimberly Golf Club, that rough diamond in central South Africa, where, in 2003, I won the Freddie Tait Putter and in 2004, the Konica at the Barney Barnato. The first was a simple putting competition, but it still counts and I was the first overseas winner. The second part of the week-long booze-up in October involved golf generally playing second fiddle. I had returned with the lads in 2006, six weeks before my stroke, but in 2008 when I was in some kind of good health, my good mate, the legend

Skitty and his wife Chris (now famously known as 'Echo' for her amazing knack of repeating all Karen's naggings of me whilst we are on holiday) asked us to join them on a holiday to South Africa. It was the perfect opportunity to return to the Barnato and later to Sun City. Add on a pre-Barnato trip to Dubai to break the journey up and the perfect social golfer trip was born. A four-day stopover in Dubai, including a round at the Emirates Golf Club, then four days in Kimberley to play in the Barney Barnato, and finally a week in Sun City, doubled up as the launch of the original *Social Golfer* book in South Africa.

Dubai

When we visited in 2008, Dubai was not then officially broke; it had also just been effectively given the keys to European golf by becoming officially recognised as the principal base, culminating with the Race to Dubai, Europe's response to the Fed Ex Trophy. So we travelled with a great deal of anticipation and expectancy; the reality, however, was a possible precursor to the problems that lay ahead for this thriving Middle Eastern metropolis.

Dubai will remain an enigma. We stayed for four days. Did I enjoy it? Well yes, but far more so than Matron, Ledge and Echo. Would I re-visit? Unlikely. The golf at the Emirates was quite fantastic but rather expensive. The hotel was magnificent, but again over-priced. The principality has little heritage of any sort and there is so much building work going on, it is a major distraction at all times. Matron possibly best summed it up by describing it as a 'work in progress and home at any time to roughly one quarter of all the large cranes in the world' – I suppose that is most apt.

A day we worried we would never see again – a trip to South Africa commences in the usual fashion.

Even laying on the splendid man-made beach of our outstanding hotel, there was the constant noise of drilling, hammering and general construction that continued the whole day. Walking along the promenade, you were hit by dust bowls which you could taste. This was not from the encroaching desert but from the general massive construction work being undertaken. Since our visit in October 2008, with the worsening world economic climate and financial problems that engulfed Dubai, I understand this may have changed, but unfinished buildings will hardly enhance this as a quality holiday destination.

Let us emphasise the positives. The weather was marvellous; October is the start of the high season which runs through to May. Temperatures average the mid-80s falling to the 70s at the turn of the year and rising gradually again to the 80s by May. June to Sepember can see temperatures approaching the 100s, hence the low season. Rain, if there is any, will generally be in February or March. So clearly, this is a sun-seekers' paradise and for golfers, these are perfect climates in which to play golf in the winter months. Most hotels are outrageously good, nearly all 5-star and some of the world's finest.

You do pay for what you get and the 'Duram Durams' (the currency of Dubai being the *dirham*) do not go a long way.

Most socialising and entertaining is inevitably in the hotels because, of course, this is first and foremost a very religious Muslim country and, as certain tourists have found out, crossing the line can be very costly.

The country has some of the finest courses on the planet as befitting the epicentre of the European game, as well as some of the most different challenges a golfer can face. Again, this can come at some significant cost. Quality does not come cheap in Dubai. There are many big name players associated with course design in Dubai – Montgomery, Els and Woods to name a few – add to that, the world-class Emirates and Dubai Creek, and it is hard to criticise this destination in golfing terms alone.

However, if as a social golfer you want more than golf, then sadly this is where Dubai starts to fall down. It was an oil state infused over the years by other Middle Eastern cultures and western influences which have overwhelmed the original nomadic Arabic heritage of this small country. There is little to get excited about except 7-star hotels, premium shopping malls, glimpsing the odd A-list celebrity and a few top-notch culinary restaurants. Again, I would suggest that most visitors with a constraint on their wallets or purses will find Dubai excessively expensive and poor value for money. Of course, this may not worry the more affluent visitors but I saw many visitors visibly recoil at the price of drinks and food in the whole of Dubai except the souks and markets where of course the underpaid underclasses meander and mingle.

When you fly into Dubai you arrive at the top notch, impressive, modern Dubai International Airport (DXB) which is only about three miles from the city centre and the main tourist districts. Superbly designed with a fine range of shopping facilities, it is certainly one of the best I have visited. On arrival, most guests who have booked into the main hotels can expect a complimentary shuttle service to be provided. I advise all visitors to book this in advance and check the exact pick-up position within the terminal. It certainly is a most cordial and pleasant way to begin your stay.

Choosing a hotel is not difficult as most offer at least a 5-star facility, most are on the beach and prices are pretty comparable between the hotels, except of course the more opulent 7-star ones such as the Burj Al Arab, the iconic, futuristic marvel that stands out over the city or the Palms which Kylie opened during our visit. A credit card with plenty of spending power is essential if you stay here.

Dubai is essentially a city that is strung along one main street, Sheikh Zayed Road. The older parts of the city, Bur Dubai and Deira, are on either side of the creek. Jumeirah is the generic term given to the beach area between Bur Dubai and Jebel Ali and many of the more reasonably priced hotels are based here. Beyond Jumeirah lies the new marina development where we stayed. It will look impressive when completed. Inland, taking over the desert, is the pretentiously titled Dubailand, the like of which would put Disneyland into shade. That is if it can be completed without bankrupting the Kingdom first.

Dubai has made an attempt to realign itself with oil which was about to run out in 2011, and then it made sense for the Emirs to replace this income with the 'easy bucks' generated from tourism. They were not aware at the time of the impending financial Armageddon ready to explode around the globe. With the major drop in property prices having driven down investment, it remains unclear whether the grand design will ever be fulfilled in this generation despite the Emirates' wealth. Dubai's financial dependence on other states in the UAE, particularly Abu Dhabi, which I am certain will in time also be its biggest competitor in tourism and golf in the area, is a recipe for long-term disaster.

We stayed at the Royal Meridian next to the new marina, a beach resort I can strongly recommend. Rooms are spacious and views over the pool and beach sensational. There is also a fine bar area to spend the evenings and several exceptional restaurants. All in all, a fine hotel.

Hotels, Dubai style.

Whilst we had few complaints about the hotel save all the blooming building work away from the grounds and the constant irritation of construction noise, it was not cheap. This proved an irritant on the first day. Regular readers will know that the Ledge Skitty is possibly the tightest man on the planet and proud of it too, so this millionaires' paradise was always going to be particularly testing for him. The first night we offered him the choice of restaurants, he chose the steak bar but developed a particularly nasty case of sunstroke when he saw the prices. I enjoyed it, but not so sure it was worth 100 nicker a piece, but Matron's reaction on being offered free cigars was particularly memorable. The next day on the beach, a hungry but recovered Ledge paid ten pounds for a plate of twelve chips at which point, he set off determined to find somewhere in Dubai he could eat or drink cheaply. It is not the destination to visit if cash is an issue, you need to be sure you can afford the visit if you want to truly enjoy it.

As we only had two full days here, we decided to play golf one day and do touristy things on the other, the perfect balance for a social golfer. Possibly the best way to get round is the open-topped Big Bus; you do get to see all you would want to see. There is a monorail due for completion and taxis were reasonably priced, but the Big Bus was our favourite. As usual, we had done our research and I will identify first what we decided was essential for us to see, then what I wish we had also been able to fit in. Both Matron and Echo insisted we see some proper Arab culture, in other words,

shopping in the gold souks in Deira, the oldest part of town. It has the added advantage of being next to the creek or river with all its local dhows etc creating an impressive vista. For shoppers, the street markets of Deira are a treasure-trove of jewellery, clothing and exotic spices. Located next to the creek, you can easily see how the city first made its name as an international trading post. The individual souks as a whole form a lattice of

Gorgeous gardens and pool at the Royal.

Just too much building work.

streets all lined with shops and providing the wallet rarely surfaces, it can be a rewarding experience. Beware there are few public toilets, we found none, which is no good for a stroke victim on water tablets. In the end, I had to ask a local jeweller if I could use his toilet which was simply a hole in his cellar floor. Try having a pee while someone is trying to flog you a fake Rolex!

The mall at the Emirates is under development and will incorporate a massive indoor ski dome of all things. It is hoped that Dubailand will become the country's greatest tourist attraction, a theme park with six individual areas: Attractions and Experience World which will include a water park; Retail and Entertainment World is a mix of entertainment, shopping and eating out; Downtown, which includes the Mall of Arabia (the world's largest shopping mall), the City Walk and the great Dubai Wheel; Themed Leisure and Vacation World which incorporates spas, health and well being in village residences, resort hotels and wellness retreats; Eco-Tourism World, a series of nature and desert-based attractions covering approximately 1.4 billion square feet; Sports and Outdoor World, the flagship of Dubai's drive to become the sporting centre of the world, will host international rugby, cricket as well as five major projects – Sports City, Extreme Sports World, Golf World, the Plantation Equestrian and Polo Club and Dubai Autodrome and Business Park which will host Formula 1 events, an ambitious project which if completed will dwarf everything else in Dubai. But watch this space,

Taking a ride up the creek on a dhow is an experience not to be missed, also it is probably the cheapest thing you can do here. The Big Bus will take you to the Burg al Arab, the Palms and World developments, worth a look to see how the other half live.

Stunning backdrop.

it is nowhere near completion and at least two years behind schedule. The developers had anticipated annual visitors totalling 15 million, which is a tall order but necessary for an outlay that is now likely to exceed $25 billion dollars. In any other country, it would have been shelved by now but not in the Middle East where to do so would be considered a national shame.

The country does have several outstanding museums I am told and quite fabulous mosques including the Jumeirah Mosque, the largest and prettiest in Dubai and the only one opened to non-Muslims. The Dubai Museum housed in the splendid Al Fahidi Fort is, I am reliably informed, the place to visit to find the real essence of Dubai. Finally, I would have liked to see the Badtakiya on the shore of the creek, a massive renovation effort intended to preserve Dubai's heritage. It is a collection of over fifty restored buildings, dating back to the 1900s, when the original Iranian traders settled. Today, they house art galleries, cultural centres and restaurants.

So to the golf, Dubai is a fantastic golfing destination with a myriad of outstanding and exceptional tracks. The Montgomery, the Els, Dubai Creek all came fantastically well recommended but we decided to play the granddaddy of them all – the Emirates Golf Club. Why? Well it hosted most major events in the area, was officially the first green course in the Middle East and its iconic bedouin tent themed clubhouse is known throughout the golfing world. It consists of two totally different courses, the championship Majlis and the new Faldo-redesigned Wadi and with as good a practice facility as you will find anywhere. It is a right regal experience.

The courses are bordered by thirty-foot trees to stop the desert sands and wild camels encroaching onto the pristine fairways. Each evening these courses require over 1.5 million gallons of desalinated water. The Majlis, or Desert Miracle course, was constructed in 1987 in just eight months and is truly

Nearly cost Skitty a fortune.

a miracle of construction and planning. Visitors should play the Majlis as it is a championship course; the 8th, 10th and 18th holes are stupendous. The 8th runs back up to the authentic Bedouin Majlis and its rough is fearsome – Skitty fell in and we struggled to pull him out. The 10th hole is a magnificent par 5, where the island green is encircled by sand, not water, although water offers the challenge at hitting 18 to a peninsular green. The Wadi is a slightly different challenge, some pleasant holes with the skyscrapers as constant backdrops. Both courses were in super condition, but bear in mind you will pay nearly £100 for any round here in Dubai. The Majlis is worth it. Enjoy your visit with a browse round the clubhouse and the pro shop which is, not surprisingly, superbly well-equipped. Prices at the 19th and in the pro shop were more realistic than in the city. Skitty, despite nearly losing himself in the desert bush, was two inches away from a hole in one. I have never seen anyone more relieved as he said he could not afford a round of drinks. A memorable day at a super venue.

Given the opportunity, I would have liked to play the unique Dubai Country Club, truly the bad bunker player's worst nightmare. This is a grassless course in the Arabian desert. Fairways are marked by green wooden stakes and within those, you play off a green carpet mat, anywhere else it is sand. Greens are 'browns' being a mixture of sand and oil; reputedly smoother than grass, they are supposed to be super to putt on. Rather sadistically for a desert course, there are traditionally-shaped bunkers as well. Opened in 1970, it was the first course to open here and remains a unique challenge, one I am disappointed to say I could not take up due to time constraints.

Return to the Barnato

Leaving Dubai, we headed for Johannesburg, then took an internal flight to Kimberley, right in the heart of South Africa. I can say unequivocally that Kimberley Golf Club is my favourite throughout all my travels; certainly not the best course, nor is it dramatic, but it has a 19th hole which is second to none and hosts the most remarkable golfing week annually, as well as being the residence of a fantastic golfing museum dedicated to the legendary Frederick Guthrie Tait. This was an important milestone in my recovery. My last visit in 2008 had been just six weeks before my stroke and on that visit, we elected to visit Cape Town and missed out on the Barnato, something I had regretted. I had played in the Barnato in 2004, winning the Friday Stableford Event (the Konica), returning to defend in 2005 when I finished fourth. Persuading the ladies to spend four days in Kimberley as opposed to Cape Town and the Garden Route was not particularly easy, but the promise of a whole week in Sun City after Kimberley had swung matters my way.

The journey began in dramatic fashion when we arrived late in Jo'burg for our connection and had

Kimberley Golf Club, home of the Barney Barnato.

to stay overnight in the airport. The next day, we had a farcical situation at the airport where the flight system showed that Echo had flown into Kimberley the previous evening and convincing immigration otherwise, despite Chris standing in front of them, was proving difficult. Also, the system showed Christine Skitt, not Christina as shown on her passport. Our trip looked like being over before it started. Then the new economic side of South Africa took over, where clearly every problem can be solved at a price. A porter identifying our woes grabbed Echo and took her to at least five different admin desks to resolve the issue and get her onto the flight. Come to think of it, these could have been his relations because with an exchange of rand, a stamp here and there, she was eventually given a boarding pass to the connecting flight. We duly arrived in Kimberley and headed to the Flamingo Casino and Travel Lodge adjacent to the golf course. The facilities in the lodge are extremely basic, quite small rooms but very clean. It is a case of you pay for what you get. Kimberley is not a tourist destination but a working diamond mining town and visitors need to realise that. It has one main attraction – the Big Hole which is quite simply a big hole left from the original mining operations in the 1900s. We were only here for three nights, playing the Friday Konica. Would I repeat my success at the Saturday closing event?

The Barnato runs for eight days and features eight individual daily Stableford events … golfers from all over Africa, some from Australia and two Brits made up a field of over 600 for the week. Every evening in the club house was fun time with local bands, drink offers and cheap food and after this, a visit to the casino – a tremendous social golfing occasion! Although it was four years since my last visit, our welcome was unbelievable. As we entered the clubhouse, we heard on the microphone, 'ladies and gentlemen, I am delighted to announce all the way from England our good friend, Ian Halliwell, is in the building', followed by tumultuous applause. I have been a proud sponsor of the museum and several artefacts I had collected were on display including a framed copy of the original *Social Golfer* book. After a special handshake from the curator, the organiser, Kimberley Dave Wilson, rushed over to shake my hand and expressed his delight at my recovery and my apparent well-being. It was truly a special moment.

Five years earlier, on Skitty's only visit, we had formed a bond with our local caddies but could not be sure if they were still around. To our delight, we heard, 'Mr Ian, Mr Steve, can we carry for you again'– it was John and his buddies. Once again, we were overwhelmed by their reaction. When

asked how they were, the response that they were still alive summed up their view on life and made me feel particularly humble after my illness battles. I gave the guys a TSG tee shirt and a copy of my book – you would have thought Christmas had come early. Remember these guys had walked four hours from the townships to caddy for a plate of hotpot and a couple of

The course was in magnificent condition.

There is always a lovely welcome from the members.

What's Matron trying to say – is this my lucky day?

The FG Tait Memorial.

The Casino and travel lodge.

Great to see John, hope he is still well and on planet earth somewhere.

Even my creative scoring can't bring about a victory this time!

quid. That night I think both Ledge and I slept very well and looked forward to the golf the next day. We even won a few bob at the casino that evening, I recall. A day that had started with us nearly losing Echo had ended with us all feeling elated and content.

The two days' golf, whilst totally enjoyable as the course is in excellent condition, did not see either of us perform to the best of our ability. However, to hear our names announced on the first tee made the long journey so worthwhile. In the Friday Konica, I again managed a top ten place out of 120 with thirty-nine points, but despite John's excellent line reading, I missed too many putts. The event had a highlight now in Barney folklore. The 18th, a long par 5 to close, has a far advanced ladies' tee which Skitty failed to clear. He promptly walks up to his ball and drops his trousers then proceeds to smash his second miles down the fairway. Our South African partners and caddies did not know what to make of it and that evening he was asked by half the golf club's female members to replicate the shot. He has never been more popular. I was quite jealous and thought I must try that sometime! Saturday saw us both with post dismal scores which was in no part due to the excesses of the previous evening. It was a memorable few days with some of the best social golfers on the planet … we will return in 2012 to celebrate Echo's 60th or at least, that's the plan. We left Kimberley content, and headed back north to the magnificent Sun City in what Echo described as a washing machine. As we took off in a horrid thunderstorm, the plane handled the turbulence as well as Skitty did the bunkers … all up and down.

Sun City

And so we moved on to Sun City, that purpose-built resort, north-west of Jo'burg in the Pilanesburg National Park. This was our third time and the place never fails to impress. The resort also put on a special cocktail evening to promote the original book, something I will be forever grateful for. The golf was stupendous as always, and our visit to the Gary Player course was particularly memorable as we were treated to playing the course as it was to be set up for the Million Dollar Challenge. There was just Steve and I playing, the TV technicians following and filming us in preparation for the Pro Event, plus a family of monkeys who seemed to take to Skitty. On the 6th, as he holed a putt, the baby monkeys all burst out in rapturous applause. They also made a bee line for Echo and Matron by the pool, pinching all the sugar from the little packets. There was a funny incident one day as all of us sunbathers by the pool watched and were enthralled as a raft of monkeys scaled the perimeter of the palace walls trying to access the bedrooms. All guests were warned to lock the patio doors, unfortunately someone had not and six monkeys disappeared into the bedroom reappearing moments later with fruit, drink and clothing, including some quite fetching lingerie. As we all fell about laughing, we suddenly heard a big shout of *sacre bleu* and something else in French which clearly indicated a family had recognised certain articles of clothing and realised it was their room being trashed. The husband, wife and two children dashed off and five minutes later appeared on their balcony to a

With the Resort Manager, Golfing Director and Head Pro celebrating my book.

The stunning clubhouse at the Lost City course.

IAN HALLIWELL IS
THE SOCIAL GOLFER

SUN CITY possibly the best golfing destination on the planet?

The golf consists of just twp courses, both totally different in style, location and playability. The flagship Gary Player is as you would expect, a true Championship test, designed in typical Player style with exceptional length, difficult carries, superb bunkering and lightning fast greens. It should be in any top 100 ratings of the world's courses, it is that good. It has an exceptional Par 5, the 9th, which teases and tantalises with the approach offering great risk reward to an island 3 tiered green, whilst 17 and 18 are as good a finish as one could wish to play. Drive over water at 17, then approach to an island green and the magificent final hole where the drive cuts off as much as the approach again, all over water as the player dare. Lush green fairways in this surprisingly barren climate give the golfer a false realisation of being in a volcano. A true test at less than £30 a round. The second course, the Lost City, offers a completely different test, being usually left to the elements it resembles more a course in Nevada. With the trademark Par 3 over the crocodile pit, superb 9th and 18th that approach the Flintstones-like magificent club house. It has a charm unique to itself and indeed is the course I prefer.

Overlooking the magnificent 9th and 18th at the Lost City course.

Most golfers are likely to have a perception of sun City as a pretentious exclusive resort for the famous and exceedingly well off. Indeed, several may be aware that the resort's flagship course, the Gary Player, annually hosts the MILLION DOLAR 12-man invitational challenge but, more likely, most will be aware that this was the base the majority of the English press and the infamous WAGs based themselves during England's ill-fated World Cup, thereby reinforcing this image of remote exclusivity. Nothing could really be further from the truth. In this golfer's opinion, the resort is possibly the finest destination on the planet, but maybe not as intimate or romantic as Cape Kidnappers and Kauri Cliffs in New Zealand, nor as great a golfing pedigree as Pebble Beach in the USA. But, for all-round value for money, great golf, exceptional food and entertainment and unbelievable accommodation, it stands comparison with anywhere. With daily flights to Johannesburg from all major cities, and cheaper fares available, Sun City really does offer golfers and their partners an exceptional value-for-money vacation.

Besides the two quality courses, the golfing facilities are second to none. A peculiar perk at both resorts is the mid-round South African buffet and beverage which is included in the price. A round will cost about £30 – inclusive of the buffet and compulsary cart. In that heat it is necessary. Caddies (or Spotters) are extra, at about a tenner, but you could save that in balls and your score would considerably benefit from their green knowledge – and they are good company too!

The Sun City Resort is located approximately two hours from Johannesburg in the Pilanasberg National Park. Limo transport can be arranged from the airport to the resort at less than a tenner each (based upon eight sharing). Being given the red carpet treatment, flowers for the ladies and champagne is a special way of starting your vacation. The resort opened in 1992 and is built in an extinct volcano in the centre of the nature reserve where the Big 5 beckon. It consists of three hotels and several chalet rentals and a week here can cost less than you would pay in Tenerife or the Costa del Sol. The pick of the hotels is the Palace, more than a 5-Star, it is certainly opulent and ostentatious, but definitely not tacky. Breakfast included can consist of pink champers, duck, caviar; it really is a delight. The resort offers far more than golf – a casino, with shows to rival Vegas or the West End, rides with the elephants, take a morning balloon ride, feed the chimpanzees or simply walk through magnificent gardens which are simply breathtaking.

With a wide range of pools in which to relax and chill included on three occasions with the Valley of Waves Water Park, it really is far more than superb golf. Top notch cuisine and wine abounds, again all a a cost which will simply amaze. I have been fortunate to visit with six different couples and no-one has ever been disappointed. For a golfer wishing to get the very best of both worlds at a price within a reasonable budget, I would strongly advise you to consider a vacation in this tropical paradise.

The monkeys get ready to strike.

Golf as good as it gets.

The Palace, opulent, magnificent, luxurious and best of all, affordable.

Two happy bunnies …

And two romantic guys!

Gary Player Country Club, Sun City.

rapturous round of applause. From the rather contrite way the children reacted, I guessed one of them was to blame. If you are able to visit, then do so, it is more than golf, it is a visual, intoxicating experience which you will not forget. I have recently completed an article for *Trade Publication* which I include as I feel this resort deserves all its plaudits.

Glorious Nailcote Hall.

The British Par 3 Championship

When I was seriously ill and was constantly being told I may never play again, this event was a target I set myself and four years on, it has become the premier highlight of my golfing year. This is much more than a golfing event, it is more a golf celebration, like a royal garden party, for four days in the splendid Warwickshire countryside at stately Nailcote Hall, where celebrities from stage, screen and sport mingle with professional golfers spanning the years. Combine this with TV coverage, the paying public, three gala evening events and it is simply heaven. Trust me, if they play golf in the spiritual afterlife, it can't get much better than this. In 2007, when I first played just three months after walking again, I partnered that fine gentleman and old pro, Bernard Hunt, coincidentally one of the last pair of brothers to play in the Ryder Cup before the Molinaris. It was Bernard who taught me the nuances of the short-course game, established the social golf concept but more importantly, kickstarted my whole golfing journey. That year, we finished a lowly sixty-fourth in the Pro Am, little did he realise that four years later, I would win the event.

2008 was quite a special year as I chose the event to officially launch *The Social Golfer* book and my Stroke Awareness campaign. It also marked the event where the Social Golfer also entered teams in the Celeb days. In the Pro Am, I had the pleasure of partnering Steve Cowle, the previous year's professional champion. This fine gentleman had also won the inaugural Trilby Tour and, whilst he did little to improve my golf, he did introduce me to my now trademark trilby. Skitty caddied for me this year and without his assistance, I am sure we

Team TSG and Rob Bonnett.

Matron doing a radio promo for the book.

TSG with Graeme Storm and Ledge the caddy.

Ian sinks for another net birdie.

would have finished in the top ten rather than twenty-fourth. He had an opinion on everything, every line of every putt, choice of balls, selection of clubs; we argued and bickered like two old ladies. We were paired on day one with French Open Champion, Graeme Storm, and Manchester United legend and lothario, Lee Sharpe. Despite the torrential rain, it was a fabulous day, Stormy and Sharpey to this day relive the banter between Skitty and I. On the 18th, Lee having had enough (his hair was out of place), swung his club so hard it slipped out of his hands, over the fence and out of bounds. Amazingly, his ball still carried 110 yards, sadly to a watery grave. Skitty, trying to impress, bounded the fence to collect Lee's club … it took longer to get back as he realised the fence was electrified. If you ever see a video of the Celeb Event where we partnered TV sports reporter, Rob Bonnet, you will see Skitty hole a monster on the 6th 'for a birdie' says the commentator, but he had already taken three off the tee. This was the year that Echo had her picture taken with everyone when she became the official BP3 stalker.

In 2009, I partnered Andrew Collinson and both he and I gave it a good shot. Andrew was second to Steve Carter after day one and we lay fourth in the team event. It meant that we went out last on day two and with all the TV coverage that went with it. Again if you see the show, you hear me a lot but do not see me. However, Matron is on every shot; I am sure the cameraman had the hots for her or Mrs Collinson. Sadly, both our hopes disappeared on the short 13th when Andrew spun back from just behind the hole to the front bunker leaving only a retreating shot and I hit the 3.30 train to Paddington. Still it was as close to real live pro tourney action as I had ever been in and it sure whetted the appetite. I also played with the most 'winningest' Senior Tour Player, Tommy Horton, in the Celeb Event and a fine experience that was. Tommy only carried a few clubs and indeed used a 9 iron at all the holes except the longer 7th and 9th.

Discussing this with Tommy who looked in my bag with my six gap wedges and pointed out what he considered a malaise of the current-day professionals who need to know the exact yardage they hit every shot. As he pointed out, in his day you had a 9 iron, wedge and sand wedge and with each club you had to be able to manufacture a variety of shots, height and distance. I saw Tommy punch his 9 iron low to the first 110 yards, high to the 8th, 87 yards. It was a supreme example of club control from one of its finest exponents. His tales of

Ian leads off the Celeb Team.

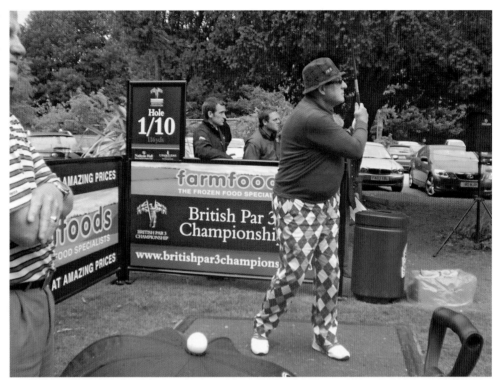

Underway, watched by Jim Lilly, 8 iron to ten feet and our second round charge is on its way.

matches with Jack and Arnie ensured both Skitty and Slasher Jones had a most enjoyable day culminating with the evening gal meal where we were joined by Mr and Mrs Horton. A splendid end to a wonderful week.

For the 2010 event, I had mentally decided to toughen up, I wanted some modicum of success from this event … three years, improvement every year, but no trophies to show for it. Prior to the event, I played for six weeks, three times a week, at Potters Wood a 9-hole par 29 short course in Wigan … I hit with short irons only, so come the event I was certainly well set up. In the Day Celeb event, I had brought together Skitty (there's no show without Punch!) and Peg-leg Roger Hurcombe, my good one-legged golfer from down south, a phenomenon whose short game I felt was well suited to this course. Also, it represented continued support from the Social Golfer to disadvantaged golfers, something I am very keen to facilitate and promote. Roger shows how simple the game can be. Our celeb was my great mate, Clive Abbott of Black Abbots fame. Clive is a low handicapper and fabulous golfer who shot level par on the day, nett four under. With Roger playing impressively and the odd contribution from Skitty and myself, we carded an impressive twenty under. Amazingly, three more teams carded this and on count back, we finished second … my first BP3 trophy. We had an amazing night at the Gala do as we celebrated long into the evening with Clive and Viv, his lovely wife, and our good ladies. Clive did an amazing acoustic to end the evening off and, despite my hangover, I was ready for the next two days pro am. It would be remiss of me not to mention the calamity on the 8th where I fell back in the bunker and, like an upturned crab, flailed about unable to stand up. Help was on hand when Peg-leg came to my rescue with his new leg, only to start to sink into the wet

Stunning, sensational, stately Nailcote Hall, home of the BP3.

The 4th, just over eighty yards, out of bounds left and behind. Our demise commenced here in 2009.
In 2010, pesky Rik put in a front bunker too.

sand as if he was in quicksand. Help was not forthcoming from Clive and Skitty, who were splitting their sides. Christine Hurcombe, Roger's wife, jumped into the bunker to pull us both out. Thankfully there were no TV cameras about.

I had originally been paired with Phil Goulding from the main tour, a former French Open champion, but he cried off to play in the Trilby Event which sadly clashed with the BP3, which had also meant my old mates, Cowle and Sharpey, were missing the BP3. My new partner was the top Midland-based Euro pro, Simon Lilly. A week after this event, he played on the main tour in the Czech Open, qualifying for the weekend and finishing in the top forty. He obviously picked up some good habits. On day one, we played with 2008 winner, Mark Mouland, and the mercurial teenage prodigy, Charlie Hull, what a fine young lady she is. Be under no illusion, this girl will reach the top echelons of the game and she deserves it. Mark was brilliant, shooting five under and leading the individual, they are net nine under leading the team. Simon and I were not much adrift on six under. I watched Mark and he rarely took the flags on, content to hit the greens and trust his putter. On day two, we were the last of the lunch pairings out … ten more pairings, i.e. twenty teams to go out in the afternoon. Simon took complete charge; our target was simple – to set a score for the afternoon starters to chase. He also asked me to try and par the holes where I had my shot, that he stressed would be the key to our success. Accompanying us around, my new caddy, Matron and Jim, Simon's Dad … it was a great team effort and we made quick inroads up the leader board as I carded six net birdies. At the close, we had posted fourteen under, two shots clear but with the afternoon leaders still to go out. You need some luck occasionally, that and my rain dance behind the tented village encouraging the storm to worsen. Throughout the afternoon, as I nervously watched the scoreboard, it became clear no-one was going to decimate our score, indeed the longer it went on, the more hopeful it looked. With just two pairs left on the 17th, we had two shots on them but bloomin' 'eck they both birdied seventeen … brown underpants job now … Simon is very laconic, I am a nervous wreck. Turns out he knew we would win on count back most likely but he didn't bloody tell me. As it happens, there's no birdies at the last. How I didn't applaud both misses I don't know, well I do, Matron was gripping me very tightly. A nervy half hour as all scores were collated, cross-checked, double-checked before victory was assured.

Day 1 Pro-Am, attired in a mellow yellow.

It was quite a poignant moment; this event means so much more to me than golf. I had donated the Stroke Awareness Cup to the PGA after it became clear that the MRC Classic would not be continued after we sold the business and this trophy was now going to be awarded annually to the Pro Am Amateur. Guess who was the first winner? – yours truly, how surreal. Add a trip to Mauritius for Matron and me, and then you may appreciate just how joyful an evening we had. There was even more success on day four as the closing team event, partnered by comic legend Jasper Carrott, when we finished fourth. I had never won a sausage in three attempts at the BP3, this year I needed a trailer to take home all the silver and glass wear. I have never been happier. Stroke victim, stroke survivor and British Par 3 winner, it doesn't get any better than this …well, maybe Mauritius … .

A final memory from this week-long pageant – I finally make my TV debut with a long chip across the final green. I am officially described by Sky Sports as sartorially elegant; the programme described me as a charismatic character … Yep, I will wear both of them. I had tried to celebrate the whole event in style and think I did, you can all be the judge. My great mate, Frank Worthington, was impressed with my caddyshack outfits anyway.

The whole event is magnificently run, a joint effort by Nailcote Hall owners, Rick and Sue Cressman, to whom not enough praise can be given for establishing this as one of the most prestigious events on the PGA circuit. Backed up by Champions plc and Mr John Heyes, this is without doubt the best event I have ever played, best organised, most enjoyable, the superlatives and adjectives won't stop flowing. The course is a little gem, even better than my eulogy in the first book. Any social or amateur golfer hoping to enjoy the feel of a professional event, sign up and enjoy the thrill of a lifetime and try and win the Halliwell Cup.

Another sartorially elegant (as per Sky Sports) outfit.

TSG sinks the winning putt on the 17th.

I receive the Halliwell Trophy from Tony Jacklin and Rik Cressman with partner, Simon Lilly, and have a few words for the TV.

The following is the official press release for the 2010 event:

O'HANLON WINS THE FARMFOODS BRITISH PAR 3 CHAMPIONSHIP

Cornwall based, PGA Professional, Richard O'Hanlon, triumphed after drama at the last hole left Nailcote's European Tour Pro's, Mark Mouland and Andrew Marshall, one shot shy of a 3 man play off.

With O'Hanlon in the clubhouse at 6 under par, Mouland missed a 6 foot putt for par which would have put him in a play off. And Marshall, who needed a birdie to make a play off watched as his 20 foot putt stopped agonisingly an inch short of the hole.

After the dramatic finish, O'Hanlon reflected on how fortunes in golf can change, 'Last year after the first day's play, I was in last place – and here I am now the British Par 3 Champion – it's amazing!'

The Championship saw several other star players in the top ten places, with 21-year-old, Oli Fisher, finishing at 2 under par on his first visit to Nailcote alongside Gary Wolstenholme and Mike Watson all in 4th place.

The Seniors' Tour No 1 money earner and course record holder, Carl Mason, finished at 1 under with European Tour players, Gary Boyd and Simon Wakefield, just behind them in 10th place. The tournament host, Tony Jacklin, produced some super golf to roll back the years and finish on level par.

Celebrating the 40th Anniversary of his US Open win, Tony was delighted but reflected that at one point when he was 3 under par and just 2 shots off the lead, his competitive instincts were really firing. 'It's so tough around here – but a great test and great fun – it's what the game of golf is all about – the fiddly bits!'

Past Ryder Cup player, Brian Waites, eliminated all the 'fiddly bits' on the first day by holing his tee shot on the signature 9th and winning a £1,500 Italian designer Fope gold bracelet.

And Tommy Horton missed out on winning the £28,000 Land Rover Freelander that Guy Salmon sponsored

Richard O'Hanlon.

on the 146 yard 7th hole when his tee shot finished just an inch away from the cup!

So the traditional wheelbarrow with £5,000 in £1 coins arrived at the presentation and the new Farmfoods' British Par 3 champion was crowned – Richard O'Hanlon.

The 'Better Ball' pairs scoring was very tight with several superb performances from some of the professionals' amateur partners. Gary Boyd and Simon Peake, Gary Wolstenholme and Sarah Herd and Andrew Marshall with Dan Holt all worked well together finishing tied for 4th on 12 under par. But hot favourites, Mark Mouland and 14-year-old partner, Charley Hull, just missed out on the title again finishing on 13 under in 3rd place with Andrew McKay and amateur course record holder, Aaron Rai, runners up on 13 under too.

It was left to a more mature partner, Ian Halliwell, teamed with European Tour professional, Simon Lilly, to produce that little bit extra to take the 'pairs' title at 14 under par. A delighted Ian Halliwell had donated a new trophy for the event and promptly won it!

A terrific group of celebrity golfers enjoyed the week and helped support the Rainbows Hospice and

Seve Ballesteros Foundation in the process. Amongst the star names competing, the large crowds which attended this year were able to enjoy seeing several new Nailcote visitors including, Sir Bobby Charlton, Len Goodman, John Conteh and Kenny Logan. And it was great to see regulars returning to take up the challenge of the Par 3 like Ron Atkinson, Lee Sharpe, Brendan Cole, Bob Champion, Peter Shilton, William Roache and Willie Thorne.

It was entertainment all the way and then the golf began!

The two charity Celebrity Am days of the championship on the 10th and 13th produced some exciting golf and the amazing Brian Close who at 79 years of age and with a handicap of just 8 won the Celebrity Trophy on both days with forty-two points on the 10th and thirty-seven points on the 13th.

Past celebrity champion, Clive Abbott, was just two points behind in 3rd place while Gary Wolstenholme lost out to Brian on a countback to be 2nd. On his first attempt at playing the course, Len Goodman finished joint 7th and Nailcote regular, Pete Langford of the Barron Knights, came in 5th with thirty-five points.

On the 13th hole, Len Goodman made it into the prizes with a 5th place finish on 33 points playing up with the crowd all the way round and even dancing with one or two! David J. Russell, Gary Wolstenholme and Warren Jacklin chased Brian Close hard, but he held on to win by two points. Sir Bobby Charlton played the event for the first time and commented that it was tougher than he had expected but that he had enjoyed a great day with his team.

The team events certainly produced some drama especially on the first Celeb-Am on 10 August. Despite some good play by the Hyland Wealth Management and Bernard Matthews' teams aided by Kriss Akabusi and Ron Atkinson respectively, and the Farmfoods' team with Gary Wolstenholme, it was left to the second team of Farmfoods, Ian Halliwell and Derek Morris, to battle it out for the top three places.

All of them finished on ninety-two points – 20 under par and on a countback, the Derek Morris team won with their celebrity, Pete Langford, assisted by his star 11 year olds – Stefan Gryla, George Gray and Eliott Garside. Ian Halliwell's team with the superb Clive Abbott were runners up and the Farmfoods' team with Tommy Horton came 3rd.

The final event of the tournament produced another really tight finish and the prize winners in 4th, 5th and 6th places were RSM Tenon with Len Goodman, Martin Ross with Jasper Carrott and Aubrey Allen with Darren Maddy.

At the end of the day, it was left to the two Farmfoods' teams and Nailcote Hall to battle it out for the final three places with the Farmfoods' team headed by Eric Herd with Gary Wolstenholme pulling off the win with eighty-three points – 11 under par. Nailcote Hall with Tommy Horton finished one shot behind and a further shot back the 2nd Farmfoods' team with Willie Thorne had to settle for 3rd place.

The Gala Dinners were a resounding success and as a result of the fundraising efforts, the various event charities have benefitted to the tune of more than £50,000. The family fun of the event was boosted by a new look tented village with chipping competition from John Letters and a golf simulator challenge. And everyone could take a breather and enjoy a free massage or face painting for the youngsters while the ladies could try products from Liz Earle and Estee Lauder in the John Lewis tent.

All in all, a great festival of golf was enjoyed by record crowds over the four days and the weather was a bit better too! There's sure to be lots more excitement and even more famous names and players coming to the Championship next year.

2010 PGA Midlands Region
Farmfoods British Par 3 Championship
Nailcote Hall Hotel
11–12 August, 2010
Simon Lilly (ENG) & Ian Halliwell (ENG)

NAILCOTE HALL HOTEL

Hole	1	2	3	4	5	6	7	8	9	OUT	10	11	12	13	14	15	16	17	18	IN	TOT
Yards	116	114	124	87	95	110	146	106	133	1031	116	114	124	87	95	110	146	106	133	1031	2062
Metres	106	104	113	80	87	101	134	97	122	944	106	104	113	80	87	101	134	97	122	944	1888
Par	3	3	3	3	3	3	3	3	3	27	3	3	3	3	3	3	3	3	3	27	54
R1	2	3	2	3	3	3	2	3	2	23	2	2	3	3	3	3	3	3	3	25	48
R2	2	4	2	3	2	2	2	2	3	22	2	3	3	2	2	4	3	2	3	24	46

SUMMARY AND ANALYSIS

Round	Date	Start Time	Start Tee	Holes	Score	-Par+	Eagles (-2-)	Birdies (-1)	Pars (-)	Bogies (+1)	D/Bgies (+2)	Other (+3+)
1	11.08.10	12:10	1	18	48	-6		6	12			
2	12.08.10	12:30	1	18	46	-8		10	6	2		
	Tournament			36	94	-14		16	18	2		

PROGRESSIVE SCORE AGAINST PAR

Hole	1	2	3	4	5	6	7	8	9	OUT	10	11	12	13	14	15	16	17	18	IN	TOT
R1	-1			-2			-3		-4	-5						-6					
R2	-7	-6	-7		-8	-9	-10	-11				-12		-13	-14	-13		-14			

SCORING STATISTICS BY PAR GROUP

Hole Par	Round	Holes	-Par+	Average	Eagles (-2-)	Birdies (-1)	Pars (-)	Bogies (+1)	D/Bogies (+2)	Other (+3+)
					PAR 3s					
	R1	18	-6	2.67		6	12			
3	R2	18	-8	2.56		10	6	2		
	Tournament	36	-14	2.61		16	18	2		

2010 PGA Midlands Region
Farmfoods British Par 3 Championship
Nailcote Hall Hotel
11–12 August, 2010
Final Scoreboard (Team)

Pos.	Score	-Par+	Name	Represents	R1	R2	Card
1	94	-14	Simon Lilly (ENG)	Wellingborough GC	48	46	»»
2	95	-13	Mark McKay (ENG)	Leam Valley GCtre	48	47	»»
3	95	-13	Mark Mouland (WAL)	Farmfoods	45	50	»»
4	96	-12	Daniel Parkin	The Belfry	49	47	»»
5	96	-12	Gary Boyd	European Tour	48	48	»»
6	96	-12	Gary Wolstenhome (BRT)	Farmfoods	47	49	»»
7	96	-12	Andrew Marshall (BRT)	European Tour	46	50	»»
8	97	-11	Richard O'Hanlon (ENG)	Lanhydrock GC	48	49	»»
9	97	-11	Neil Briggs (ENG)	European Tour	47	50	»»
10	98	-10	Tony Johnstone (SAF)	Zimbabwe	50	48	»»
11	99	-9	Tony Allen (BRT)	Maxstoke Park GC	50	49	»»
12	99	-9	Tom Whitehouse (ENG)	European Tour	50	49	»»
13	99	-9	Scott Henderson (SCO)	Kings Links GCtre	49	50	»»
14	99	-9	David J Russell (ENG)	Archerfield Links	46	53	»»
15	100	-8	Mike Watson (ENG)	Weymouth GC	50	50	»»
16	100	-8	Iain Pyman (BRT)	North Region	48	52	»»
17	100	-8	Oliver Fisher	European Tour	48	52	»»
18	101	-7	Malcolm Gregson (ENG)	Carlyon Bay GC	53	48	»»
19	101	-7	Mark Smith (BRT)	Stamford GC	51	50	»»
20	101	-7	Tommy Horton (ENG)	Tommy Horton Golf Ltd	50	51	»»
21	101	-7	Mark Booth (BRT)	Whittlebury Prk G&CC	49	52	»»
22	101	-7	Ian Walley (BRT)	Shirland GC	49	52	»»
23	101	-7	Benn Barham (BRT)	Chart Hills GC	46	55	»»
24	102	-6	Richard Strange (BRT)	Norwood Park GC	53	49	»»
25	102	-6	Simon Wakefield (BRT)	Wychwood Park GC	53	49	»»
26	102	-6	Carl Mason (ENG)	Fox Club, Florida	52	50	»»
27	102	-6	Tony Jacklin (ENG)	Jacklin Design Grp	52	50	»»
28	102	-6	Dave Dixon (BRT)	European Tour	51	51	»»
29	102	-6	Maurice Bembridge (BRT)	Seniors Tour	51	51	»»
30	103	-5	Mark Sparrow (ENG)	Himley Hall GC	55	48	»»
31	103	-5	Mathew Morris (ENG)	Walmley GC	54	49	»»
32	103	-5	Brian Waites (ENG)	Minehead & W Somerset GC	51	52	»»
33	104	-4	Liam Bond (BRT)	Marriott St Pierre Hotel & CC	55	49	»»
34	104	-4	Ben Challis (ENG)	Lea Marston Hotel & GC	54	50	»»
35	104	-4	Gordon Brand (ENG)	Hollins Hall	52	52	»»
36	104	-4	Tim Rouse (ENG)	Northants County GC	52	52	»»
37	104	-4	Steve Carter (ENG)	South Staffordshire GC	50	54	»»
38	104	-4	Kevin Spurgeon (ENG)	Ferndown GC	50	54	»»
39	105	-3	Brian Rimmer (ENG)	Little Aston GC	51	54	»»
40	105	-3	Shaun Webster (BRT)	Champions UK	50	55	»»
41	106	-2	Richard Booth (BRT)	Hale Golf Club	54	52	»»
42	106	-2	Daniel Lowe (BRT)	Sandwell Park GC	52	54	»»
43	107	-1	Jason Groat (ENG)	Denver GCtre	56	51	»»
44	108	Par	Ian Proverbs (ENG)	Walsall GC	54	54	»»
45	108	Par	Stephen Bennett (ENG)	Waltham Windmill GC	52	56	»»
46	108	Par	Warren Jacklin (BRT)	Barden G & CC	51	57	»»

47	109	+1	David Hutton (ENG)	West Region	58	51	»»
48	109	+1	Gary Emerson (ENG)	Remedy Oak GC	56	53	»»
49	109	+1	Chris Rose (ENG)	Feldon Valley GC	55	54	»»
50	109	+1	Craig Swinburn (ENG)	Notts GC	53	56	»»
51	109	+1	Siôn Bebb (WAL)	Vale Hotel Golf & Spa	53	56	»»
52	109	+1	Graeme Storm (BRT)	European Tour	53	56	»»
53	110	+2	Malcolm McKenzie (ENG)	Hillsborough	56	54	»»
54	110	+2	Simon Lynn (ENG)	Trentham Park GC	51	59	»»
55	112	+4	Gary Alliss (BRT)	Ladbrook Park GC	57	55	»»
56	112	+4	Jason Powell (WAL)	Hinckley GC	54	58	»»
57	114	+6	Chris Gane (ENG)	European Tour	61	53	»»
58	114	+6	Andrew McArthur (BRT)	European Tour	56	58	»»
59=	DSQ	-	Andrew Collison (ENG)	Bungay & Waveney Valley	50	DSQ	»»
			Dennis Durnian (ENG)	A6 Physiotherapy	54	DSQ	»»

The PGA headquarters, Port St Lucie.

The Florida Open Golf Championship for Golfers with Disabilities

Since my stroke, I have become a supporter and advocate of events which epitomise the essence of sporting competition, but in particular, to highlight the sporting endeavour of remarkable individuals who overcome severe disabilities to participate and often achieve significant success in sport despite these considerable disadvantages. I am particularly fortunate to be able to regard many of these rather exceptional individuals as friends. I include the article on the 2009 event by my good friend, Joe Stine, which I won and which gives a true impression of the individuals who make up this special occasion. Sadly, I was unable to defend the trophy in 2010 at the magnificent PGA complex at Port St Lucie on the exceptional Wanamaker Track, designed by George Fazio. This was frankly immaterial as I got to spend the weekend with my great mucker and inspiration, Charles Brugh, and met so many other inspirational characters who put my problems into their proper context. There is always someone much worse off than you, whatever your problems or issues, that's for certain.

The PGA complex consists of three super courses and would rank as a great destination for any golf vacation. In August, it can get a tad too hot – bloomin' hot golfing in 120 degrees ain't fun! That's my excuse for my failure and I am sticking to it. The PGA Resort is also the home to quite a magnificent history museum which is a must-see for any anorak of the game. The Ryder Cup was on display before it was sent to a wet Wales to be reunited in its European home as I told all my American friends at the time.

As well as Charles Brugh in the USA, I have also become great friends with Peg-leg Jake and Roger Hurcombe who has become a regular member of the SG Team in competitions in the UK. A fine gentleman, competitive and an exceptional low-handicap golfer, I am proud to have him as both a friend and colleague. These two guys represent all that is good about sport and all that these competitions mean to many in their situation. A desire to be competitive, no matter what your

The contestants at the 2010 event. Disabilities don't discriminate in age or gender.

Charles, look how serious my mucker is too. On his way to breaking 120.

Cor blimey, Roger is carrying his bag. I'm pushing a trolley, somewhere!

personal trials is, I believe, a natural human desire and I am proud to support that in my small way.

These two extraordinary characters are not unique, as I met many like them on my travels, but they are both very special to me and inspirational to my continued well-being. I will return to these guys later with a look at their disabilities and recovery and the part that golf played in that recovery.

Above & right: Trophies at the PGA Museum, US Open, US Masters, Ryder Cup, et al.

The 4th Annual

Florida Open

For Golfers With Disabilities and/or Mobility Challenges

by Joe Stine

Golf has long been known for its ability to heal, the mind, body and spirit. Nowhere is this made more apparent than at the Florida Open Golf Tournament for Golfers with Disabilities and/or Mobility Challenges.

The 2009 open tournament was very much an inspiring success and a lot of fun for everyone involved. The annual open tournament took place on June 14th, 2009, and for the fourth year in a row was hosted by the generous folks at Kissimmee Bay Country Club.

A diverse group of golfers showed up and participated, rallying to raise awareness for the accessibility issues concerning golfers with disabilities and/or mobility challenges, but more importantly they came to have fun while playing golf. Participants of the 4th annual tournament included golfers of all levels of abilities as well as disabilities.

As in previous years, several members of the pres-tigious Eastern Amputee Golf Association competed in the 2009 open tournament, some of whom wore prosthetics and some who didn't. But make no mistake; this all inclusive tournament was not just for amputees. There was also an eclectic collection golfers participating that were mobility challenged from the effects of such conditions as strokes and paraplegia.

In a conscious effort to be all-inclusive, golfers without disabilities were encouraged to play in the open tournament, along with their friends with disabilities, and were eligible to compete for the Overall and Low Gross Awards. Everyone with a USGA Handicap was also eligible to compete for the Low Net Awards. As always the player with the lowest gross got the honor of having their name inscribed on the permanent open tournament trophy.

Sponsored by Florida Golf Magazine with some ini-

tial 'much needed' guidance provided by the National Alliance for Accessible Golf, the goal of the open tournament is to "have fun playing golf, while raising awareness of accessibility issues concerning golfers with disabilities and/or mobility challenges."

The National Alliance for Accessible Golf (accessgolf.org) is an organization focused on the inclusion of people with disabilities into the game of golf. The Alliance is administered by a Board of Directors representing the major golf industry organizations in the United States. These organizations provide services for people with disabilities, and individuals and others who advocate for the inclusion of people with disabilities into society.

Kissimmee Bay Country Club should be commended for being at the forefront of this type of event. Kissimmee Bay Country Club's owner, Bill Stine, who is a former president of the Florida Golf Course Owners Association told us that Accessibility for mobility challenged golfers is considered 'business as usual' at Kissimmee Bay.

'Bridgeburg Golf, makers of 'The Turf Chopper' single rider golf cart, helped to raise awareness by sposoring the 2009 Florida Open for Golfers with Disabilities.

(Sitting on left) Port Orange resident and stroke survivor, Jim Sylvester was sponsored in the open tournament by The Golf Club at Cypress Head.

The Golf Club at Cypress Head sponsored a golfer in the 2009 open tournament.

The Golf Club at Cypress Head, an Arthur Hills designed municipal course in Port Orange, Florida, should also be commended for their part in sponsoring a golfer in the 2009 Florida Open Tournament for Golfers with Disabilities.

When asked about the company check that was used to pay the tournament's fifty-dollar entry fee, Jim Sylvester, (pictured above sitting with his wife and friends) a stroke victim and an avid golfer from Port Orange said "The folks that run the Golf Club at Cypress Head are very conscientious of mobility issues concerning seniors and golfers with disabilities. This was the fourth year in a row that they have sponsored a player in the open tournament.

The Golf Club at Cypress Head deserves special recognition for sponsoring a player in each of the four annual events.

"Addressing the needs of golfers with disabilities is more than just the right thing to do, it's good business."

Making an investment in golfers with disabilities is a hot new trend in the business world. According to the 2002 census bureau report, one in five U.S. residents has a disability. That's about 18% of the U.S. population or 51.2 million people. More and more people, such as inventors, designers and golf course owners, are making an effort to address the needs of golfers with disabilities. This tournament lets everyone have a lot of fun while raising awareness of those issues.

One innovative company that has helped to raise awareness of the issues concerning golfers that are mobility challenged, by sponsoring the 2009 all inclusive open tournament is Bridgeburg Golf. (www.bridgeburggolf.com)

The compassionate folks at Bridgeburg Golf are the makers of the 'Turf Chopper'; a new three wheeled single rider electric golf cart that weighs only 150 lbs. This new addition to the golf cart arena is compact, quiet, affordable and easy to operate. (See the full-page ad on the back cover.) Not by coincidence the name was chosen because its unique design resembles a three-wheel motorcycle "chopper". But that's where the comparison ends.

Billed as "a next generation golf cart," the Turf Chopper has revolutionized the single-rider concept that is beginning to reshape the industry, and priced at less than $2000, it offers a cart that's price-point is far below many current options available.

Weighing in at a mere 150 pounds without rider and clubs, the cart exerts less weight per square inch than conventional and other single rider carts and leaves no discernible footprint. This is a definite plus for greens-keepers and course maintenance.

Many Florida golf courses, like Kissimmee Bay Country Club, will now allow golfers with disabilities to ride these types of lightweight single rider carts onto the putting greens. For many mobility challenged golfers it is the only way they can get out and play golf.

The tournament director and the GM of Bridgeburg Golf, both rode Turf Chopper single rider golf carts in the 2009 open tournament and they performed flawlessly.

Born out of necessity, the Turf Chopper's inventor experienced debilitating back pain while playing his favorite game. He loved golf but said walking 18 holes was out of the question and riding in a conventional cart only made matters worse. Being determined and resourceful, he set out to build a cart that would adapt to his needs; after several attempts the prototype for the first Turf Chopper came to fruition.

In 2010 Bridgeburg Golf will once again be a sponsor of the Florida Open For Golfers With Disabilities and/or Mobility Challenges. They have commited to bring a dozen Turf Chopper' single rider golf carts for players to use during the tournament. The 5th annual open tournament will be played at PGA Village on August 28, 2010 at the prestigious PGA Club in Port St. Lucie, Florida.

'Bridgeburg Golf, makers of 'The Turf Chopper' single rider golf cart, and Titleist will be two of the sposors of the 2010 Florida Open for Golfers with Disabilities.

Virgil Price, a St Petersburg resident and Treasurer of the National Amputee Golf Association (NAGA), dominated the inaugural tournament in 2006, winning 1st Place overall, scoring a gross 72 on the challenging 18 holes at Kissimmee Bay.

Mike Hudson shot a 75 to win 1st place Overall in the 3rd Annual Florida Open Tournament for Golfers with Disabilities and/or Mobility Challenges held on 7/14/08. Born with only one hand, Mike Hudson is a Volunteer Golf Instructor in Pasco County.

Tampa resident, Monroe Berkman, a polio surviver, won the 2007 Florida Open Tournament for Golfers with Disabilties, playing every shot, including sandtraps from his SoloRider Adaptive Golfcar. Berkman, who shot 80 had no problems hitting out of the bunkers using his stand-up seat to support him during his full golf swing.

Stroke survivor, Ian Halliwel came all the way from England and shot a 74 to win 1st Place Low Gross in the 2009 Florida Open Tournament for Golfers with Disabilties and/ or Mobility Challenges. Now his name is also permenantly inscribed on the prestigous Open tournament trophy.

Bridgeburg Golf GM, Mike Mazza presented the open tournament trophy to the 2009 1st Place Winner, Ian Halliwell.

For some of the participants the annual golf tournament is a chance to look within and hopefully widen the scope of their abilities. For others it's more of an opportunity to look outside of their own selves and learn by focusing on the issues concerning their fellow golfers. Stroke survivor, and this year's 1st place winner, Ian Halliwell did a little of both.

Ian Halliwell who had initially lost the use of the left side of his body, due to a stroke, said that he was most positively influenced and encouraged to win by his playing partner in the tournament who was a Traumatic Brain Injury survivor. "I am humbled in his presence," said Halliwell of his playing partner, Charles Brugh. "I hope we remain good friends, in good health, and that I can be a little part of his continued remarkable story.

Meeting people like Charles (aka Brew) makes my campaign to raise stroke awareness all the more worthwhile. I hope that he his able to join up with me when I hit Florida on my Round the World Trip next year."

Halliwell who had come all the way from the U.K. to play in the tournament, shot the 'Low Gross' score of 74 to win 1st Place in the all inclusive, 2009 open tournament. Now his name is permanently inscribed on the prestigious open tournament trophy along with the three previous winners.

Ian Halliwell, has dedicated a large portion of his life to raising stroke awareness by telling others how his recovery was facilitated by golf. Ian also has spent a great deal of his time tirelessly fund-raising around the world for The Stroke Association. (www.stroke.org.uk) by organizing celebrity tournaments and by publishing a book entitled 'The Social Golfer'.

The Social Golfer started as a travel and golfing journal published to raise funds for The Stroke Association and grew to include the Social Golfer web-site and blog (thesocialgolfer.blogspot.com) where you can follow Ian's tireless fund-raising golf trips around the world.

Prior to his stroke in December 2006, at age 48, Ian was an avid golfer and had enjoyed many golfing trips to the Costas, Tenerife, Tunisia, and South Africa. Playing to a handicap of eight, he still harbored dreams of retiring and trying for his card on the Seniors Tour, but those dreams were dashed just days before Christmas of 2006 when he suffered a major stroke which caused total disability to the left side of his body, leaving him unable to speak or move.

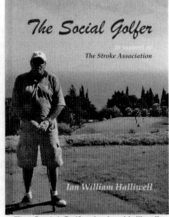

The Social Golfer, by Ian Halliwell

"I still have aches and pains," says Halliwell in his book. "My left side is still slow in relation to the rest of my body. My leg causes grief periodically. When asked by the doctor how I feel, I usually reply, 'Uncomfortable, not ill,' to which he often replies, 'We cannot do anything about discomfort, it comes with the territory.'

Later in his book Halliwell, who went from an 8 handicap before his stroke to a 17 handicap after his stroke said, "With golf, my swing is now much more secure without the rotating hips of my left side." He also states, "Golf is such a big part of my life and has been the catalyst for much of my recovery."

In regard to the stress of taking golf too seriously, Ian now says, "Since my stroke, my golf game has not worsened at all. Indeed, because of my medication, I presume, I no longer fret over four footers. I simply hit and if it goes in, that's great, if not, so what. My score is irrelevant. I now play the way the elders intended golf to be played. You start at A and end up at B and play wherever it rests in the meantime, with no drops, and no preferred lies. Seven is not a dirty number, taking seven is better than not playing at all.

I love playing and being in the company of good players - you cannot fail to admire their skill and technique. Mulligans," he goes on to say, "are a thing of the past. Every shot is important; you never know, it could be your last so enjoy it."

Halliwell's book details his amazing and inspirational recovery and return to the golf course after just over a year. The book also details how he is heeding Pro Golfer, Bernard Hunt's sage advice to "become the best damn social golfer on the planet".

"I know that there are many people out there who feel beaten by a stroke," says Halliwell in his book. "Progress can be so slow and frustrating that it often seems easier to just give up. Golf helped me focus on my recovery and I'm hoping that my journal will help others find their own motivator."

So far 'The Social Golfer' has raised over £20,000 for The Stroke Association, and has just been added to Amazon and WHSmith's on-line stock and all profits are being donated directly to The Stroke Association.

Around The World in 80 Days: 2010 a Golf Odyssey

As an experienced charity author, Ian will be following in the footsteps of the Jules Verne character Phileas Fogg in 2010 with an exciting announcement of his next major fund-raising event. Around The World in 80 Days: 2010 a Golf Odyssey is the latest plan by the golf enthusiast to raise money for charity.

Ian, who has already raised over £20,000 for The Stroke Association, plans to travel the world from January 2010 to March 2010 playing golf at some of the most illustrious golf courses in an attempt to continue raising much-needed funds for both The Stroke Association and The Multiple Sclerosis Society.

"Both The Stroke Association and The Multiple Sclerosis Society have been extremely helpful to myself and my family," stated Ian. "We received invaluable support from The Stroke Association following my stroke in December 2006, and want to help raise funds for The Multiple Sclerosis Society in recognition of my wife Karen's illness."

Ian's literary skills will again be in use as he intends to write a follow up to his recently published book, The Social Golfer, which will be documenting the trip but also rating the different golf courses he plays.

"I will be fortunate enough to play at courses such as the Ko Iau Golf Club in Haiwai and the legendary Pebble Beach and Cypress Point Golf course as well as competing in The Wrest Point Masters in Tasmania and The Edwin Watts Tour in Florida," said Ian. "And I would like to share my experiences with other people as well as following the Social Golfer format by rating each course, and of course, all proceeds raised will be donated to charity."

Excerpts from 'The Social Golfer' Blog
www.thesocialgolfer.blogspot.com

The Social Golfer is a travel and golf journal, website, and blog written by avid golfer and stroke survivor, Ian Halliwell, about his recovery and tireless fund-raising around the world for The Stroke Association. (www.stroke.org.uk)

Written Tuesday, 23 June 2009
THE 2009 FLORIDA OPEN FOR GOLFERS WITH DISABILITIES AND/OR MOBILITY CHALLENGES

Last year I was most fortunate to play in the 2008 event at the magnificent Kissimmee Bay Country Club. This event features golfers from all over the USA with a variety of handicaps that have amazingly not stopped them participating in – and more importantly – enjoying golf. They epitomize all I try to ensure the Social Golfer promotes: total enjoyment and social interaction through golf.

I was fortunate to be in a foursome with two winners: Mike Hudson, a low handicapper with just one arm, and Renee Russo a sprightly golfer with a prosthetic leg following an amputation when she was a young lady in her 20s. I met many golfers with significant physical handicaps; double amputees mixed with fellow stroke victims and heart attack patients. The event encompasses all that is good about golf and is the perfect remedy when I occasionally still feel sorry for myself.

Getting encouragement on the way around

So, it was with great pleasure and anticipation that I returned on Saturday for this year's competition. Last year the event had over 40 participants, sadly this years was less well supported, partly I think because of the oppressive heat wave we are currently enjoying. I guess even for these most-keen of golfers, 18-holes in 100 degree temperatures and intense humidity is not pleasurable. Still, the course was in pristine condition and all set for a magnificent day's golf. I was in a threesome with Tom, a retired American History teacher from The Villages, in North Florida. Naturally I asked him what history! Tom had sadly lost his leg over 40 years earlier in a freak accident (in the 8th grade) playing gridiron. A lifetime without a limb. Still it ensured I did not moan about my stiff left leg.

The true spirit of golf and how to overcome difficulties

Tom was very keen and competitive and an enjoyable companion during the round: he pushed me to deliver all the way. Our third member was a young man called Brew, who had been involved in an automobile accident 19 years-ago. He was still being treated and had obviously been in quite a bad way and had only recently taken up golf to supplement his ongoing recovery. He played the entire round and each shot with an enthusiasm I found spiritually fulfilling, I became his unofficial caddy, reading putts, recommending clubs and generally encouraging this remarkable young man.

It has been said life and a round of golf can be compared to an amusement park: each hole and each day are different but there to be enjoyed. Brew clearly had more than his share of ups and downs, and difficult times, but I have rarely completed a round feeling quite as content as I did this one and that was before the score. Brew now knows many English golfing terms including: hit it hard... find it... hit it hard again... whack it... cracker... give it a welly...

Because I was so relaxed and the course set up particularly lenient in view of the difficulties some players

would have (and bear in mind all the events I had played were off championship tees) suddenly playing off the front tees made the course so much easier. I shot 40 out and with the aid of two chip-ins on the back nine level par 35 for 75, to finish the winner by 6 shots. The main source of my success was the support given by both my partners and organizer Joe Stine who all constantly encouraged me during the round as they realized I was in contention.

I gave a gift of my book to all competitors and had a book signing after the cup presentation. The book was well received by all. Whilst unbelievably proud to become the 4th winner and first overseas champion, I will take from this day far more than a golf success. My sincerest hope is that on that day I encouraged Brew to continue his golf journey. I hope to keep in touch and anticipate the pleasure he will have if and when he breaks 100.

"Brew" (Charles Brugh)

Finally, I leave this trip with the story of the guy who inspired me most. I thought I had it difficult till I read this, and I offer it as encouragement to all individuals who suffer illness and disability, and to all of us who are feeling down because of the economic climate as a reality check as to what is important. From Brew:

"I'm unclear what I've told you previously about me and my injuries (I have declarative & procedural memory deficits). Your remarkable recovery from stroke is truly inspiring. I am amazed and impressed. I have already directed a stroke survivor's family to your web-site (the stroke survivor is still unable to communicate). Like you, the survivor was an avid golfer pre-stroke.

I always enjoy any activity in which I choose to participate. Having said that, I'd like to explain my additional motivations for avid participation in adaptive athletics in general, and specifically the great sport of golf (!) I am a severe Traumatic Brain Injury survivor. Due to diffuse axonal shearing, MOST structures in my complex neural network were greatly impaired. Resulting from a near-fatal automobile accident in March of 1990, I've used diverse adaptive athletics to recover from MASSIVE brain damage for almost two decades.

For the last 19+ years I've retaught myself to walk, talk, swallow, feed myself, bathe myself, read, write, THINK, I was legally blind for a period, I was paralyzed from the neck down at one point, the eclectic list is long and sordid. I have no doubt your experience with stroke produced similar challenges.

I'm rebuilding my once decimated brain, neuron by

neuron – synapse by synapse. I am doing so through copious independent study on numerous topics, and ardent participation in multiple diverse athletics. Rigorous engagement in adaptive sport promotes regrowth of neurons (neurogenesis) and rewiring (neuroplasticity) of my once decimated brain.

    Written in late 2007 as part of a successful grant request from the Challenged Athletes Foundation, the aforementioned document is as concise a summary as I can write about my journey pursuing excellence through adaptive sport.

    I attempted golf soon after I was released from the rehabilitation hospital. In '91-'92 the golf swing was far too complex for my damaged brain to comprehend, let alone execute! I have worked, hard, for the last 19+ years to rehabilitate so I may return to the great sport of golf.

    A multi-sport athlete, I could have chosen to apply for a number of 'tools' (sports equipment) to further my neurologic rehabilitation. I chose golf. Armed with a generous Challenged Athletes Foundation equipment grant, I selected, and was custom fit, for 2008 Ping G10's. As a survivor of severe brain trauma, the great game of golf is a pinnacle of mind/body integration. The Florida Open for Golfers with Disabilities, in which I had my #1 English caddy guiding and encouraging me, marked my official return to golf.

    I consider golf the equivalent of a graduate degree from a prestigious university for neurologic rehabilitation. Though an avid golfer pre-TBI, I know I'm a 'newbie' to golf and have much to relearn and perfect. I'm thrilled, after almost two decades of intense rehabilitation, to have finally begun my reintroduction to golf. I intend to go as far as I can through golf.

    As you can see in the aforementioned document, my experience with adaptive sport as therapeutic modality is extensive and diverse. The title sums up my use of adaptive sport to pursue rehabilitative excellence. Though I have much to relearn, I have (finally) reached a point where I may again pursue the great game of golf! 'The life we lead creates the brain we have'.

Charles Manning Brugh, ('Brew')

Charles Manning Brugh, AKA 'Brew'

Without incredible challenge, a person is unable to achieve incredible success. This I am sure you will all agree is a tremendous story and truly reflects what the human body and mind can achieve. My achievements pale into insignificance. I am humbled in his presence, I hope we remain good friends, in good health, and that I can be a little part of his continued remarkable story.

Meeting people like Charles (aka Brew) makes my campaign for stroke awareness all the more worthwhile. I hope that he his able to join up with me when I hit Florida on my Round the World Trip next year.

Ian Halliell, 'The Social Golfer' June 2009

Don't miss The 2010 Florida Open for Golfers with Disabilities and/or Mobility Challenges!

    The 2010 Florida Open for Golfers with Disabilities and/or Mobility Challenges is scheduled for August 28, 2010, with a shotgun start at 8am sharp. It will be held at PGA Village at the prestigious PGA Golf Club, located at 1916 Perfect Drive, Port St. Lucie, FL. 34986

    Representatives of the, Adaptive Golf Foundation of America (AGFA), the U.S. International Council on Disabilities (USICD), Eastern Amputee Golf Association (EAGA), National Amputee Golf Association (NAGA) and the National Alliance for Accessible Golf (NAAG), are scheduled to play in this all inclusive open tournament.

    So, if you would like to play golf, while helping to raise awareness for the accessibility issues concerning golfers with disabilities and/or mobility challenges, come and play in The 2010 Florida Open Tournament for Golfers with Disabilities and/or Mobility Challenges.

    For more info you can view the entry form on-line at: www.floridagolfmagazine.com/open or call Florida Golf Magazine at 863-227-2751.

Charles Brugh, aka "Brew" competed in the 2009 Florida Open Golf Tournament for Golfers with Disabilities and/or Mobility Challenges and very much inspired everyone he met, especially the tournament champion, Ian Halliwell.

Written in late 2007 as part of a successful grant request from the Challenged Athletes Foundation:

I, Charles Manning Brugh, am a survivor of a near-fatal automobile accident that left me with severe "permanent" brain damage. As a Traumatic Brain Injury survivor (comatose 2 weeks), I've been forced to rebuild my entire persona – mind, body, and soul. Of my own volition, by promoting and enhancing neurogenesis and neuroplasticity, I have determined how to affect the wholesale remapping and restructuring of my intricate neural network. I use diverse adaptive athletics and copious independent study to effect phenomenal neurologic regeneration. Essential to sustained rehabilitative success is physical, psychological, and cognitive fitness. Inherent multiple challenges of adaptive sport promote health and fitness in these critical attributes concurrently. Traumatic Brain Injury (TBI) continues to challenge in ways I never knew possible. I spend an inordinate amount of time, effort, blood, sweat, tears, pain, and money rehabilitating my cognitive, physical, and spiritual health. Am I "all better"? Far from it. However, I continually improve – with limitless potential.

Adaptive sport is phenomenal therapy. Substantially enhancing quality of life, the athletic challenges of adaptive sport are central to my determined efforts to prevail over near-fatal Traumatic Brain Injury (TBI). Extensive and diverse, my expansive personal experience with adaptive sport and purposeful outdoor endeavors span nearly two decades. Since my motor vehicle accident of 21 March 1990, my athletic/therapeutic repertoire includes:
Adaptive Golf – Adaptive Water Skiing/Knee boarding – Sailing; in 2004 I lived on a 100ft, hand-built, 3-masted, wooden tall-ship for 5 months anchored in the ports of Jonesport, Rockland, and (briefly) Cutler, Maine – Climbing walls (indoor & outdoor) – Multi-day bicycling tours – Sea-kayaking trips – White water rafting trips (multi-day) – Canoeing trips (multi-day) – Camping (throughout central and north Florida, Michigan, and the Colorado Rockies) – Horseback Riding – Adaptive Surfing – High & Low Ropes Courses – Fishing (fresh water and salt water) – Off-road Mountain Biking – Rock Climbing – Parasailing – Adaptive Alpine Skiing – Wheelchair Rugby (Brooks Bandits/United States Quad Rugby Association – Atlantic South Division) - Wheelchair Tennis (First Coast Tennis Foundation/Brooks Wheelchair Tennis League) – Competitive Handcycling – Adaptive Rowing (Jacksonville University/Brooks Adaptive Sport and Recreation Program)

Neurophysical skill needed to compete in adaptive sport is extensive, and, at times, overwhelming – particularly for a Traumatic Brain Injury survivor such as myself; timing, eye-hand coordination, balance, information processing, fine and gross-motor skills, communication, visual-spatial relations, attention, judgment, memory, perception, and reaction-time are all required cognitive abilities. With enough purposeful effort, repetition, and focused attention, cognitive and neuromuscular skills are reacquired and enhanced. I am rarely satisfied – constantly I raise the bar. I fondly refer to this as my 'achievement addiction'. While I never subject others to the same level of scrutiny, in any endeavour I hold myself to the highest of standards. I am my own worst critic. I am my own best critic.

I possess an aggressive spirit. I am also highly competitive. For the first 17 years, multiple physical and cognitive deficits necessitated competition primarily against myself in unrelenting efforts to rewire and reconstruct my being. For nearly two decades, I have used adaptive sport to promote and enhance neuroplasticity and neurogenesis in my traumatically injured brain. I have progressed to a point my rehabilitative focus again includes competition against other athletes. Competition brings out the best in me. Training, rehabilitation, and competition are complementary endeavors. For this reason, athletic training, practice, and competition are central to my continued rehabilitation. I now practice and compete with others challenged by disability – fantastic! Coupling self-directed neuroplasticity with the diverse cognitive and physical challenges of adaptive sport, I am overcoming severe, "permanent" brain damage to a degree few thought possible. I make remarkable progress applying my God-given intelligence, talents, and tenacious determination, to many adaptive sports. The life we lead creates the brain we have.

Charles M. Brugh

Trouble at Hilton Head – should I take a drop?

The Edwin Watts Amateur Golf Tour

One of the big disappointments I felt as I recovered from my stroke was that my long wished for dream to play on a golfing tour would never materialise. As my mentor, Bernard Hunt, sagely pointed out, this was never likely anyway, but the disappointment lingered a long time, despite the many competitions around the globe I had been fortunate enough to be invited to. In the summer of 2008, I came across an amateur tour based in and around Orlando which operated under the banner of the golfing mega store, Edwin Watts. Basically, my enquiries showed that the tour operated like our own football league. Golfers were split into five separate divisions (or flights as they are referred to in the States). These are championship, then A, B, C and D dependent on flight. You compete against your own peers on a regular basis, but successful golfers will be moved up in the same way as promotion in our leagues. You also get a *bona fide* USGA handicap too, regularly updated after every event.

I registered and played two events in 2008, at Falcons Fire and Victoria Hills, two exceptionally fine tracks as are all the event hosts I was to become aware of. I was made particularly welcome by Tour Director, Tom Mirus, and all the players. The events do make you feel like you are actually playing a tour event. I rejoined in 2009 and my intention was to compete in as many events as I could early in the season to

Team Orlando 2010 – we finished third out of more than twenty-five cities.

ensure I finished in the top ten of the flight which would result in an invitation to the National Final at Hilton Head Island in South Carolina.

Again, the tour took in some of the best courses in and around central Florida. Playing in D Flight, I finished third at Duran, second at Metro West and third at Stoneybrook West, but approaching the first major of the year at the magnificent southern Dunes, I was still not sure of a top ten place as this was likely to be my last ranking event of the year. At Dunes, I came from six shots down on day two to complete an unlikely comeback and win the event, secure my invitation to Hilton Head and win vouchers which enabled me to buy Matron a full set of clubs. This was some experience in itself as she was still undecided as to whether she was right- or left-handed. In the end, as she putted right-handed at Crazy Golf, we chose a right-handed set which still, some two years later, need christening. She does play golf in a totally appropriate way, sitting in the cart drinking wine and dropping her ball on the green to putt out, not for her any carries over water, bunkers etc.

My last event on tour was the two-man scramble played at my local course, Championsgate National where I was paired with big hitting, young Lonnie Loretta, son of US Senior Open Champion, Larry, a fine young man with an immense pedigree as well as drive. This event is always played on Father's Day weekend and Championsgate (that weekend being US Open weekend) was chocker, with no free tee times. Lonnie, travelling from the coast was late – he had not realised it was

Randy, Alberto and Champ James from the EW Tour.

a shotgun. Five minutes before the off, the starter advised me that a young lady would partner me if Lonnie didn't turn up so that I could be in the competition. As it was my last day, I was doubly disappointed until one Michelle Wie walked round the corner and said, 'If he doesn't turn up, can I join you?' Unfortunately, who blooming drove into the car park – his timing absolutely unreal. Michelle signed my card then headed off to the driving range and Lonnie couldn't understand my disappointment at his appearance. In fairness, his play was awesome, we took his drive on 17 out of 18 tee shots and I saw parts of the course I did not know existed. We won by two shots, a fine end to my season.

So I headed to Hilton Head in October, relatively confident, but I soon realised how difficult this would be. We played the Shipyard Course off the Tips and my 5 wood was bruised for days with all the approaches it had to complete. Penalty drops next to Gators did not help, and the Shipwreck wrecked the entire Orlando squad's chances. The next day, we all improved at the Fazio but I was less than impressed with my forty-seventh place. I had expected and hoped for a top thirty. The whole event was top notch. The location was sensational as a golfing resort. It made me determined to return and I will write about Hilton Head separately.

The guys at the Nationals.

I knew that a return in 2010 was unlikely because of my commitments. I was scheduled to play in just three events: the tour opener at Black Bear and the majors at Grand Pines and Mission Inn. I was placed in all three, runner-up twice and third in the first major at Grand Pines. The points gained in the majors secured me a seventh place and an invitation to Hilton Head again.

Staying in a purpose-built villa with flight champion, James Rearden, we had a fantastic week, but once again fell foul of the difficult challenge that the Fazio and Oyster Reef presented. I did finish in the top thirty (twenty-ninth) and top scored for

The superb Fazio signature 16th.

Orlando as we finished third in the team event, so some modicum of success. Clearly, I need to go up a notch or four if I am to succeed at this level. Once again, a fun-filled week, intense competition and many new friendships made.

As I write, I am unsure as to how many events I will play in 2011 as the Nationals unfortunately clash with the Barney Barnato and I want to return there soon. However, the USA Nationals remain a challenge unfulfilled and I will return to improve on my past two results and meet up again with some fantastic social golfers from all over the USA.

Hilton Head Island

A boot-shaped island of just over 34,000 residents plays host to over 2.5 million visitors a year, many down to tee off on the vast number of manicured lush courses. Hilton Head is a semi-tropical paradise of salt marshes, lagoons, sandy beaches, moss-draped oaks and magnolias. Conveniently located to enjoy the majesty of Savannah and the intimate smaller towns of Bluffton and Beaufort, the island is truly a social golfer's paradise. Whether it is wildlife and the beauty of nature, historic downtowns with quaint antique malls, eco tours or fishing, this island has it all. Add a dash of dynamic night life and fine restaurants, all at prices that appear significantly cheaper than mainstream America, it is no

wonder the island is so popular, particularly in the high season that runs from Memorial Day to Labor Day, the end of May to early September.

The island is shaped like a boot and split into several different areas based on the old plantations. The toe being the Sea Pines where Harbour Town is for golfers with its famous lighthouse and world-famous course that hosts the PGA event, the Verizon. The ball of the foot is the Palmetto Dunes Resort, where we stayed whilst playing the Etour National Finals. The heel is the Port Royal plantation with the Hilton Head plantation and Palmetto Hall, host of the Oyster Reef course, at the back of the boot. There are also smaller areas: Windmill is on the tongue, where the causeway joins the mainland or lowlands to the island; Shipyard and Wexford separate Sea Pines from Palmetto Dunes; Indigo Run and Long Cove straddle the creek that runs down the centre of the boot from the Lace End to the heel. Getting round is easy as a ring road effectively runs around the centre, off-shooting periodically onto the estates.

To the north of the island lies Beaufort, Bluffton to the west and Savannah, a must-see if you are in the vicinity, to the south.

The island is so stunning and natural that it is a place that Richard Attenborough would never tire of as it is a nature lover's wonderland. Besides a

Harbour Town marina.

plethora of charter sea-fishing available, kayaking and rafting is also particularly popular. You can meet the local Atlantic dolphins or maybe you are up to an alligator encounter (I was not), which locals tell me is highly recommended and can be found at the Sea Pines Resort. It is run by an experienced staff of naturalists and you are apparently aboard a safe, (so they say, but then they would, wouldn't they!) twenty-one foot electric boat. You will get to see from close proximity, the natural habitat of this exceptional creature of the wild. Bird watching, twitter trips abound, Bill Oddie would love this place.

You will notice the absence of street lighting that is because it is the natural habitat of the sea turtle which can be attracted by the lights and that is why after dark, there is little light anywhere in the resorts. Sunsets are spectacular from just about anywhere on the island. Restaurants, particularly fish ones, abound and I did not encounter a bad one on either trip. I can wholeheartedly recommend the Black Marlin at Palmetto Bay marina, Frankie Bones on main Street and Marleys at Sea Pines main gate. The best pubs I found were within a hundred yards of each other, Casey's American Sports Bar and the British Open pub, both on and near Highway 278 in Wexford. The British is a must for all golfers and UK visitors, particular those who, like me, are pining for English beer, Boddingtons or Strongbow cider, and good old-fashioned fish and chips.

In the first year, I stayed at the Palmetto Dunes Resort, a superb location, great rooms, fantastic restaurants and the great service you would expect from the Hilton Group. For a beach holiday, this stands comparison to any I have stayed at. The second year, James and I stayed in a villa. This would be ideal for a family or couple(s) looking for a cheaper option.

There's plenty of high-quality shopping and several gorgeous marinas. As I have said, as a social golfer's destination, it offers so much more than golf. I do intend to take Matron back and I could enjoy this place with or without the golf.

The Palmetto Dunes Resort, fantastic location, ideal beach resort on Hilton Head.

The mansions of Beaufort.

The location is convenient from both a golfing and travel perspective from the mainland and it would be a loss if the visitor simply stayed put on the island despite its many charms. With more than 300 years of history, Savannah is a visitor's dream. There are many great and different ways to experience the city. Whether it be a walking tour, (naturally not my favourite), carriage tour, trolley tour, water tour (not Matron's favourite) or a bus tour, you are sure to discover that the city is full of history, beautiful architecture and fascinating stories on every street corner. Its charm, beauty and history will be highlighted no matter which tour you choose, they all bring the past back to life.

You can take a tour of the movie sites, sit on the bench where Forest Gump told his box of chocolates story. It has been a location for over seventy-four movies. It also has a world-renowned culinary reputation and unsurprisingly, fine food abounds. Experience River Street fronting the river, where the old brick houses and warehouses dating back to the 1800s now house trendy shops and restaurants – it is the city's premier shopping destination.

Whilst not famous, Bluffton and Beaufort offer their own charm in a much quainter, intimate way and should not be overlooked. Indeed, Beaufort was voted by *Life Magazine* as the most romantic city on the east coast. To my UK readers, city is a loose term; it is no more than a rural town. Abundant art galleries mingle with antique shops and trendy boutiques on Bay Street. The calm waters of the Beaufort River offer a perfect vantage point for a tour of historic Beaufort and its environs. See the gigantic houses with gothic columns and expensive lawns rolling on the water's edge.

Bluffton is only ten minutes from Hilton Head and is a quaint, old town with a thriving art district and antique and craft centre. In October, there is always a major three-day art, craft and antiquities fayre which Matron, I know, would have thoroughly enjoyed. It has many nineteenth century historic antebellum homes to tour and many old churches which are superbly maintained. The farmers market every Thursday in summer is a big draw. With many food vendors, well-being seminars and demonstrations and live entertainment, located at the end of Wharf Street on the river – the setting gives it an enviable ambience that totally lends itself to this perfect small town.

There are many historic forts in the area relating to the key role they played, in particular during the Civil War. Fort Howell on the island on Beach City Road remains the most intact.

The area is also home to the Gullah culture pertaining to the Angolan slaves who were origin-ally brought here over 300 years ago. It is a particularly interesting and unique culture, now protected by state statute. Their descendants are called Geechee whose story is different in that when the Civil War ended and the slaves were freed, the plantation owners, who could not pay for their labour, sold their lands to their slaves and left. With no bridges

Historic Bluffton.

You are never far from aquatic leisure pastimes at Hilton Head.

and little contact with the outside world, these islanders made a living by simple fishing and farming. Isolation allowed the islanders to maintain their culture, heritage and language and today, from sweet grass baskets to local food to performing arts, the Gullah culture is an intricate part of everyday Hilton Head life. At Sea Pines, there is story-telling around a Gullah campfire. In June and July, there are Gullah food festivals with special singing festivals in the Gullah church.

Golf at Hilton Head and surrounding areas

Firstly, it should be said that if you are staying on Hilton Head with its multitude of splendid tracks, that within less than half-an-hour, particularly down the Bluffton Corridor, there are many more exceptional golf courses of similar character and quality to those on the island itself.

On the island there are over twenty courses so the golfer has so much choice.

The Hilton Head Island area is one of the nation's foremost golf meccas. Is it any wonder that *Golf Digest* readers named Hilton Head Island No. 10 on its list of the world's best golf resorts? With spectacular oceanfront courses, challenging riverside courses, courses that meander through the centuries-old maritime forests, courses beside vast tidal marshes or with Low country flare, sparkling lakes and lagoons, and courses designed by the PGA Tour's most noted players, Hilton Head Island is sure to provide you with a memorable golf vacation!
[www.hiltonheadgolf.com/hilton-head-golf-courses]

The ultimate resort to look for your preferred course on … as it says, a golf mecca.

Any golfer must make an effort to play the daddy of all the course – the Harbour Town Golf Links. Host of the Heritage PGA

The iconic, mega photographed 18th at the Links.

The Gary Player-designed Hilton Head National at Bluffton.

Event since 1969 and whose champions read like a who's who of the golfing good and great – from Arnie, the first victor, to Jim Furyk, the 2010 champion. Since 1969, the only major winners not to play in the Heritage are Ian Woosnam and Paul Lawrie, such is its legacy and popularity. Golf here does not come cheap, but then again the quality and the experience is worth it.

At the National Finals, I have had the opportunity to play the Fazio, Shipyard and Oyster Reef.

All were in majestic condition at the end of October, all were an exhilarating challenge and the green fees were well worth the money. From my observations and discussions with fellow golfers, this is indeed the norm you could expect from golf on the island. The golf is difficult, be under no illusion these are champion tracks with many tee box options.

Stunning golf awaits at Oyster Reef.

These houses are on the left of the green at 17. Famously, my Orlando mate, Dana Turgeon, hit them both twice with his tee shots on a practice round in 2010. Amazingly, he avoided the windows. I think it is the sign of a great player who can prove the first one was not a fluke. Even the effective Mr Reload was of no help this time.

From my observations, I believe the other best course on the island, and the next one I want to play, is the Golden Bear Course at Indigo Run. I understand that this is very much a course which uses water, bunkers and difficult greens as its defence but, at 7,000 plus yards, Jack Nicklaus's design seems to pack an all-round punch.

The Bluffton Corridor runs east from the Interstate 95 along US 278 to Hilton Head Bridge. Most visitors will use this corridor if travelling by car. There are ten outstanding golf courses open to the public here, all of which are of the same quality as on the island, but green fees tend to be significantly lower. There are also several nine-hole executive courses for that quick round.

Go to www.hiltonheadgolf.com for information on all courses.

Stunning rugged scenery at Royal Hobart.

The Wrest Point International Masters, Hobart, Tasmania

Sitting in the hospital in early 2007, as well as feeling sorry for myself after my stroke, I also lamented the fact that my sudden illness had caused me to miss out on a once in a lifetime trip down under to play in this prestigious event. As I recovered and got back to some normality, I set my stall on making up for this disappointment by ensuring I would be well enough to compete in 2008. (I wrote about this trip in the first *Social Golfer* book). Well, I was well enough to compete in 2008 but not significantly fit enough to do myself justice and participate as keenly as I had always imagined I would. I wrote then that I fully intended to return sometime in the future and it was always likely that I would make room for a return at the start of the round the world trip to attempt to put right my previous poor performance.

This event truly encapsulates all that a social golf event should. Classes split into age, gender and ability ensure you are competing against your peers. In 2008, at the age of 49, I was placed in the under 50s so arguably I was at the wrong end of my grouping. This time at the age of 51, in the 50s to 60s category, I would be one of the younger players, hopefully an advantage. Based at Wrest Point in the Hobart Festival Month of January, over 700 golfers, mainly from Australia and New Zealand, are joined by several international competitors and their spouses to enjoy the unique hospitality of this splendid island in beautiful summertime down under. The competition, four Stableford rounds at the Royal Hobart and Tasmania golf courses, is supplemented with two gala meals with sparkling entertainment and 19th hole offers every evening. The whole event, superbly organised and managed by Go Golfing Australia, run by Mr Peter McCartney, is now in its tenth year explaining the immense popularity of this event. Indeed, besides the golf, this whole event has a vibrant social scene which is synonymous with the event and why so many return year after year. It was great to see faces from the last two years, even better were all the comments made on how much fitter and better I looked, all I needed to do was transmit that out onto the golf course.

From the day one the 'meet and greet', Karen and I were made very welcome and our week here was certainly the perfect anecdote to any fears I had that my recovery was not now permanent.

Getting ready to rumble at Royal Hobart.

The splendid iconic Wrest Point Tower.

And so to the tournament … I am a firm believer that any golf competition is only as good as a combination of several important ingredients. Firstly, your fellow competitors, and here this has few peers, fostering a quite unbelievable camaraderie. Secondly, the courses, and this year once again Hobart and Tasmania were again in quite excellent condition. Finally the organisation and, without question, *Go Golfing* have few peers in this respect. Add fine weather and great socialising and the social golfer is in his element. In 2008, I simply never recovered from a day one mauling of just seventeen points, so it was with some trepidation I approached the first tee at Royal Hobart. But I played steadily, compiled thirty-two points to be tied third after day one, but a whopping seven behind the leader and runaway Tasmanian bandito, Peter McClennan. Day two was not as successful, possibly because of the extra-curricular activities the night before, and because of a nightmare start at the first at the slightly easier scoring on the day.

The first hole at Tasmania Golf Club is only a 310-yard all downhill, slight dogleg to the right. It is protected all the way down by a row of pine trees, separating it from the driving range. I am bold, in good form and go for the green with a slight fade to get round the corner of the dog leg. I overdo it and fly over the pines onto the range. I motion to reload, but I am advised that it's not out of bounds and I will be able to chip back onto the green. Great, that's a let off, except I play with a yellow ball and the range balls are all yellow too, so it was like searching for a needle in a haystack. One white ball later and no points atone for the easiest holes. Sadly I compounded this on the easiest stroke index 18, short par 3, hole 5, just a little flick which

Great guys but no-one wanted to talk cricket.

In the middle El Bandito, Peter.

I put into a bush and decided I was either Tiger Woods or Phil Mickleson at the Masters in 2012. Same result – nil points – just 28 for the day. In the end those would cost me second place.

Back again on day three, I certainly played my best of the week. Angry and now sober after yesterday's debacle, I compiled thirty-five points, third best on the day and back into the top ten. The 'Bandit' shot another forty, at this stage I have to say he can't half whack a ball and is fantastic company on the course. In 2008, Andy Flintoff's Ashes campaign had been a 5-0 disaster and I got absolutely ribbed silly. This year was payback time, but my antipodian chums were suddenly off cricket. On the way back from Tasmania, our coach droped some people off at the Bellerive Oval where the Aussies are thrashing Pakistan in the Test Series. As the coach pulled up and doors opened, there were several thousand Aussies queuing to get in. I couldn't resist shouting out 'Ricky, where's the Ashes?' Before I was lynched, the coach driver started back for Wrest Point and I was peppered with crisps and nuts from all around the coach. Happy days!

In the final round, I reverted back to day two form and carded a disappointing twenty-nine points for 124 over all, and a fifth place final position, a significant improvement. As it turned out, a par 3 at my last hole would have put me into second place, still twenty-four points adrift of 'Al Capone', so close, yet so far. This hole inflicted carnage on my foursome. Surrounded by bunkers, all four hit into a bunker and there was little sand left when we had finished. Indeed, my bogey after leaving one bunker for another was the only ball that found the green. Medal play and we could all still be there.

Not the success I had hoped for or anticipated but a massive improvement which, according to my many friends and Matron, truly reflected just how far I had come in the two years since my last visit and three years since my stroke. I am still in touch with many in Australia, particularly Paul and Steve, despite Steve being a Stoke City fan hailing originally from the Potteries.

2012 – I will be back fellas … providing England still have the Ashes!

Our hopes are bunkered.

Final night camaraderie, great guys, great event and I will return in 2012.

Terrific Tasmania

Karen and I returned to this tranquil, tantalising, ecological, stunning paradise and it has to be said had a devil of a time, if you will pardon the pun. An island about the size of Wales or Florida, with only half a million people (of which half are centred around the southern tip, in and around the state capital Hobart), it naturally remains pretty unspoilt. It is, of course, a hell of a long way from anywhere except mainland Australia and does have that end of the world feel about it. The journey was long, tedious and difficult, although it is well worth the trip because most visitors would be entranced by the natural beauty and historic significance of the place. For golfers, there are a plethora of fine courses. The journey from the UK would take over twenty-four hours flying time, making a stopover absolutely essential. This year, we chose Singapore before flying on to Melbourne to change for a final hop – another one-hour flight over Tasmania to Hobart. Australia truly is a big, big country; you get some idea how big when you consider that four hours after leaving from Singapore you fly over Australian Territory and yet it is still four hours from Melbourne. That's the same as flying from the UK to Tenerife.

Miles of unspoiled beaches, some of the best on the planet, historic monuments which date back over three centuries to the island's colonial past, ensure that the visitor has a myriad of tripping options open to them.

I wrote about Hobart in the first book so this trip I decided to see much more of this fantastic place, its extreme habitat and its historical character as well. Fortunately, most places can be easily accessed from Hobart which retains a prominent place in my affections as one of the greatest places to visit, particularly in January, the Summer Festival month.

The festival is a month-long extravaganza of sport, usually a Test series, tennis (the world's best

Rugged beauty, teeming with wildlife that is unique to this island.

The harbour at Hobart.

women were in town), music festivals, craft and art fairs; the place teems with activities and there is nowhere better than Salamanca Square for wining and dining.

The harbour, superbly located, remains the focal point of most activities in the city and adjacent to this is the uniquely titled Old Woolstore Aparthotel. No prizes for guessing what this multi-award-winning establishment was previously used for. It is particularly noted for its outstanding buffet breakfast. For a sea city, Hobart is also, and rightly so, regarded as a garden city. It is an ideal base from which to see the majority of the attractions in the south of the island, although any visitors should also tie in a trip to the north of the island, ideally using Launceston as a base for visiting the attractions on the north coast. Hobart to Launceston is about three hours by car. A breaktaking stay in Hobart and Launceston would allow the discerning tourist to virtually cover the entire island as well as all the best golf courses.

A visit to Port Arthur, an historic convict site, considered to be Tasmania's premier tourist attraction, is without doubt a must see. The packed parking lots for cars and buses certainly bear testimony to that and a swelling crowd at the visitor centre offered further proof. One could spend many hours, if not the entire day, here exploring the penal settlement that was only closed in 1877 and which once housed as many as 2,000 convicts, soldiers and civilian staff. Some of the buildings have obviously been ravaged by time, some gutted by fire; the wide-

Port Arthur.

ranging site has undergone significant restoration work which is ongoing under a government-backed conservation scheme.

It is hard not to be drawn into the era as this place oozes nostalgia. A novel quirk is that on arrival all visitors are given a playing card which equates to a particular convict and you can then trace his or her history and, in particular, the reason for his or her incarceration. The five of spades equates to one James Hall, a house breaker from Bermondsey, who was given fifteen years for stealing goods worth five shillings. Aged 19 when transported, this was effectively a life term as he could never afford the transport back to the UK if he survived his sentence. Sadly, James died of TB after just eight years down under. This does give reality to the visit that is particularly intriguing. There are guided forty-minute tours and a twenty-minute mini harbour cruise to the Point Peur boys' prison and the Isle of Dead Cemetery where I find Hall's grave. There is also a ghost tour for the not so faint-hearted.

Golfers should take the opportunity to play the Tasman Golf Club, not to be confused with the Tasmania Golf Club, outside Hobart. This 9-hole course is a tight, tree-lined course with punishing rough, but the main reason for playing it is the stunning views of the Great Southern Ocean and rugged Tasmanian Peninsula. Also, the Par 3, 136-yard 8th hole will live long in the memory, where you hit off a cliff, over a yawning chasm with a drop of over 200m to the ocean below, to a sausage-shaped green. It is remarkably similar to the 16th at Cypress Point, but as this is Tasmania, it is not as popular or widely known.

Russell Falls.

Continuing northwards through the unspoilt interior of the island towards Launceston, one can visit the tiny township of Bothwell and visit the Australian Golf museum and the famous Nant Distillery. Imagine the Scottish Islands without the snow and you have an idea of the topographical nature of the countryside and why so many wineries and distilleries flourished here. It is also home to the Ratho Golf Links, Australia's first golf course and the first in the entire southern hemisphere. Prominent Tasmanian golfer, Peter Toogood (what a great name for any sportsman) set up the museum in 1996 and, from humble beginnings and with considerable support from many Australian notables such as Norman, Baker Finch and Thomson, it has become a treasure trove of golfing memorabilia and history. Of course, as a golfing anorak, I loved this place. The museum is a must visit for golfing historians or anyone fascinated by the development of the game. There are a host of displays – covering clubs, balls, even clothing – which show the changes through the ages which are as revealing as they are riveting. The museum is open seven days a week, from 9 a.m. to 4 p.m.

The Nant Distillery was established in 1821 and guided tours are available every day except Sunday, from 10 a.m. to 4 p.m. The distillery was restored in 2005 to full working capacity and in 2010, the first batch of whisky was distilled – and very, velly, velly nice … HIC, HIC it is too. The production steps really are quite fascinating, from grinding the grain (in the newly-restored flour mill) to seeing the grist being placed into barrels for fermenting. It is a long, involved process before the final product can be poured, but it is amazing to think this process has not changed for 200 years.

Golfers must visit the Ratho Links, a unique 15-hole layout. Designed back in 1822 by the Reid family from Scotland, it remains as it was originally set up two centuries ago. This is how golf was played in the great days of the nineteenth century and how Tom Morris, Willie Park, Freddie Tait, John Ball would have played. Indeed, borrow some old mashies, nib licks and gutta balls to really get

The unique Ratho Links.

a feel for golf of yesteryear – amazing. The greens are square, so they can be easily fenced to keep the sheep off. It is a working farm and a local rule states a ball striking a sheep can be replayed without penalty. This island never fails to amaze.

Launceston and its surrounding areas have a quaint beauty, which, given its name, appropriately reminded me of the fishing villages of Cornwall. Colourful houses overlooking the ocean mingle with tea houses and local pubs where once again the local fare will make sure the visitor does not go hungry. As in Hobart, boat trips are a popular attraction and a good way of seeing the rugged coastline. Dependent on the time of year, dolphin trips and whale watching are possible. For the golfer, this area is particularly well served. Within easy reach is the Launceston club, Tasmania's oldest 18-hole club. Although nestling in the suburbs of the city, and I use that word loosely, the course has serenity because of its design and layout. Natural bush, backed by clusters of eucalyptus, black wood and wattle trees, intermingles with the many bunkers and occasional water hazards to make this a dangerous track if you're much off line. The signature hole is the 17th, a par 3 of over 170 yards which is played over a deep gully to a small, but well-bunkered green. The hole, the Spion Kop, was named after a Boer War battle, not designed by a Liverpool fan as I had originally thought.

From here, you can play the Country Club of Tasmania, just ten minutes from the city centre. A

modern, purpose-built country club in the American style of resort and course design. The course, designed by Peter Thomson, is a fine one and is exceptionally well-maintained. The resort has undercover driving-range facilities, tennis and squash courts, horse riding, a spa and an indoor pool, plenty of bars and restaurants as well as a casino. It is clearly popular with many Victorians who hop over from Melbourne by ferry.

Golfers who visit Launceston must

The Country Club of Tasmania.

The new Lost Farm course – a stand-out design .

play Barnbougle Dunes, possibly the finest course in the world built in this century. This rapidly developing site now has a sister course, the Lost Farm, thus making it an even better prospect for the discerning golfer. In the first book, I covered my original visit here and nothing has changed – this remains one of the world's greatest courses, now a fine resort and if possible, a must play for any golfer who has the opportunity.

As I have said, Tasmania is a long way from anywhere except mainland Australia, but if you love golf with a competitive edge, and travel, then head off there in January, play the Wrest Point Masters and stay on to enjoy this often mysterious, always enthralling and compelling historic island … and the golf ain't too shabby either!

Floridian Charity Events

Based in Orlando and, on the strength of my ongoing charitable commitments, I have been fortunate to have been invited to participate in, as well as sponsor, several golfing events here which are of particular interest to me. As these events are usually four-man Texas Scrambles, I have also met many great social golfers on my travels which is an added bonus to the golf. If you live in Orlando, the grand-daddy of golf in the town is Arnold Palmer and the chance to stay, play and meet the great man at Bay Hill was inevitably going to be something that I could not miss. The Formet Foundation (in honour of the deceased Orlando main circuit judge) is a charity based on helping sick youngsters and their families. I had donated several *Social Golfer* books and general social golfer promotional gifts, tee shirts, mugs, etc, together with general golfing memorabilia, to the auction and in April 2009 had the good fortune to play in this prestigious event.

Bay Hill is everything you read about and more. Luxurious, historic and a golfer's dream. We

The Formet Ladies.

stayed in a room overlooking the 9th green which, until I later visited Pebble Beach, was the closest I had been to a PGA Pro lifestyle. The course itself was good, but maybe I expected too much … four exceptional holes, fantastically maintained greens, but not the drop dead gorgeous that I had anticipated. Still, it was a memorable weekend. With the Cunninghams, we carded a sixty-three, but were well off the pace as can happen in scrambles. I holed a birdie putt on the excellent par 3 17th and my approach at the 18th, made famous by Tiger in subsequent Bay Hill invitational events, will long live in the

memory as will of course meeting the great man, '… hit it hard, find it, hit it hard again' was his advice to me and is now my trademark after dinner speech story.

My only success in Florida Scrambles came at the Toys for Tots at Mystic Dunes in the annual scramble, raising funds and Christmas toys for those less

With the Cunninghams on the 17th tee.

fortunate. With a guy I have become great friends with, Scott Ramey, we ate up the course that day courtesy, if I say so myself, of a red hot putter.

I particularly like supporting youth charities and I was proud to sponsor the Lakeland Youth for Christ event at the popular Bridgewater Golf Course. Sadly, again a score in the low sixties could not prevail but I unveiled my snazzy, now always worn, 'John Daly Loudmouth' attire and again had a memorable day.

Another great day was at my local course, Ridgewood Lakes, when I played in the US Marines Event. This was made particularly memorable because I was joined by my good friend from the UK, big John Roberts, host of the annual Tenerife

The guys at the Youth for Christ, sponsored by TSG.

Event. Again, it meant establishing new friendships like Fred Geier, but what really set this day off was the marching of the band and playing of the National Anthem and JR singing about Manchester United to the Marines' marching tune. No success, but great enjoyment had by all at a super venue.

Having just seen Europe defeat the USA to reclaim the Ryder Cup, takes me to my winning performance in the Cyder Cup, representing a European team against the USA team, at Celebration Golf Course. Run by the local Irish bar, the cup is an annual competition between US residents and European residents. Faced with an eighty-yard approach at the 18th to a green surrounded by thirty spectators and one down was a spine-chilling feeling, nailing it to six feet and then having to go for the match winning half was a sensational feeling, quite inexplicably so perhaps ... OK, Cyder not Ryder, but trust me, it really was the real thing to me.

The Cyder Cup.

Bridgewater Golf Course hole 6.

The Celebrity Circuit

I have been fortunate here in the UK to have been invited to play in many celebrity events where I have been able to use the Social Golf concept to support golfers with disabilities and involve them in the SG team at these prestigious events. In 2010, the Social Golfer team featuring fellow stroke victims, the Ledge, Steve Skitt, and Peg-leg Hurcombe (who, with his new artificial leg did the double of the Show Am title at Henley-on-Arden), my great mucker the legendary, Lothario (a great chef as seen on *Come Dine with Me)* at England footballer Frank Worthington's Annual Charity Do at the West Midlands Golf Course. Frank, who has had more clubs than allowed in his bag, is one of the great guys on the celebrity circuit and has long supported my event, so it took little persuasion to support his.

No matter what the competition, it is pointless entering if you have no intention of winning. I

have organised several tournaments in aid of the Stroke Association, ably supported by many of the Celebrity Golf Tour, and, with fellow Lancastrian, Steve Parry, was fortunate to win the Northern PGA MRC Pro Am at Carden Park. This was not due to me, but Steve carded sixty-eight to win the £5,000

I show Frank how to putt and dress.

Peg-leg, Skitty and the Ledge.

Joys of winning.   *The girls enjoy the victory as well.*

event 1st Prize, although I could claim that my birdie at the 16th was the team-winning effort as we clinched a one putt victory.

In 2010, I also ran my own Social Golfer Open down at Hever Castle in Kent, in conjunction with the Social Golfer interactive web site, www.thesocialgolfer.com. We attracted over fifty golfers, sadly I could not do a Tiger and finished fifth, but again a great day during which money was raised and some humour as I tried to organise it without Skitty, presenting the prize to the runner-up having lost the winner's scorecard.

My visits to Tenerife have become particularly poignant for me. It was my last big trip before my stroke in 2006 and so, when I returned in 2008, it marked a big stepping stone in my recovery. My mate, big John Roberts, had always invited about twenty golfers from Lancashire but in 2008, he merged his competition into one run by the local hostelry in Golf De Sur, the Wild Geese – call in,

Above right: Teeing off in my own event … proud day.

Above right: Here's one you could have won – runner-up, Tom Hurcombe (Roger's son) being wrongly presented with the trophy.

Right: The winner, Andrew Siggs.

Memorable day at Golf De Sur with George, Paul and Stan … first title since my stroke.

Since the wins in 2009 and 2010, I have not enjoyed the same success but using the social golfer connections, have become a supporter and sponsor to the event. Great people, a fabulous charity and a worthy cause which I am proud to be associated with.

you are sure to receive a warm welcome. This event would be day one of the JR Classic and would involve over a hundred golfers individually and in teams of four participating to support the local children's charity for disadvantaged and disabled children. In 2008, I had a remarkable day, buoyed up by the reception I received. I was quite outstanding, shooting seventy-nine, and cleaning up the individual title whilst leading my team to success.

Whilst individual success is extremely satisfying, winning with friends and enjoying their camaraderie is what social golf is really all about. Having fun whilst participating, then finding out you have been successful, is a quite exhilarating culmination to any event. I have been most fortunate in that regard.

Above: Dave Ward fails to reach the ladies' tee and pays the penalty.

Right: Another victory speech, Dave has his trousers back on.

The G Tour 'Race to Cyprus, 2011'

I had been searching for an amateur tour similar to those in the States, more so after my local club, Standish Court (now known as Standish), went belly up for the second time in twelve months. I

happened upon this superb Stableford event consisting of twelve individual competitions at mainly prestigious De Vere resorts from the website www.gtour.co.uk. Over 180 players participated which was some achievement for the organisers. From these, the three best individual scores formulated into an order of merit. I played four events, never out of the top fifteen, including a fifth place at Oulton Hall and second place at Mottram Hall. These results catapulted me to fourth position in the overall order of merit and winner of the Birdie Order of Merit for golfers with handicaps of plus fifteen. It was with some confidence that I headed to Belton Woods in November for the top fifty finals, the top ten to head off to Cyprus for the grand final. Belton had happy memories for me as I had won Bunkerfest II there in May and won a superb remote control Stewart trolley. Sadly, despite returning

Left: Realising I have won.
Above: Son, Paul, and fine guy, Robbie Earl.
Right: Being presented with my trolley.

from Florida in great form, this mid-November date resulted in the course being a buggy-free zone due to the weather which in truth was not too bad. It was disappointing because carrying my bag left me extremely tired and in no position to really challenge and I trailed in seventeenth. I had phoned to check buggies were on and taken my match bag, not my lightweight portable, which taught me to always have a lighter-weight bag in the boot. Still, I have to say this did not really dampen my year on tour, I made many new friends, particularly Steve Howarth and John Moore, who both qualified for Cyprus. Colin, Simon, Darren, *et al* are to be congratulated on the way they organised this tour. If you are keen on competitive golf, this is the place for you.

The SDGP Scottish Open and the World Team Cup

I had been invited by my good friends, Roger Hurcombe and Tony Lloyd, to represent England against Scotland, Wales, Ireland and a Rest of the World team in Glasgow. Prior to the event, I was asked to play in the Scottish Disability Golf Partnership's Scottish Open. Staying at the magnificent Westerwood Resort just outside Cumbernauld, it brought home to me again how many fine places there are that I had never heard of. I had donated a copy of the original *Social Golfer* book to all the competitors and was delighted with the response I received.

So, in early July, I ventured north of the border to north Glasgow to play in the SDGP Open and then represent Team England in the Disabilities World Cup … eight days of constant golf helped by superb, rather unseasonable Scottish weather where for the whole time it was shorts and tee shirts all the way, apart from one day when tee times were put back an hour.

The SDGP Open was played at the splendid Dullator Carrickstone course. An impressive thirty-six hole club in pristine condition, befitting this prestigious competition. The parkland course features two distinct loops on the new course, the first eight holes featuring blind holes, long carries, undulating greens and particularly punishing rough, where scoring for all in the Stableford format was particularly difficult. The opening hole, a difficult par 3, really sets the tone but the par 3 on the fifth – 170 yards of carry wreaked havoc on all three days, with five balls lost and just one point scored – I hated that hole. The back nine, the older-established course was a far more enticing prospect, with wider fairways, more bailouts, flatter greens and this is where everyone seemed to prosper. On days one and two, the back nines (over twenty points) gave me a three-shot lead going into the final round. Sadly, playing first out, I probably concentrated on keeping young Adrian Canny at bay rather than compiling a winning score but, in my defence, I had some bad news overnight from back home with the bereavement of a friend, so my mind was not totally on the job in hand. It was fair to say however, with scores of thirty-five and thirty-seven in rounds two, Colin Brock's thirty-nine made him the deserved winner and the runner up was Andy MacDonald, also with thirty-nine, both worthy scores which even at my best

Third place at the SDGP Scottish Championship.

would have proved difficult to match. Third place and a lovely crystal trophy for my debut on this tour was fair reward and I was well pleased with my form going into the World Cup.

We then moved down the road to the splendid Westerwood Resort for a four-day Ryder Cup format. I offered to be paired with Team England's totally blind golfer, Peter Hodgkinson, and, together with his wife and guide, Margaret, we formed an unlikely undefeated partnership of two wins and a half which helped propel England to fifteen from eighteen points and a healthy lead going into the twelve-match singles. Playing with Peter was a wonderful experience. On day one, by some strange chance, we were first off in a greensomes, where you both drive and then choose one play alternate. Peter was extremely nervous and so was I, but I had one of those moments when we won the toss and I said we would go first. Even Roger was surprised and, in front of a large gallery, I told Peter that we were about to make a statement of intent and I absolutely leathered my drive 240 yards to the marker at the dog-leg first. I had told Peter I would leave him to it, that lasted all of one hole, when I realised he had two great attributes, he could always be relied on to hit his 6 iron straight and over 100 yards and he was very reliable and confident on the greens. The guy was superb and when a point was needed on the last day, he delivered. I will never forget his and Margaret's joyful faces as they left the 18th and climbed the clubhouse stairs to the rapturous cheers of all the competitors. The Scots gave us an almighty scare on the last day, but Peter and I secured

*With the World Cup
(rear Peter Hodgkinson).*

the two victories at the end to both remain unbeaten and, surprisingly, we had been an integral part of Team England's world success. It was particularly memorable because of the magnificent hosting of the event by the SDGP and the camaraderie of the teams.

Team England.

Venice.

2. Travel Broadens the Mind

After starting the long journey to recovery after two major illnesses, I have given myself small goals and targets to assist in the ongoing recuperation. I also believe that anyone faced with life-threatening conditions will inevitably make resolutions that you think will be easy to keep as you regain your health. Prior to my brain tumour operation in 1996, I had six months in which to prepare and get myself very fit to get through ten hours of surgery. I promised myself that I would keep up the training regime but sadly this did not last. I also promised myself that my financial affairs would be up-to-date and easy for Karen to cope with in the eventuality of any problems (this was to became a major problem for Karen when I had my stroke in 2006). The other resolution I made, and the only one I kept, was that the world is a big, fine, wondrous place and that there were many places I needed to see and visit before my time on planet earth was over. My second illness made all three resolutions more significant and, this time, I was able to keep them. I am still not as fit as I ought to be, but I am getting there. I am more financially organised and I have been round the world, yet there remains so much more I wish to see and enjoy. Whilst many of my travels are inevitably golf orientated, Karen and I have visited many places where my clubs did not tag along. Naturally, for research purposes I always examined the golfing potential, but mainly these visits were for social enjoyment and that is what I hope this section of the book will accurately portray.

Since my stroke in particular, travel has become increasingly difficult, although an important part of my life – simply getting through an airport is so much more stressful for me. My mobility has been a constant issue, yet with Karen's unstinting support and, more importantly, an understanding of my problems and difficulties, we have seen places we previously had only dreamed of or read about. We have images locked in our heads that hopefully will stay forever, whether it be an historic site such as Chichen Itza, or a modern wonder such as the Sydney Opera House. There is little to compare with that first thrill when you realise that you are actually following in the footsteps of history and are standing on perhaps the point where Cæsar was murdered or the pleasure gained from knowing you may be sitting on the actual steps at Alcatraz where Al Capone would have sat during his incarceration. You may be looking at Sydney Harbour Bridge or the Golden Gate for the first time and this gives an unbelievable warm glow. Visiting the fountains at the Bellagio in Vegas, the USS *Arizona* Memorial in Hawaii, Ground Zero in Manhattan or simply tobogganing down from Monte in Madeira are all tummy-tingling moments that I will take with me to my grave. Travel has given me some of my most treasured memories. It gives us such an understanding far beyond the confines of our own existence and experiences. Nearly losing one's life twice has simply increased the desire to encapsulate as many memories as I can of this spectacular planet and its differing cultures.

Madeira

Nineteenth-century poet, Coleridge, wrote in 1825, 'I should think the situation of Madeira the most enviable on the whole earth. It ensures almost every European comfort together with almost every tropical luxury.'

If your idea of a holiday paradise is lying on a sunbed by a pool, then Madeira 'the Island of Flowers' would be wasted on you. However, if you appreciate breathtaking, unspoilt natural beauty, coupled with lots to see and do, fine wine bars and restaurants, then you simply must put Madeira on your list of places to visit. Often referred to as the floating garden of the Atlantic, this Portuguese island is situated 378 miles off the coast of Morocco, and enjoys a fabulous year-long climate with temperatures averaging between 18 and 24 degrees.

Madeira is a fascinating blend of contrasting and unlikely ingredients, a destination that will no doubt remind you of other far flung destinations, yet at all times remaining unique. The steep terraced hillsides with their flourishing banana crops may put you more in mind of Bali or St Lucia. English roses and perennials grow in profusion alongside Asian orchids, giving a kaleidoscopic colourful setting. The island's fragrant eucalyptus woods recall Australia, whilst the gorse-covered moorlands of the central plateau could be anywhere in the Scottish islands. Nature's profusion is all the more enjoyable when accompanied by the civilised comforts that this modern destination now affords with many 5-star hotels and excellent food and wine available. Madeira, blessed with all this, really is such a delightful and satisfying holiday destination.

The flight into the airport sets the scene of the holiday with a thrilling, heart-stopping landing on a runway that is perched on stilts, precariously hanging over the cliffs falling down into the Atlantic Ocean. Indeed, if it's too windy, flights are often transferred to the nearby smaller sister island of Porto Santo and then you are ferried back to the main island, a sensational and different way to start any vacation.

Funchal Airport.

Most hotels are based around the fascinating, enchanting capital of Funchal in the south of the island. It is an enthralling small city with an extremely relaxed cosmopolitan feel. Tourists mingle easily with the very friendly, welcoming residents and unlike most capital cities, the crime rate in Funchal is almost zero. There is a wide range and variety of cuisine available here, with hundreds of restaurants, taverns and bars offering *al fresco* dining from many types of cultures, though thankfully it's not the type of place where you could get a full-English breakfast every ten yards.

The locals love to eat out and there are a vast number of high-quality restaurants to choose from. There is, so the locals say, a local speciality dish for every day and you can believe it. Visitors to the island constantly compliment the quality of the local cuisine, and there are many local dishes on offer

Funchal city centre.

to preserve the local heritage and satisfy the curiosity of its visitors. However, international food is also easily available and the British influence is still a part of Madeiran life – one can have a local *pastel de nata* (custard tart) or a scone with jam and cream!

Madeiran food is akin to Portuguese food. There are plenty of seafood and fish dishes – tuna, clams, swordfish, oysters, mussels and cod. Typical Madeiran specialities include, *bolo do caco* which is locally-baked bread which is scrumptious when served hot with parsley and garlic butter. Another favourite is *sopa de tomate e cebola* which is tomato and onion soup. A fish speciality is the *espada* or black scabbard, unique to Madeira and particularly delicious, whichever way it is cooked.

There are several excellent restaurants in Funchal and many others scattered all over the rest of the island as well. Fish dishes such as *escabeche tuna*, tuna steak and scabbard fillet and meat dishes such marinated meat and the traditional *espetada* (beef seasoned with spices, garlic and laurel leaves, then cut into cubes and grilled on an open fire), served with the usual fried corn and delicious *bolo do caco* bread are must haves for visitors to Madeira. Discos and wild night-life it is not, but for high quality *haute cuisine*, Funchal certainly is memorable.

A fabulous day out is a trip up to Monte, the mountain which overlooks the capital. You may take the cable car up to take in the

Tropical gardens at Monte.

Toboggan ride, Monte.

fabulous, spectacular views, then maybe visit the colourful, yet idyllic tropical gardens and palace located at the mountain top or visit the ancient church of Nossa Senhora. However, your return journey has to be on the ancient transportation method of tobogganing down the mountain, which dates back to the 1850s as you slide at speed through the narrow winding streets on a wooden sledge pushed and steered by two locals dressed all in white with their trademark white straw hats. Ernest Hemmingway, not a man known for expressing strong emotions, described the ride as one of the most exhilarating experiences of his life. Although it has to be said that the speeds the toboggans now reach are considerably lower than they used to be as the cobble roads are being replaced by tarmac. The longer ride (far better value and views) will cost about twenty euros per person and tips are expected, as is the souvenir photo you will certainly be hounded to buy. Most visitors consider this the essential Madeiran experience.

The vibrant market in the centre of Funchal is well worth a visit to gauge the feel of the place and, as you make your way round, the stallholders are sure to offer you their tasty wares. You will probably never have realised that fruit could taste that good. Not surprisingly, the Botanical Gardens are some of the finest on

Above & left: Funchal market.

the planet. In July, Funchal comes alive with vintage-car rallies, jazz festivals and live music and dance. Whilst the whole of Madeira is really one vast botanical garden, where plants grow in the most extraordinary profusion thanks to the combination of fertile volcanic soils, sunshine, regular rainfall and high humidity. If you are at all interested in plants, then the Jardin Botanico really is a must visit. Even if you are not a plant buff, you will certainly enjoy the magnificent setting and views.

There's plenty to see outside Funchal, the bus routes and services are excellent and very cheap, car hire if you are experienced in foreign driving is the best way to get around, however coach tours are particularly good value. Most trips will take you through the lush, mountainous interior to the north of the island that boasts some stunning, sensationally rugged coastlines and is the wettest part of the island – you actually drive under gushing waterfalls. The flowers on this part of the isle are stunningly beautiful, many unique to Madeira. Gardens are amass with colour virtually the year round. Located at the junction of the island's spectacular north coast road and the main road south is a small charming town of Sao Vincente. About one kilometre out of town are the Grutas de Sao Vincente (the caves of Sao Vicente) where you can trace the island's volcanic history and walk through

a series of lava tubes measuring about 1,000 kms. They are a visual delight with dramatic rock pools, streams and *café au lait* coloured walls, they are one of Madeira's most popular and natural wonders.

The island is a mecca for walkers and hikers who particularly love the island's 2,500 kms long irrigation system. The *levadas* are small, man-made canals which transfer water from the north and the interior to the country's capital and drier south. Walking the *levadas* and, along the way, visiting the gardens, observing its wealth of folk traditions and customs and meeting its hospitable and easy-going people, will provide a complete change of scene and pace of life for most visitors,

Grutas de Sao Vincente.

yet most are certain to leave feeling both inspired and relaxed. The native forest area of the Laurissilva is particularly stunning, whilst the views from the Nuns Valley, a small village nestling between two almost perpendicular mountains in the heart of the island, will leave you breathless.

To cater for the family market, the island has developed a new aqua park at Santa Cruz, just 30 minutes by bus from the capital. The Madeira Theme Park at Santana is really only suitable for under 11s, but there are dolphin trips as well as turtle and whale outings available from Funchal harbour which are sure to appeal to teenagers. Madeira does however remain an island targetted at the mature, more discerning holidaymaker. Either by accident or design, this clearly works for Madeira.

A day trip to the flatter more arid beach island of Porto Santo is a perfect way to end your trip to this majestic island.

Terracing on the precipitous volcanic peaks of Madeira.

Porto Santo.

Finally, as a golfer, it would be remiss of me not to mention that the island hosts several outstanding, great-value golf experiences in the typical Portuguese tradition of quality courses. Palheirro Golf, just 10 kms east of Funchal, is a magnificent cliff-top course with views back over the city and the bay. The Santo de Serra, a 27-hole championship course, regularly hosts the Madeirian Open on the European tour and offers any golfer a challenging day. On Porto Santo, Seve designed two courses which are as good as any on the Mediterranean mainland.

In 1921, the then ultimate discerning guide for travellers, *The Travellers Gazette* described Madeira as 'this flower-bedecked isle under Ionian skies' – nothing much has changed.

Santo de Serra.

Barcelona

In April 2008, just sixteen months after my stroke, I turned fifty and Matron arranged, all by herself, a long weekend break away in the Catalan capital, Barcelona. This was a first for her, I had arranged all our holidays pre and post stroke. She did a marvellous job from the choice of hotel, right on Las Ramblas, to hiding the fact that our mates, Ledge and Echo, would join us without me knowing. She had hidden my golf clubs sadly, so I did not get the opportunity to play the highly rated PGA Catalunya but that just means I will visit again in the future.

We arrived in Barcelona in the early evening and checked in at the Hotel 18 which is right at the top of Las Ramblas. This new, modern, boutique hotel was fabulous, its location could not be improved and its roof-top bar, pool and patio offered unrivalled views of the city. Well done, Matron! Since Barcelona is a city where everyone stays up late, we had time to enjoy a drink in a sidewalk café and a short walk around La Ramblas before turning in.

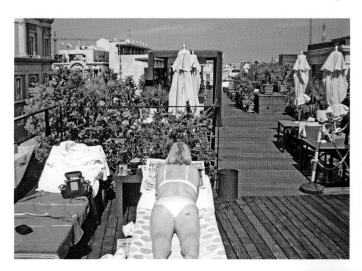

The beautiful rooftop patio.

The next day was St George's Day and Las Ramblas came alive. This festival is very popular in Barcelona. It is the second most important national feast in Catalonia, where the day is known in Catalan as *La Diada de Sant Jordi* and it is traditional to give a rose and a book to a loved one. Flower stalls, book stalls and street entertainers – it was a wonderful sight. The date of 23 April was not only famous because of the legend of St George, but also because it is the anniversary of the death of two great writers: Cervantes (of Don Quixote fame) and Shakespeare.

These great writers have passed into history for their great works, becoming important symbols in their respective countries. One way of acknowledging the work of these geniuses was to call this date the Book Day which is how it came about. On 23 April, books are sold in the streets on long stalls prepared specially for the grand occasion.

St George's Day entertainment.

Many people take advantage of this day, even though they may not normally be regular readers, to buy and enjoy a book. It is one way of encouraging people to read. This is also a popular date to launch new novels onto the market and many authors take advantage of this to promote their new book, indeed it is something I may consider one day. The town was particularly busy as the Champions League semi-final first leg between Manchester United and Barcelona was taking place, United winning 1-0, much to the chagrin of the locals. It was also the Formula 1 weekend and a Tennis Masters event. Our hotel had many sporting stars and me this week – I didn't feel out of place at all, neither did Matron as she hadn't a clue who anyone was.

The next day was my birthday and I thought Matron had lost the plot as she was on the phone constantly, saying she was talking to the kids. We seemed lost in Barcelona, walking aimlessly around. Little did I know, the Skitts were in town and they were trying to meet up. After a while, we entered

My birthday singers.

a café bar and had a little snack. As I am sitting there, two local musicians came to our table and thinking they want paying, I shooed them away.

Then I realised they were playing *Happy Birthday* and, standing behind them, were Ledge and Echo. I still did not grasp what was happening and I said to Matron, 'They are crap, don't give them any money.' 'Tight sod,' said Ledge which was when I realised they were there. 'What you doing here,' I ask stupidly. It's funny because for the previous couple of months, Steve and I had been at loggerheads at work and quite frankly had several major disagreements and many unpleasant arguments. Still, true friends are hard to find, and despite this, our two buddies had made every effort to get over to celebrate my birthday. I was totally shocked, bemused but very grateful that they had joined us and we had a great time. The thing about Echo, she always researches where you visit, so we had a walking tourist guide with us, plus she takes copious photos of absolutely anything … so we would have many reminders of this trip. She also knew all about the bus trips around the city.

She informed us that one of the easiest ways to tour any city for the first time was to go on a hop-on, hop-off bus. In Barcelona, it is called the *Bus Turistic*, and it has two main routes, red and blue. We were able to buy *Bus Turistic* tickets at the hotel. It cost us four euros at the hotel to buy a bus package, but we then saved six euros on our bus tour at the bus stop, twenty-one euros without the hotel package and fifteen euros with. Every little euro helps.

We got good seats on the double-decker bus before 10 a.m., sitting upstairs in the open air and we rode the whole red route (almost two hours) without stopping. We got off at Casa Batllo, one of the architect Gaudi-designed houses that is a UNESCO world heritage site. Before touring the home, we had a snack at a sidewalk tapas bar / café and listened to an excellent street entertainer from West Africa who was singing 'easy listening music'. I love the atmosphere of a cosmopolitan city like Barcelona! After our snack, we walked across the street to the Gaudi-designed home which was built for the Batllo family in the early 1900s, and had an enjoyable tour (with headphones). The fee was expensive (13.5 euros with our bus discount), but it was fascinating to see this amazing example of Gaudi's work. There

Top right: Gaudi's unfinished catherdral.

Right: Beautiful Barcelona.

Below left: Street artists on Las Ramblas.

Below right: My 50th birthday portrait.

More Las Ramblas entertainment.

Human statues, La Ramblas.   *The quay at Barcelona.*

was not a straight wall in the place and the windows, walls, and ceiling were all whimsical and interesting.

After touring the Casa Batllo, we rode the red route bus to La Sagrade Famillia, Gaudi's famous unfinished church. They have been working on this masterpiece for over a hundred years, and it may be another twenty-five before it is finished since they are only using donations. It is definitely a 'must see' in Barcelona.

We hopped back on the red bus and rode around to where it met up with the blue route. We then headed down Las Ramblas where I had a painting done which looks absolutely nothing like me. Ledge and I 'tap up' and the girls get serenaded and we spent late afternoon on the quay and beach. A beautiful city with a beach – just can't beat it!

All that was missing was golf, and I knew I would want to come back and play the PGA which was about one hour out of the city. This home of the PGA qualifying school has two courses that are now considered some of the best in Europe. The Stadium course is a spectacular and imposing course that has been consistently ranked among the ten best in Europe since it was opened and was recently voted #88 in the world, #3 in continental Europe and #2 in Spain. As the venue for numerous PGA

events, it is also routinely singled out for praise from the professional playing fraternity. Be warned however, the beauty of the course can distract from the many dangers waiting to do serious damage to your scorecard. It makes no concessions with its trees pressing onto fairways, strategically placed bunkers and the lakes that come into play on no fewer than seven of the toughest holes. This is why players return time and again to test themselves. It is rare to find so many memorable holes on one course and, despite the many ups and downs, tees are elevated and very few fairways are uphill. The stunning dogleg of hole 6 is one of them and it demands nothing less than a driver and total commitment.

For a slightly less difficult challenge, go to the equally beautiful, but kinder, Tour course. Dominated by pine trees and lakes, the course is shorter and a little less difficult to play than the Stadium course, yet the Ángel Gallardo and Neil Coles design ensures that it remains a

challenge for players of every level. Most of the holes feature wide fairways and strategically placed bunkers, which can be forgiving of a less than perfect shot. Another feature sure to focus the mind is that it seems you are never far from a water hazard.

Barcelona is truly one of the great cities of the world. Its animated citizens, its eccentric architects, the collages of mosaics really do give this city a truly unique flavor. It has to be the ideal short vacation, less than two hours flight time from the UK.

Venice

Due to my stroke the previous Christmas, I had been unable to take Karen anywhere for her fiftieth birthday. We did manage quite a nice little break in Cornwall but after my fiftieth in Barcelona, I was acutely aware that I had not reciprocated equally and by her birthday in 2009, I had started to feel significantly better and arranged a mini-break to Venice. Now if there is a more beautiful, romantic, gorgeous destination on the planet, I need to know, because in my opinion, this picture postcard iconic city, trumps even Rome and Paris for elegance, class, charisma and charm.

When you arrive at the airport and have to travel to your hotel, this will involve water travel. The local water buses are plentiful and relatively cheap, but to impress I opted for a personal water taxi. It was a fine way to travel, with a running commentary of the many noteworthy sites, but at ninety euros as compared to ten euros, I am not sure it was worth it. We were staying on the Lido on the south Lagoon. The reason, quite simply, was that it has the only beaches in Venice and more importantly, the only golf course. A no brainer then, really. This uniquely romantic city has been built entirely on water and has managed to survive into the twenty-first century without the use of cars. Narrow alleyways and canals meander between sumptuous palaces and magnificent churches, colourful markets and quiet idyllic backwaters, often unchanged in centuries. It truly offers an awesome line-up of sights for visitors and for first timers, it can be slightly mesmeric.

St Mark's Basilica.

Views come with a cost and some service.

It was a Venetian called John Cabot who, in the pay of Henry VII, believed he had found the northeast coast of Asia when he landed in Newfoundland and claimed it for England, effectively establishing the first American colony. Other famous Venetians include Marco Polo, Vivaldi and the legendary Casanova. Truly a place steeped in history, but it is the architecture that stands out in the city, a picture opportunity at every turn.

We took the water bus to the north lagoon island of Burano, a haven for artists with brightly painted houses and it is noted for its fish dishes and lace-making. We returned via the larger island of Murano which has long been synonymous with glass-making. In the 1500s, the islanders developed new blowing and fusion techniques and so skilled were the craftsmen and so closely guarded were the trade secrets, that tradesmen would migrate only under the threat of death. A visit to the glass museum was a must as some of the pieces were absolutely sensational.

We did, of course, have to be serenaded in a gondola on the Grand Canal, the main artery of central

The quaint island of Burano.

Venice. It is not cheap, about a hundred euros for a full fifty-minute trip, but certainly worth it. To see the Rialto Bridge, the Bridge of Sighs and watch how the gondoliers navigate those narrow waterways and to see the commercial use of the waterways was an awesome experience.

Have a glass of wine in St Marks Square but, like Rome, if you can see something like the Doges Palace whilst imbibing, you will pay more for it. Views here do not come cheap.

The Lido beach with its twice-

The Lido beach.

Church of San Giorgio Maggiore.

daily raked and manicured sand and rows of multi-coloured bathing cabins and beach umbrellas is where Venetians spend their summers and most weekends. It is a classy, smart, clean and friendly place to sunbathe.

The golf course is perched on the southern end of Lido Island right on the Adriatic Sea. Legend has it that Henry Ford, President of the Ford Motor Company of America, was the *deus ex machina* in the creation of a golf course on the Lido in Venice, a wonderful 18-hole course located in the Alberoni area. Ford stayed at the Hotel Excelsior in 1928 with his golf bag and clubs, only to discover that there was no course on the Lido, nor anywhere else in Venice, to enjoy a game which at the time was much in vogue in America, but practically unknown in Italy. Ford complained about this to his friend, Count Giuseppe Volpi di Misurata, a enthusiastic man who was president of the 'Italian Company of Grand Hotels' (C.I.G.A.), and convinced him to find a

The famous Rialto Bridge from our gondola.

suitable location on the Lido on which to create a golf course equal to the elegant structures already present on the island.

Count Volpi was also the ingenious creator of many cultural and social events, namely the Venice International Music Festival (1930), the Venice Film Festival (1932) and the Venice Theatre Festival (1934) which still take place every year or every two years. Speaking of the film festival which draws

stars from all over the world, it should be mentioned that the prize for the best male and female actors still bears the name Coppa Volpi, in his memory.

Volpi and Ford spotted a suitable location at the Alberoni, in the extreme south of the Lido, near the mouth of the port of Malamocco. The area of approximately 100 hectares presented natural features similar to those of many Scottish links, where

sand and wind would surely make the game equal to that in the best British tradition. Many world famous professionals have played on this course as well as the Social Golfer – among them, Arnold Palmer (who still holds a 5 below par record), Severiano Ballesteros, Tony Jacklin, Lee Trevino. The course has many peculiar features. There is the wide selection of trees that flank the fairways and make the game even more difficult, including cluster pines, weeping willows, poplars and mulberry trees that make the course green and practicable all year round. Then there is the self-draining sandy foundation, capable of absorbing a great quantity of rain in a short space of time. Other difficulties are the *bora* or *sirocco* winds that require sudden changes in game tactics, as well as the intrinsic difficulties of the course. All these elements make Venice golf club one of the best and most challenging of Italian courses. Numerous species of animals are to be found there: blue heron, pheasants, ducks, nutrias. The course is amazing and the setting sublime. At times, there is a links feel because of the wind and you are so close to the sea. Given the location, the price is not that high, at sixty euros the green fees are great value for money. The course is well-groomed, but not as manicured as you would expect

from a high-end course. Yet, that is one of its charms, it has the beauty and location of an élite golf course, but you don't always get the perfect lie and the grass is not always golf-course quality grass. It is challenging and interesting and I highly recommend it.

Bergen

What is special about this small town port on the North Sea coastline? Well, besides being stunningly beautiful, it was home for twelve months to our youngest daughter, Tanya, on an exchange from Leeds University to Bergen University. During her year away, she turned twenty-one, so mother and I used this special birthday as an opportunity to visit her and enjoy a break in a country we had never visited or before then, ever been inclined to visit. Tanya had warned us that it was outrageously expensive, but what the heck, you are only twenty-one once. It was a pity that our visit was in February because Bergen hosts Europe's most difficult and challenging golf course, Meland, but it only opens in May. Never mind.

Norway is now rated the most prosperous nation in the world. How is it that our little North Sea neighbour has achieved this while big old Britain is wallowing in national debt and economic turmoil? The answer is simple – oil and gas. The Norwegians have simply used their revenues far better than we have. Those old enough will remember the promises of the 1960s and 1970s that oil would change Britain for ever, we would be wealthy, poverty would be non-existent – what happened, where did we go wrong?

The birthday girl, Tanya.

Exporting oil at $70 a barrel has turned Norway into the wealthiest nation on earth. Today, Norway is a society which, on paper at least, enjoys the greatest affluence the world has ever seen. Its GDP in 2005 rose to £35,800 per head (that's for every one of its 4.5 million population), leap-frogging past both Switzerland and the United States, and way ahead of Britain's £21,000. This year, it will reach dizzier new heights. Forget public

borrowing and the national debt – they don't exist. Instead, there is a huge tax surplus, and the national debt has been paid off.

Bergen airport terminal is spanking-new, enormous and eerily quiet; all signs of prestige spending projects funded by easy money. The efficient on-time bus service into the city centre is the first warning of price shocks to come; £10 return for a 15-minute trip, but at least the ticket seller smiles. In oil-boom Norway, one might expect rows of Dubai skyscrapers, swaggering executives and a glut of big 4x4s. Instead, Bergen is more like Wigan town centre on a quiet shopping day. There are little outward signs of a well-to-do affluent society. Perhaps the shops are quiet because, unless you are on a Norwegian salary, the prices are eye-popping. Even the well-off Danish on day-trips gasp. Norwegians, meanwhile, pour over the Swedish border every weekend just to pick up groceries. And when they fill up their (heavily-taxed) cars, the price they pay at the pump is amongst the highest in Europe. Rather like whisky in Scotland, there is no discount on petrol just because they make it there. But don't be fooled by the sky-high prices; even after taking them into account, Norwegian incomes still top the table on a 'purchasing power parity' basis. Though food and drink (especially wine) is at times gobsmackingly expensive, other goods are on a par with Britain. Housing in the major cities (despite recent rises) is cheaper than the UK. So where's the money going? Is the government splashing out on schools, hospitals and lavish welfare projects? A brief visit suggests spending is indeed up – a new cancer wing here, a fancy new school gym there – but nothing that shouts boom-time.

Everyone in Bergen seemed happy and smiling. It was a most noticeable fact perhaps because unemployment here is, after all, the lowest in Europe. On a claimant-count basis, it is around 2.5%, close to half the level in Britain. Another sign of contentment and economic security is the country's fertility rate. Norwegian mothers have more children per head than anywhere else in Europe, except Iceland and Ireland. Norway has among the highest level of females in the workforce. Squaring the circle is maternity leave that stretches to 42 weeks on full pay.

But visitors are still left scratching around for signs that they are really in the richest place on earth. Where are the Ferraris and Porsches? Why, in a country almost smug about its superior welfare standards, are there an uncomfortably large number of beggars and rough sleepers around the central station? The answer lies in a remarkable decision taken many years ago to ring fence the flood of oil revenues from the North Sea. Every dollar earned is swept straight into what was once called the State Petroleum Fund but is now called the Government Pension Fund. The truth is that Norwegians are simply not spending their oil windfall, but putting it aside for the future. What's more, none of the money is allowed to be invested in Norway. The fund has ballooned in size and recently became the world's biggest pension fund, for the first time outstripping Calpers, the $200bn Californian fund.

We stayed in the quite splendid Strand Hotel overlooking the harbour and market place. This unique place has a special part in Norwegian literature folklore as it is reputed to be the home of Varg Veum, the hero of Gunnar Staalesen's immensely popular private investigator novels, who is immortalized in bronze on the sidewalk in front of the hotel, where the detective's office was also supposed to have been. In fact, the hotel bar had its own Veum section, full of various memorabilia not just from the novels, but also props and stills from the popular films and TV show. And of course the bar serves Veum's favourite drink – Simmers Taffel aquavit.

For us, however, it was the hotel's location that made this a splendid base for our vacation. The cost of the place soon hit us as we ventured into the city's Irish Bar, every city has one, doesn't it? Here I ordered a pint of Caffreys and it cost me over a tenner, needless to say, I was soon searching for the cheapest bottle of local brew. As we arrived, it started to snow, proper snow, not like ours in England, but beautifully white, soft and fluffy, great for snow balls and guess what, it did not bring the town to a standstill. Karen and I watched from our balcony as smooth running Norwegian efficiency kicked in, with the minimum of fuss and with everyone clearly knowing their role. Several road diggers entered the square and quickly cleared all the roads and pavements, then salt and sand, readily dispersed onto

the pavements and come morning, there was a city ready for action. It was very impressive – in the UK, wet leaves stop the trains. The city's location is awesome, we meandered through the old town, with its colourful wooden buildings gleaming in the mid-morning sunshine. In the afternoon, Tanya took us up the cable car with the impressive twenty-six degree track to the top of Mount Fløyen; here you have great views of the city and waterways below. The next day, we visited the King's Winter Palace and, covered with thick snow, it really was a winter wonderland. I am pretty sure that few people

would consider Bergen as a destination for a break, but trust me, despite the cost, it is well worth a visit and quite unforgettable.

The owner of the Strand was a keen golfer and gave me plenty of reasons to want to revisit in summer. There are about half-a-dozen courses within a few hours of the city but two within a reasonable distance, the 9-hole Bergen golf club and the highly-rated and recognised Meland golf course. I have standing invitations of both of these which I intend to take up in the near future.

Golf in Norway has recently become more popular and now Norway offers numerous golf clubs and golf courses. In some parts of the country, golfers can even take part in exciting competitions of ice golfing and golfing in snow, providing a unique challenge for any type of golfer. The typical

golfing season in Norway ranges from early May until the snow comes (mid/late November). Golfing in many locations is possible twenty-four hours a day between the middle of May until the end of July. This is due to the phenomena of the midnight sun. With a stroke rating of 151 from its back tees, no other European course can

compete with this (the highest possible rating is 155) and thus Melands par-73 course has been crowned Europe's hardest test. The playing area is fairly generous but nearly every hole runs through a corridor of trees and creates problems in the mind.

In addition to its distractingly beautiful setting, with both mountains and sea as neighbours, Meland golf club has a very aesthetic design. You would not be the first to slow your pace and let others pass you on holes 8 through 13; the view towards the city of Bergen and its seven mountains, perhaps capped with snow even in May, is exceptional and well worth missing your turn at the tee.

Historic Scotland
The Birthplace O' Golf

by Joe Stine

Picture below is a photo of an 1836 Survey of St. Andrews' Old Course which is on display at the World Golf Hall of Fame in St. Augustine Florida. Back then, St. Andrews' narrow nine hole track through the thorny gorse bushes, had no double greens and actually only had ten holes, eight of which were played twice. To play an eighteen hole round, it was necessary to play the same holes, going out and coming in. So, the 1st hole was also used as the 17th hole.

Golf's history is still being written, but unfortunately the record of its origin is an incomplete collection of documents and artifacts. One thing that is certain is that golf began in Scotland. For it is in Scotland after all that golf has its roots and its soul. It's also where the 'grande auld geme' is understood and appreciated 'jist a wee bit' differently than anywhere else in the world.

Florida Golf Magazine decided to visit some of the oldest golf courses in the world. With this goal in mind, we undertook an extensive tour of the country that touts itself as being the birthplace of the game we love.

Map of Scottish golf courses, from golfvacationsscotland.com

To anyone planning a golf vacation to Scotland, we would recommend the use of an experienced and reputable travel agent. We did some research and contacted a company called golfvacationsscotland.com to help us organize a tour of some of Scotland's truly historic golf courses, and their guidance proved to be invaluable.

After speaking with a very personable Irish chap named Eamonn Kennelly at golfvacationsscotland.com, it became evident that we could not visit every old golf course in Scotland, so we decided on whirlwind tour of eight historic courses in ten days. The folks at golfvacationsscotland.com made all of the travel arrangements and helped us plan an itinerary around an eclectic cross-section of historic Scottish golf courses, which included in order, Gleneagles, Brora, Royal Dornoch, Carnoustie, Crail, St. Andrews, Kingsbarns and Prestwick.

The historic Gleneagles Hotel

We started our Scottish golf vacation by flying into Glasgow International Airport. From there we rented a car and drove to the historic and luxurious Gleneagles Hotel. They have three courses at **Gleneagles**, the Kings, Queens and a new course designed by Jack Nicklaus called the PGA Centenary Course, but we were there to play the historic King Course design by Open Chapion, James Braid in 1919

James Braid's plan for the King's Course was to test the best players' shot-making skills over the eighteen holes. When they play the King's, the world's greatest golfers admire the cunning and craft with which he achieved that goal.

You find out all about it with your first approach shot. If you have driven straight and long from the tee, you will have what looks like a simple pitch to the elevated green. But you must be sure to select the correct club, because the shot is always a little longer than you think, with the wind over the putting surface often stronger than you can feel it from the fairway.

Selecting the right club for each approach shot is the secret on the King's. It is certainly one of the most beautiful and exhilarating places to play golf in the world, with the springy moorland turf underfoot, the sweeping views from the tees all around, the rock-faced mountains to the north, the green hills to the south, and the peaks of the Trossachs and Ben Vorlich on the western horizon.

The 5th Hole at Gleneagles, designed by James Braid

Gleneagles (Kings Course)
The Gleneagles Hotel
Auchterarder, Perthshire
Founded 1919
Course Architect James Braid
Moorland
Par 71, Length 6790 yards

Facilities:
Pro Shop Yes
Carts Yes
Caddies Yes
Pull Trollies Yes
Catering Yes

After staying two nights at the Gleneagles we drove to Tain, Ross-shire, and stayed at a marvalous Bed and Breakfast that is owned by the Glenmorangie Distillery callled the Glenmorangie House, www.theglenmorangiehouse.com

While there we played two old courses, Brora and Royal Dornoch. The course at **Brora Golf Club** was also designed by James Braid. Braid won The Open Championship in 1901, 1905, 1906 and 1908.

Brora Golf Club was established in 1891. In 1923 James Braid, five times Open champion and prolific design of golf courses, the most famous of which is Gleneagles, visited the course and redesigned the 18-hole layout whid has stood the passing of time and remains a fair and challenging test of a true traditional links course.

Brora Golf Club	Facilities:
Brora, Sutherland	Pro Shop Yes
Founded 1891	Carts Yes
Course Architect James Braid	Caddies
Links	Pull Trollies Yes
Par 69, Length 6110 yards	Catering Yes

The 9th Hole at the Brora Golf Club, designed by James Braid

As with all seaside links there are some very special places throughout this course; the panorama of seascar and landscape from the second tee, the proximity of the sea to the 9th green and the beauty of the 13th green, one of the jewels in Braids crown. Brora golf course represents all the attributes of a traditional Scottish Highland links, with a classic layout, and well worth a visit when in this part of Scotland.

The following day we played **Royal Dornoch Golf Club** which was designed Old Tom Morris. Dornoch, pronounced with a soft 'h'.

Royal Dornoch Golf Club is said to have the northernmost Championship course in the world. It is of such high quality that many professionals hone their game at Dornoch leading up to the Open Championship each year. Its isolation is the main reason for it not having hosted an Open Championship.

Royal Dornoch the 5th, 6th and 11th

The course is a typical old links with nine holes running away from the clubhouse and nine holes coming back. When the gorse bushes are in flower, it is a magnificent sight and its proximity to the ocean affords water views on all holes.

Most tees at Royal Dornoch are elevated high above the level of the fairway allowing the wind to take your ball at its whim and adding to the challenge. The greens are generally long and narrow and some are quite undulating. The putting surfaces are wonderful and will reward a good stroke.

It is no surprise that Royal Dornoch is regularly rated among the top 20 courses in the world, and after you play there, you are certain to agree.

Royal Dornoch Golf Club
Dornoch, Sutherland
www.royaldornoch.com
Founded 1877
Course Architect Old Tom Morris
Links
Par 70, Length 6,514 yards

Facilities:
Pro Shop Yes
Carts No
Caddies Yes
Pull Trollies Yes
Catering Yes
Major Events: British Amateur

The next day we drove south to St. Andrews where we stayed at the beautiful Old Course Hotel overlooking the Old Course. www.oldcoursehotel.co.uk

The next day we drove south to St. Andrews where we stayed at the beautiful Old Course Hotel overlooking the Old Course. www.oldcoursehotel.co.uk

The Jigger Inn and the Old Course Hotel

While staying in St. Andrews we played three courses, the first being Carnoustie. The **Carnoustie Golf Links**, like St Andrews, is a public golf course. The Championship course has hosted several Open Championships, most recently in 1999. Sadly, that tournament will be best known for the 72nd hole antics of Frenchman, Jean Van de Velde, where he had a triple bogey including a visit to the Burn to force a playoff with Justin Leonard and the eventually winner, Paul Lawrie.

The Carnoustie Clubhouse

The course is widely thought of as the most difficult Open venue. The wind plays a big part in the way the course is played and a calm day here is uncommon. The holes are generally long and are so well bunkered that position off the tee is paramount to a good score. Carnoustie has no weak holes and requires a well-rounded game to score well. Accurate chipping to the large greens is crucial and it is best to avoid the bunkers as they are deep and well placed.

The finishing holes are as good a collection as you would find anywhere. The 16th is a punishing par three of over 250 yards to an elevated green. The 17th is a par four where it is possible to cross the burn three times during the journey to the green, and the 18th is a difficult driving hole across the burn and the approach must also carry the burn as well.

Carnoustie was designed by Alan Robertson in 1842

Carnoustie Golf Links
The Links,
Carnoustie, Angus
Founded 1842
Course Architect Alan Robertson
Links
Par 72, Length 6,941 yards

Facilities:
Pro Shop Yes
Carts No
Caddies Yes
Pull Trollies Yes
Catering in the Hotel complex
Major Events: Open Championship (6 times)
British Amateur (4 times)
Dunhill Links Championship (European Tour)

Swilcan Bridge crosses Swilcan Burn on The Old Course in St. Andrews. St Andrews Links Trust Photo

The **Old Course at St Andrews** is loved or loathed, appreciated or misunderstood, but as the birthplace of golf, it is universally respected.

Standing on the first tee of the Old Course at St Andrews is the realisation of a dream for many golfers, yet with the widest fairway in the world ahead, it's amazing how many are overwhelmed by nerves and put forward a less than ideal beginning to their round.

The subtle bumps and hollows make for uncertainty on every shot, the placement of the bunkers and other natural hazards and the varied slopes and swales on the massive double greens make for a golfing experience without peer.

The golf links at St. Andrews is where the game of golf developed for over six centuries. Hacked through the gorse bushes originally known by locals as the thorny whins, the Old Course has staged more Open Championships than any other golf course and has provided the backdrop for some of golf's most memorable moments.

The 17th green on the Old Course, dubbed the Road Hole.

Pictured above is the green of the 455 yard dogleg right Road Hole of the Old Course. Drive over the dark green sheds on the right side if you dare, and you are still left with a difficult shot into a shallow green set at 45 degrees to the fairway. Play it long, and the ball will lie on the road that runs behind the green. Play it short, and the notorious Road Hole Bunker lies in wait.

Our caddy told us that the prudent shot is to the front right corner of the green.

The Old Course, St Andrews
St Andrews, Fife
Founded 14th Century
Course Designer Unknown
Links
Par 72, Length 7,115 Yards

Facilities: Pro Shop Two Clubhouses (Links and Eden), both with Pro Shops
Carts No
Caddies Yes
Pull Trollies Yes (after midday)
Catering Yes (In both clubhouses)
Major Events: Walker Cup, Curtis Cup, Open Championship (26 times), Amateur Championship (15 times), Dunhill Links Championship (European Tour)

The day after playing the Old Course we made our way to **Kingsbarns Golf Links**, and were we ever glad that we did. Known as the Pebble beach of Scotland, its vistas or breathtaking.

Unknown to most people Golf has been enjoyed over the links land of Kingsbarns since 1793. This links served the golfing needs of the locals and holidaymakers until the onset of the Second World War when the Links was mined in the national security defence effort and it quickly reverted to rough pasture.

It's not surprising that St Andrews locals believe the links at Kingsbarns will be added to the Open Championship rota in the future. Only six miles from St Andrews, I agree that Kingsbarns is one of the finest new courses in the world. If you haven't heard of Kingsbarns before, you will know all about it in years to come.

Having converted an old nine-hole course into the magnificent creation took a great deal of imagination and foresight, and the results are almost beyond belief. With the sea visible from every hole, the holes are aesthetically stunning and magnificently designed to ensure ease of play from several tee locations. The greens are undulating and roll fast and true.

The 15th, a par three along the water, is as spectacular a short hole as you will find anywhere. The final hole demands great courage with the final 50 yards being over a valley with a burn waiting below to swallow your ball

A small number of courses are worth raving to your friends about, and this is certainly one of them. You will love it!

Kingsbarns Golf Links, called the Pebble Beach of Scotland, has to be seen to be believed.

Kingsbarns Golf Links
Kingsbarns, Fife
Founded 2000
Course Architect Kyle Phillips, Mark Parsinen
Links
Par 72, Length 7,126 yards

Facilities:
Pro Shop Yes
Carts No
Caddies Yes, on prior application
Pull Trollies Yes
Catering Yes
Major Events:
Dunhill Links Trophy (European Tour)

Located 10 miles along the Fife coast from St Andrews, the Balcomie Links at the **Crail Golfing Society** is the 7th oldest club in the world.

Crail is one of the old, classically designed courses in Scotland. The sea comes into play on a number of holes, where a decision to gamble with the beach or take the easier dog-leg has to be made. Positioning of the tee shot is more important than length on most holes and some of the finest short holes to be found on any course will be a lasting memory.

This course was first used permanently by the Society in 1895, when it was opened by Tom Morris who stated 'there is not a better course in Scotland'. The Balcomie course had been in existence long before this and there is a record of a society competition being played in September 1857.

3rd green looking to 4th green of Crail's Balcomie Links

Crail Golfing Society
(Balcomie Links)
Founded 1786
Course Architect Old Tom Morris
Links
Par 69, Length 5922 yards

Facilities;
Pro Shop Yes
Carts No
Caddies On application
Pull Trollies Yes
Catering Yes

Sahara bunker and 17th Green at Prestwick

The **Old Course at Prestwick** was the original host of the tournament that became the Open Championship, the most sought after prize in world golf. It was used for the first 12 Opens and has hosted the tournament on 24 occasions in total.

It is not long enough by today's standards to be on the current Rota of Open courses but remains a fine example of traditional Scottish links golf. In places, it is a tight and testing layout, where position rather than power is prized. In fact, on some holes, length can get you into more trouble than more conservative play.

At first glance, Prestwick appears conservative and at peace with its place in the history of golf, however in fact it is a relaxed and friendly club that enjoys hosting golfers from all around the world. Visitors are encouraged to use their temporary membership to its full capacity, and enjoy the full lunch in the lavish Dining room or just a snack in the relaxed Cardinal room.

Cardinal Bunker and 3rd Hole at Prestwick Golf Club

Prestwick Golf Club
Links Road,
Prestwick, Ayrshire, Scotland
Founded 1851
Course Architect Old Tom Morris
Links
Par 71
Length 6,544 yards

Facilities:
Pro Shop Yes
Carts No, Pull Trollies Yes
Caddies Yes, on application
Catering Lounge, Bar & Dining room is available. Jacket, Collar & Tie required
Major Events: Open Championship (24 times)
Amateur Championship (10 times)

Prestwick is arguably one of the most important old Scottish courses in the history of golf, second only to the Old Course at St. Andrews. If you golf in Scotland, it would be a mistake to not play Prestwick.

Vancouver, the Olympic Flame.

3. Around the World in Eighty (plus a few) Days

Originally, after the success of the first book and the popularity of the social golfer concept, I had a whimsical idea that I could follow in the footsteps of that famous traveller from literature, Phileas Fogg and travel the globe in eighty days, with Matron as my Passepartout, with the intention of playing some of the most venerable courses on the planet. It was anticipated that this trip would form the basis of the follow-up book. However, so much had happened pre and post the trip, that it was clear that the trip was only a part, albeit a substantial one, of my ongoing story and recovery. Also, despite Nicola, my PA's best efforts, she was unable to complete the journey in eighty days exactly, due to the constraints of flight timetables, my demands to play in competitions along the way and to see the Winter Olympics in Vancouver. So what, it took a little longer. Unlike Fogg this was not part of a wager, so I tagged on a few extra places along the way. Essentially, my brief to Nicola was that I wanted to play again in the Wrest Point Masters in Tasmania, visit Kauri Cliffs and Cape Kidnappers in New Zealand, Koolau in Hawaii, Vancouver for the Winter Olympics (and play golf somewhere in British Columbia, so I could boast that I had played golf at the Olympics). I also wanted to play Pebble Beach, visit Vegas, move on to the Edwin Watts Tour Opener in Florida and at the same time to celebrate my mucker, Brew's, twentieth anniversary of his near-fatal automobile accident. It says much for Nicola that she managed to pull all this together and give us the holiday of a lifetime.

In December 2009, the month leading up to our trip, the planning, excitement, research and work needed in order to leave my businesses for a three-month spell had left me feeling as good as I had for years. As a stroke survivor, I had to accept that things could never return to pre-stroke days, but in December, mentally at least, old Ian was back. I felt I was back in a time warp, I had high enough energy levels to do a full day's work and even continue into the night. I was abuzz with anticipation. I have since spoken about this to fellow stroke survivors and I am sure that recovery is aided by the stimuli of achievement, be it work, sport or leisure. I think it is essential that, however big the challenge, travelling the world, playing golf or walking to the shops, the brain will encourage the body to complete the task in hand. Too often, I think, ennui sets in, together with an acceptance of inactivity. I encourage all survivors in the support groups I am involved with, to set little goals and challenges and most say that in the pursuit of these, there is usually a corresponding improvement in well-being, no matter how successful or not the outcome is.

I had been told I would not walk again, never mind swing a club and here I was three years later, embarking on my second long trip since my stroke and this time fulfilling a life-long ambition to travel the globe. To complete the journey with my soulmate and partner made the trip even better. We were to see some wonderful places, meet many interesting characters, play some super golf courses and at the end of the journey, we both agreed, what a wonderful world this was.

And so, on 2 January 2010, at 9 a.m., we left Manchester for Singapore.

Singapore, a tropical beachside paradise.

Singapore

We had chosen Singapore for a stopover for a couple of reasons. Firstly, we had been to Dubai many times before and had already visited Hong Kong, leaving this as an obvious choice as we could then fly by splendid Singapore Airlines to Melbourne, via Singapore. Secondly, Singapore has two world-class golf tracks at Sentosa and Teneh Merah, so it was a no-brainer.

All I knew about Singapore prior to the trip was that this city state, hub of commercial activity and gateway to the Pacific, was famous for its draconian rules, particularly the chewing gum ban. It had, of course, played a major role in the Second World War and I was intrigued about its war history and colonial past. I looked forward to a cocktail at Raffles, but had little expectation or anticipation of what else to expect. Certainly in the past, Singapore had a reputation of being bland and boring, but I had been told by visitors that since the millennium, it had undergone a major renaissance of epic proportions. The waterfront had been revitalised, new casino resorts, a Universal Studios theme park and an exploding arts scene centred on the recently developed esplanade.

We arrived at Singapore's futuristic modern international airport, probably, no certainly, the best organised I have travelled through. The journey from the airport to our hotel on Siluso Beach on the island of Sentosa at the southern tip of the city gave us a first-hand glimpse of the cleanliness and orderliness of this cosmopolitan melting pot of asian and western cultures. Traffic was busy but not chaotic, there were never any queues, no beeping of horns, no rubbish in the streets. It was difficult to comprehend we were in a city which, after Hong Kong, has the second highest population density in the world with over 6,000 people per square kilometre. The difference between here and Hong Kong was already becoming apparent.

We arrived tired but enthralled at the superbly located Siluso Beach Eco Resort to be greeted with a message from home; my mother had suffered heart failure and was critically ill back home in Wigan. During our stay in Singapore, we did not unpack in case we had to return home quickly. Indeed, it was only on the last of our five days here that we decided to carry on the trip after speaking to a slowly recovering mum in the UK who pointed out there was nothing I could do to help so I may as well continue the journey. Mothers sure do have a way with words!

Our first experience of Singapore hospitality came that first evening. We were sitting in the bar having a quiet drink, contemplating a possible early end to our adventure when the waiter asked us why we were not heading off to the later establishments. Pointing out that I was anticipating a call from the UK in respect of my mother's condition, he simply placed his mobile on the table and said, 'You can use my phone, Sir. Phone up now and check everything is OK.' Naturally, I thanked him and said I had a phone and would phone later due to the time differences. I was just impressed that he would entrust his phone to a complete stranger without any regard to cost. This was not to be the only example of a unique brand of hospitality, courtesy and respect that was clearly shown to all visitors.

Sentosa is a separate island at the southernmost tip of Singapore, indeed it is the southernmost point of continental Asia. It is where most locals go to spend their weekends and has the best, if not the only beach in the city area. It has become a major resort and recreation area after its previous life as a military base. The fall of Singapore is well documented, but I still find it quite incredulous that the British garrison here had all its guns positioned out to sea to fend off the anticipated Japanese invasion, whilst the crafty Nippons merely advanced from the rear through the Malaysian peninsula, famously many on push bikes. Previously, it had been known as Pulau Blakang Mati, meaning island of death, referring to its chequered past as a haven for pirates and the underclasses of Malaysian society which invariably led to many outbreaks of disease on the island. After the British left in 1968, the government felt that an island of recreation needed a more appropriate name, i.e. Sentosa, meaning island of peace and tranquillity. This may have been the case in the 1970s, but whilst parts are still quite serene, beautiful and tranquil, the peace has generally disappeared as western commercialism has rampantly blossomed.

The Siloso Beach resort is superbly located just a mere cricket pitch from the beach, across the small coast road that runs along the length of the island. Regular free buses run along this all day and passes are given for the duration of your stay by the hotels on the isle. The Siloso Beach is certainly not a resort with many amenities at all, except the superbly landscaped pool area, which is probably the finest hotel pool that we have ever encountered. The restaurant is basic cafeteria fare, a small but friendly bar and the rooms, despite outstanding views over the beach, are quite small by any standard. This hotel is all about value and location and on both counts, it rates highly. Visitors do need to realise you are in the tropics and this hotel is set in a tropical rain forest so expect plenty of little friends. If you cannot cope with bugs at all, stay in the city, they are hard to avoid in Sentosa. A good mosquito spray repellent is essential. Sentosa is an ideal base for a trip to Singapore in that it is only a hover rail trip, five minutes from the mainland and has many fine tourist attractions which certainly enhanced our visit. Also, it has possibly the finest golf course in Asia, say no more!

The beautiful landscaped pool at the Siloso Beach resort.

Soon the main tourist attraction will be the Universal Studios development which will simply dominate the northern part of the isle overlooking the Singapore channel back to the city. The 5.5 billion development, Resorts World Sentosa, will include the Universal Studios theme park, casino, oceanarium, marina and luxury resorts and will go head-to-head with a similar development on the mainland at Marina bay. There is no sign of the economic recession here. It is certainly massive, pretentious possibly, but it does not look out of place, it has to be admitted.

At the moment, the principal tourist attraction is the Mount Imbiah lookout, with its centrepiece, the Carlsberg Sky Tower which you can ascend in the disc-shaped, air-conditioned cabin which slowly spins up the central column some 430 feet. The views from the top are simply sensational. There are many nature trails through the park which give an unrivalled opportunity to observe the outstanding tropical flora and fauna as well as the many small animals such as long-tailed macaques, squirrels, geckos and spotted doves. All lead back to the splendid Merlion, the 120-foot half lion and

View from Skytower, the Serapong golf course and the new Universal Studios.

The view over the Singapore Channel to the city.

The Merlion – you can walk to the top.

half fish creature that has become the tourist symbol of Singapore. For thrill seekers, there is the Sentosa luge and skyride, as well as the 4-D cinema. There is a splendid waxworks museum, the Images of Singapore which takes visitors through Singapore's complex and diverse history with multi-media shows and walk-through settings with live actors. A little *kitsch* at times, it is nevertheless, enjoyable. Finally, for nature lovers, there is the butterfly and insect kingdom which is exactly as it says; the first kingdom has over 1,500 live butterflies from over fifty species that flit and flutter between the lush tropical plants in a large enclosed garden – positively therapeutic. The adjacent kingdom has more than 3,000 bugs, including some of the world's largest and rarest creepy crawlies. Guaranteed itchy times!

Underwater World, on the far western side of the island, is one of Asia's best aquariums and a must visit if on Sentosa. You can dive with the sharks – if you are brave enough; I gave that one a miss. Also on the western side is Fort Siloso, the only remaining preserved coastal fort, used as a prisoner-of-war camp during the Japanese occupation – it offers a one-stop overview of this island's role in the Second World War. A tram takes visitors from the foot of the hill through a series of films and exhibits detailing the fort's history. The displays at the adjoining surrender chamber take you through the years of the war with films, mementos, and wax figures depicting the British surrender in 1942 and that by the Japanese in 1945. Different, maybe not everyone's cup of tea, but historically, it was fascinating.

Finally on Sentosa, right on the beach, is the interactive water show, Songs of the Sea. This night-time multi-media spectacle with a live cast and rousing music is on twice nightly and combines shooting jets of water, bursts of fire, dazzling pyro-technics and clever computer imaging. This is definitely not just for the younger ones, trust me.

The beach at Siloso is as one would expect, clean, tidy and at the weekend, mega busy as the local city inhabitants

Gorgeous nature trails of Imbiah.

flock to this idyllic mecca. During the week, it is much quieter. There are a number of bars and restaurants but you will not find much *haute cuisine* here. Also, unless it is a weekend or a holiday, the nightlife here ends rapidly after 10 p.m. We enjoyed being based here but, after two days and with the news from home that my mother was improving, we decided to visit the city on our remaining nights in this thriving metropolis. It is weird being on such a pleasant beach and peering out to sea, seeing ships entering and leaving Singapore harbour all day long. It is just full of ocean-going vessels bringing goods to and from the city. Singapore

Well worth watching, the magical enchanting Songs of the Sea.

has no natural resources and as such is entirely dependent on this trade. It is now the busiest harbour in the world and the largest container depot. Despite this, there is no intrusion and it hardly diminishes the beach-side experience at all. Conversely, it seems to enhance it.

View from our hotel room.

English is spoken everywhere, although not surprisingly in a country which is over 65% Chinese, mandarin is heard everywhere. The local dialect most commonly used is a hybrid cross of English and Chinese, called locally Singlish Speak. If ever a language can be described as relaxed and animated, malleable, frank and affectionate, it is this dialect. It is peculiar to Singapore hence the term – the agglutination of the 'head' of Singapore and the 'tail' of English. Amazingly, I could understand this, as to me it was similar to north of England slang. For example, if in Lancashire someone said, is there 'any udders', this would mean, is there anything else or an alternative. Similarly, 'can I hepchew' means can I be of assistance. 'Owd on' means wait a minute. I was in my element conversing with the natives and introducing my own phrases, such as 'I'm clempt' meaning I am rather hungry, which you never know, may take off. The language is not championed in the corridors of academia or echelons of power and business, however, the student, politician or bank manager would certainly use it at home or in the canteen. It is a homely language that departs from English in structure and syntax, but is still ultimately English with a slight fracture – which due to the fact that locals speak at breakneck speed can, to the untrained ear, sound like a foreign language. Don't worry, every Singaporean understands the Queen's English as well.

On any map, Singapore is simply a dot at the tip of the peninsula of Malaysia. Despite original fears for its survival, this 267-square-mile island has blossomed into one of Asia success stories. Partly due to the entire population's *kiasu* attitude, afraid to lose or afraid of failure, an island with no raw materials and no significant internal market was surely destined to be a political, economic and geographical absurdity. Singaporeans grasped the opportunity big-time and, not content with being the best at something – best airport, best airline, there is a relentless drive to the biggest, best or tallest. Singapore now has the world's biggest fountain at Suntec City. It has the highest observation wheel, beating the London Eye, with the Singapore Flyer. It is a national obsession of the whole populace to prove themselves to the rest of the world. Perhaps it is the years of colonial rule, the upheavals of the Second World War or the eclectic mix of Asian and Western cultures that produces this desire. This is a dynamic cosmopolitan city where all cultures seem to mesh together giving a unique vibrancy wherever you are. With such a varied range of cuisines, clothing, religion, it is a kaleidoscopic melting pot without any edge at all. It may appear western in outlook but in reality, the state ensures old eastern values dictate and underpin everyday life. Confucian precepts still temper ideals of personal freedom, and respect for one's elders and, as in our case, visitors to the country, rank very high.

This is a country famed for its moral conscience and social campaigning. The chewing-gum ban is legendary, but for me the problem with dealing with urination was the best example of handling a social problem. In a country where the high-rise block is the principal means of accommodation, there was apparently a serious problem with young males using the lifts as toilets. So, every lift in Singapore has been fitted with urination sensors which pick up the offending fluid and immediately locks the lift so the offender can be literally caught with his trousers down. Similarly, it is an offence (but I am not sure how it is enforced) not to flush the toilet on each and every visit.

A monorail takes you across from Sentosa to the mainland via the ultra imposing Vivo City shopping plaza with a fine promenade overlooking the harbour front. From here, there are ample cheap taxis to head deeper into the city and an excellent bus service. Again, Singapore hospitality came to the fore. Karen and I were looking at the bus map trying to ascertain the precise bus on which to head into the city when a young local lady introduced herself and spent the next ten minutes going through all the alternatives open to us. After a few minutes, her friend advised her that their bus had arrived. She cast a withering look at her colleague and simply carried on her explanations, missing her bus in the meantim.e. I can assure you that would not happen in the UK. Several times in and around the city when we were looking at our maps, we were approached in a kindly and pleasant manner by a variety of Singaporeans, male, female, old and young who were only too pleased to be of any assistance in getting you to your destination. In Vivo City, there are several outstanding

restaurants overlooking the harbour with its art displays and interactive shows. The best is the aptly named Carnivore Brazilian Churrascaria, a meat lover's paradise, where friendly knife-wielding *passadors* make the service an integral aspect of the dining experience. The marinated, chargrilled, succulent meats keep on coming until

View from Vivo City boardwalk back to Sentosa and the new Universal Studios.

your tummy is fit to explode. Lunchtime or evening, this busy enterprise will not fail to impress.

Singapore is awash with fine culinary experiences. There are, I would suggest, few places in the world where life revolves around food like it does in Singapore. Locals seem to converse about food like us Brits discuss the weather. They will debate where to get the freshest seafood, hottest chilli sauce, and food is a major focus in Singapore where everyone from all aspects of life seems to have an opinion and are remarkably critical on all matters culinary. Indian, Chinese, Thai, Malay are naturally very popular bur pernakan is regarded as Singapore's most indigenous cuisine. It can be best described as a mix of Malay and Chinese spices, commonly known as *rempah*. This nose-tickling mixture gives the cuisine a distinct aroma and flavour. The national dish seems to be fish-head curry, which is what it says. Despite the somewhat unappealing sight of a giant fish head in a thick sea of gravy, flavoured with curry powder and tamarind juice, it does give a most delicious and satisfying taste sensation – if you appreciate curries, of course. Locals wax lyrical about the eyeballs of the fish head although after slurping the gravy, Matron gave it a complete miss. Wherever you are in Singapore, you will only ever be a sand wedge from a fine restaurant; they are on every corner. Around Marina Bay and the North Quay on the Singapore River, around Raffles' landing site, there are a mixture of bars and restaurants where you can while away the balmy tropical evenings. Second to food is shopping, the locals clearly love retail therapy and malls are everywhere, but the joy of shopping, I assume, is the diversity. From swanky air-conditioned malls to steamy bazaars, ethnic neighbourhoods to huge department stores, it is a duty-free paradise. Orchard Street is the Regent Street or Fifth Avenue of the city, and I did well to keep Matron from the credit card whilst walking down this street.

A visit into the city is not complete without firstly a visit to one of the many food centres where an astonishing variety of dishes are cooked on the spot. Locally called hawker foods, these are usually elegant centres which vary in ambience but they do offer multi-ethnic Singapore cooking at its best, a fraction of restaurant prices. Secondly, a Singapore sling at Raffles hotel is a must.

Sir Thomas Stamford Raffles, what a glorious name, with a name like that, you are destined for greatness. Raffles' machiavellian plans in the early 1800s

The Queen of the East.

allowed him to establish a trading post for the British East India Company and from his detailed plans for its development, modern Singapore, the Lion City, had its earliest history. The Raffles Hotel and its long bar where it is obligatory to have a Singapore Sling, a classic drink of gin, cherry brandy, lemon juice, sugar and club soda. Delicious it sounds and delicious it is. You enter via its cast iron porticoed entrance along Beach Road (the hotel originally faced the beach before substantial land reclamation). This leads into the lobby with its marbled floors. Opened in 1887, the grand old lady of the east has seen its fair share of kings, queens, presidents, prime ministers, movie stars and doyens of literature, as well as ordinary people, attracted to this splendid icon of tropical elegance and style. If you visit Raffles, just five minutes away is the Chijmes, formerly a gothic convent, which has now been converted into a collection of alfresco restaurants, pubs and art and handicraft shops. It is a

Matron refuses a sling, prefers the strawberry daqs!

splendid place to spend the evening. Finally, a ride on the Singapore Flyer is a must for any visitor. At 165 metres, it is the world's largest and a thirty-minute ride gives some stunning views of the city in good weather.

There are plenty of fine museums around the city, the best being the Asian Civilisations Museum located next to the magnificent new Parliament House. There are eleven galleries over three floors and it has a sizeable collection of artefacts pertaining to all aspects of Asian history. There are interactive displays which enhance the whole experience. It is located on the river bank next to an outstanding restaurant, Siem Reap II, specialising in Indo-Chinese specialities and the Trendy Bar Opiume where the trendy of the financial district often spend the early evening hours after a day's hard graft or, if you are in need of a British beer, walk over the bridge to the Black Penny, Victorian London pub and also enjoy fish and chips in a newspaper.

There is a thriving art and culture scene based around the esplanade and we particularly enjoyed early evenings overlooking the harbour, sitting at the Society Bistro at No 1 Fullertons or the Palm Beach Japanese restaurant. This city does rock after dark. Come dusk, pubs shift gears, clubs rev up, their music, theatre and dance come alive on stage. There is something for just about everyone, whether a night at the opera or a pub crawl. The options are truly plentiful. This city does have a party soul. Classy and opulent in parts, tacky in others, but with a vibrancy and decadence which is uniquely Singapore.

Both Karen and I agreed that for a stopover to Australia, this was a better base than even Dubai and Hong Kong and we do hope to return.

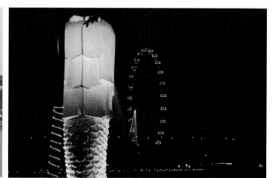

Above left: Singapore river with its array of bars.

Above right: Singapore at night, the famous Singapore Flyer.

Right: The imposing arts centre on the esplanade.

Golf in Singapore

With Singapore quickly becoming an Asian hub for golfers around the region and around the world, golf courses are springing up across the country like wildfire. Even in the land-scarce tropical island, there are more than fifteen golf and country clubs in the city state and there are no fewer than twenty-five golf courses in Singapore.

Mention of a golf course to any Singaporean with golfing experience and the Laguna National Golf and Country Club comes to mind. Situated at the corner of the island off Changi Coast Road, the Laguna consists of two championship 18-hole courses, the Masters course and the Classic course. Having hosted big-name events in the golf tournament, namely the Caltex Masters (with Ernie Els and Nick Faldo) and the Singapore Masters, the Laguna National is one of the premier golf courses in the city state. Both courses were designed by the world renowned Dye Design, and the Laguna National has won several accolades and is ranked one of the best in the world by several digests. To top it off, the Laguna National boasts a three-tiered driving range to improve your swing. Home to one of the richest tournaments worldwide, the Singapore Open, the Sentosa Golf Club runs two world class 18-hole courses, the Tanjong and the Serapong course. Located on the resort island of Sentosa off the southern tip of Singapore, golfers will be taken away from the hustle and bustle of city life and thrown into the tranquil peace that Sentosa is famous for. The Tanjong course is known to challenge even the most hardened golfers with its barrage of natural hazards and its narrow landing areas on fairways. Overlooking the South China Sea, the Tanjong course provides golfers with scenic beauty and endless fairways. Just be sure to avoid the monstrous towering trees when you tee off! The Serapong course is an absolute gem to behold for any golfer in the world. It hosts the annual Singapore Open and has been awarded the highest honours in the golfing scene. Awarded the accolade of #1 course in Asia and the #1 host venue in the Asian Tour by the *Asian Golf Review* and the *Asian Golf Monthly*, the Serapong course is a definite visit for travelling golfers around the world.

Located strategically in the heart of Singapore's central business district, the Marina Bay Golf Course opened in 2006 for public use, making it entirely accessible for anyone and everyone with a passion for the sport. Laden with bunkers (over ninety of them) the Marina Bay Golf Course will provide even the champion golfer with plenty of excitement. With the scenic view of the Singapore business-district skyline looming in the distance, golfers will not only be entertained by the challenges of the course, but will also be provided with a spectacular field of vision.

Finally of note, there is the prestigious Tanah Merah, host of the HSBC Women's World Event, with its two highly-rated tracks – the Gardens, rated best in Singapore if not Asia, and the Tampines which is no slouch itself. For the discerning golfer, you would be likely to play one of the above if you visited Singapore, but I am assured the standard is extremely high on most courses. Obviously, the principal tracks mentioned here come at a premium which equates closer to the prices in the UK and USA for top rated courses i.e. about £100 plus or $200. As my visit was short and had the cloud of my mother's illness hanging over it, I had decided that I would play at the Sentosa golf as I was based there and I obviously wanted to play the championship Serapong course. I was not to be disappointed.

The Sentosa is an imposing golf club; the sheer size creates an impression of opulence and stately magnificence, the like of which I have rarely seen. It takes over the west side of the island totally, the two courses climbing the hillsides and running down to the coast and the Singapore river. The clubhouse is majestic in old colonial style with a modern pro shop, top-rated restaurant and changing rooms which would not be out of place in a 5-star luxury hotel. However, I do not think you would get many of the locals playing here. On the day I visited, the place was overrun by Japanese tourists

or business people. The car park was awash with BMWs, Mercedes, Bentleys, the odd Porsche, Ferrari and even a Roller. Still, I was made very welcome and soon found myself transported down to the first tee of the Serapong, past the splendid practice facilities and the second clubhouse which acted as a 19th for players who wished for a break at the turn. A course with three clubhouses, that was a first. Greeted at the tee with, 'you're more stylish than Poulter is …'

Yes agreed, but I think he really meant more outrageous. The opening hole is a straight away par 4 to a green set under a display fountain, the first sign of the sheer beauty of the place. The second is a downhill par 3 of about 160 yards, to which I hit a tee shot to 40 feet and three putted. The putt I had left had four subtle differing breaks so I repeated my putt four times and never got close. This was to be a recurring theme, superb greens which had outrageous yet subtle breaks, very difficult for a tyro to read. No wonder this is a championship course. From here, the course meanders downhill through a series of par 4s and Par 5s … all great tests in their own right, with grand views of the city and the Singapore river. Manicured bunkers and fairways just lend themselves to a thorough golf test but a most enjoyable golfing experience. It is understandable that this track is rated as one of the best in Asia. Round the turn, the course runs parallel to the river and these holes are without doubt, the making of this course, where water is constantly in play with little bail-out up the mountain. The final four holes head up towards the clubhouse. Only 17, a small par 3 really disappoints. Sixteen to a lake protected green is a beautiful par 4 and 18 a long narrow, well bunkered 5 to a green surrounded either by water or sand is a fantastic finishing climax to a splendid afternoon's golf. Future visitors will also have the extra panorama of the new Universal Studios being built next to the course. Whilst at the moment it does not look intrusive, only time will tell and noise may certainly become an issue. The Serapong certainly is impressive, majestic and beautiful. This is a course I would consider it an honour to play again. It was a great start to my golf tour of a lifetime. My only disappointment was my inability to play elsewhere in Singapore.

First hole green with display fountain.

Hole 2, I would still be there trying for a birdie, truly difficult green.

*Above and right:
The course meanders serenely
down towards the river.*

*Below: 13th, difficult par 4
along the river.*

Par 3 14th, all carry over 200 yards.

No bail out right, jungle left, great test.

Universal Studios fun after the golf.

Stunning 16th green.

The final approach to 18, a truly magnificent ending to a wonderful round of golf.

Sydney

From Singapore, we headed out to Tasmania for my return to the Wrest Point Masters, covered earlier. As you can no longer fly directly from Tasmania to New Zealand, we had an opportunity for a few extra days in the wonderful 'land down under'. During the first trip, we had stayed in both Melbourne and Sydney and initially, I thought of stopping over this time in one of the other major cities. Perth was the one I fancied, but it is easy to forget just how big Australia is. Hobart to Perth is like flying to Tenerife from the UK. The garden city of Adelaide and the highlife of Brisbane, with the possibility of visiting the Great Barrier Reef, were also alternatives but Karen really fancied returning to Sydney for a longer stay, as she had clearly fallen for this sprawling metropolis and the vibrant waterfront, in particular. I preferred the chic, more sophisticated Melbourne and still do, but I have to say that this time I enjoyed my seven days in Sydney far more than our first visit, as we got to know the city, its attractions and its people far more than our previous three-day stay.

Sydney is, of course, the largest city in Australia and the state capital of New South Wales. The city contributes approx 25% to the country's total GDP, a measure of its importance and status to this fledgling nation. To many Europeans and North Americans, Sydney is quintessentially Australia and Australia is really Sydney and a bit of outback. Multi-culturalism is evident everywhere. In early 2011, British Prime Minister David Cameron announced that multi-culturalism in the UK had failed. In the USA, there is a similar feeling, yet here in Australia it has been successfully embraced, the city's rail transport website for example offers navigation choices in more than eleven different languages. The citizens are known for their pro-environmental perspective and the Sydney skyline where simple buildings sit comfortably among expressionist constructions is an ongoing example of this feeling. It is a party town, nestling around a beautiful natural harbour with stunning beaches and gorgeous parks, it really is a city of well-being. Indeed the travelling website *Forbes Traveller* recently graded Sydney as the second happiest city in the world, beaten only by Rio, deffo on my agenda – the Para Olympic Golf in 2016 maybe! Third was Barcelona, fourth was Amsterdam and fifth was Melbourne. I am on the same wave length as *Forbes* and it says a lot about the Aussies that they have two major cities in the top five and yes, the citizens of Sydney do seem happier (or is that livelier?) than Melbourne – more party animals, I think.

So we arrived in Sydney on Sunday 17 January and headed straight to the Rocks, a must visit neighbourhood of fine sandstone buildings under the imposing Harbour Bridge, a major historic centre of Victorian Australia which was superbly renovated and re-developed in the 1970s as an importnant recreational area with a mega-busy pub life at night.

Karen had researched a bit about Sydney; well, she had read a travel guide on the plane and was determined to have more of an input into the planning of this visit. So, over a glass or two of South Australia's finest, we planned our stay. She wanted to spend a day at the city's world famous Royal Botanical Gardens, the first as it turned out, of many superb ones we would visit on this round the world trip.

Last time we had visited Manly Beach, so this time she wanted to visit Bondi Beach, arguably the

SYdney Harbour Bridge.

most famous beach in the world, with over 50,000 sun worshippers a day at the height of summer, all of them bikini-clad Antipodean beauties – I was up for that. The famous Taranga Zoo was also on her radar whilst I wished to head to Darling Harbour to see the aquarium and spend a day in the modern leisure oasis of a different kind. With street entertainment, Chinese gardens and the Zaafran Asian Fusion restaurant which we had visited the last time and which had created such a lasting impression, it was a must visit again on this trip.

Friday would be reserved for golf already pre-arranged at Moore Park, in the shadow of the famous Sydney cricket ground, and so we headed back to our hotel, contented and happy to be back down under.

So after a gorgeous eggs benedict breakfast on Sydney Harbour, there really can be nothing better than taking a cappuccino with the Harbour Bridge to the left of you, the Sydney Opera House to the right and watching those yellow harbour boats come and go, from and to the suburbs. The only downside (but it is fun) is trying to eat your muffins without a ginormous seagull getting it first.

As per Matron's Sydney itinerary, we headed off to the Royal Botanical Gardens. These beautiful gardens, established in 1816, make a sweeping curve from the Opera House to Woolloomooloo Bay. It really is a most gorgeous spot, full of majestic trees, spacious lawns, bird-filled ponds and ornamental flowerbeds. If you're particularly lucky you may see the girls from Aussie Aerobics taping a show. It really is a truly pleasant way to spend a day, invigorating, interesting, beautiful, historic,

The Royal Botanical Gardens, so close to the city centre.

Flying foxes resting in a tree, looking like a collection of broken umbrellas.

the adjectives abound. There is a large colony of fruit bats (aka flying foxes, wingspan over one metre) which give a remarkable display considering the location and with the backdrop of the city skyline. The tropical centre with its spectacular rose gardens and impressive cacti collection really was enthralling, even to someone like me who is not particularly into horticulture. Karen and her new camera never stopped clicking. There are also examples of how the Aborigines used to live before we Brits arrived. It is no wonder the gardens are so popular as they are such a tranquil base in the centre of a pulsating city. In a society where myriad cultures co-exist in apparent harmony this is the cornerstone of Sydney's

culture and mentality. 'No worries' is the catch phrase that sums up a liberal people intent on enjoying each day as it comes. Nowhere is this better expressed than in the Botanical Gardens whilst sipping a Chardonnay, watching the fruit bats glide serenely overhead. Oh happy days …

Sydney has a wide variety and choice of restaurants and whilst we tended to gyrate towards the Rocks after a day of walking around the Botanical Gardens, we both agreed that we should find somewhere closer to our hotel, the Menzies on Carrington Street, and a fine one it is too, located on the main road to the harbour. Opposite the Menzies is a stylish brasserie, called Steel, which quite frankly would not be out of place in New York, London or Paris. Quite tastefully

Original aboriginal hut.

designed, featuring much interior steel sculptures and ornaments, it had a fine choice of Australian fare to boot. I can highly recommend this to any visitor. It was a perfect end to a perfect day – no worries!

The next day, towels in hand, we headed out to Bondi, the beach which has defined the Sydney

lifestyle. Bondi is Aborigine for 'breaking waves'. Hence the popular surfing on the beach. Going to Manly beach, you needed to take a boat, to get to Bondi, you need a train or bus – either way it is about thirty minutes from the centre of the city, through, it has to be said, some of the less salubrious areas. The journey was nevertheless enjoyable and an important aspect of the Bondi experience as many passengers were carrying their surfboards with them and pleasingly often wearing very little.

Magnificent cacti garden.

Bondi Beach.

Bondi Beach is anything but a romantic stroll in the moonlight, sandy spot. It is the closest ocean beach to the city and at first glance, could easily be dismissed as a tacky tourist trap. However, don't be misled by appearances: there is a reason why many die-hard Sydneysiders would not live anywhere else and why this place is so venerated by Australians everywhere. Everything you hear, read and see about Bondi is true, including the fact it is generally too noisy and overcrowded and, because of its popularity, generally over-priced, but it is also the funkiest place in town, boasts many of the city's best eating and drinking holes, some exceptional clothing shops and is where Sydney's beautiful people are to be seen.

And there's the surfing, man! By the way, there is a most pleasant municipal golf course at Bondi which actually is the site of several unique and splendid ancient aboriginal rock engravings.

We eventually found a little piece of beach fit for gentle sunbathing, very difficult with the surfer dudes, loud ghetto blasters, frizbee throwing, etc. Once again a rustic northerner like me regretted the beer and pie belly … we did look odd, white, overweight and old, surrounded by these fit, stunning Aussie guys and gals. We managed two hours, too hot, too noisy and too obvious that we were pommies. We set off to look at the rest of Bondi. The main thoroughfare from the bus station to the promenade is the

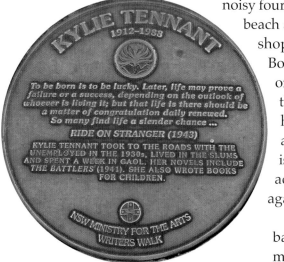

A mantra for life on the Writers Walk. As a stroke victim, this is particularly poignant and relevant.

noisy four-lane Campbell Parade which really runs parallel to the beach and is lined with bars, restaurants, swimwear and gift shops. This leads onto the promenade which houses the Bondi Pavilion with more cafes and bars and then right onto the beach itself. Hall Street which climbs away from the beach up to Bondi Junction is really the villagey heart of the beach area with everyday necessities such as banks, post offices, more cafes and bars. Off this area is Gould Street with many splendid clothing shops and, according to Matron, very reasonably priced. Then again, she would say that.

Bondi was different, enjoyable but once again looking back, the old man in me preferred Manly, Bondi was more Benidorm to Manly's Marbella, I guess, but I sure enjoyed the day and could imagine having a great time there if I had been thirty years younger … We returned to the city and arrived back at Circular Quay again. All trips in Sydney start and end here, whether by train, boat or bus. The quay (more of a semi-circle) really is the hub of Sydney's ferry system which operates from under the Harbour Bridge at the Rocks to the majestic Opera House, a quite supreme vista from any angle. A must see and quite refreshing as well as interesting is the Writers' Walk. As you walk around the quay, there are a series of round, manhole-size plaques set into the promenade dedicated to a famous writer offering a brief quotation on human nature and Australia in general. Look out for Germaine Greer, Barry Humphries and Clive James. The quay features an array of Sydney's finest restaurants, many centred directly in front of the Rocks at the Mai Overseas Passenger Terminal or, to you and me, where the massive cruise ships dock for Sydney. Two of the best we have tried and can recommend are Quay and Aria – don't Aussies keep things simple? Quay is the home of one of Australia's Gordon Ramsey equivalents, Peter Gilmore, and is exceptional and it is where after a clean-up, we spent our third evening in this splendid city.

The next morning, we set off for breakfast at the Quay prior to our day trip to Taronga, a 'zoo with a view'. This is a seventy-four acre site on the hillside at Bradley's Head, directly facing the Opera House, Harbour Bridge and the city from South Sydney – simply a superb location. We nearly didn't get there as Matron had not realised it was a boat trip, albeit only twelve minutes across the river.

However, fortified by a fine breakfast, we boarded the *Taronga Flyer*. You can acquire your zoo tickets at the quay which does simplify matters. The trip gives spectacular views of the harbour and stops at the small fortress island of Fort Denison which had served as a prison in Victorian times. Famed for its lack of amenities, the only food was bread, water and biscuits. Ironically, it now regular hosts weddings and is renowned for fine catering, and

The much discussed elephant enclosure.

brunch at the café is always well attended.

The zoo itself is relatively new having been relocated from Moore Park where, coincidentally, I would be golfing on our last day. All the animals arrived by ferry – the story goes that Jessie the elephant walked through the city to the quay and gingerly boarded the ship, watched by hundreds of locals. 'The animals walked in two by two … the elephant and the kangaroo,' the original version, I wonder. The zoo had just opened the contro-versial, much delayed Asian Elephant Rainforest, which had been plagued by many rows over the wisdom of turning more elephants into zoo exhibits. In truth, this is something I can easily

Such realistic enclosures.

connect with as there is something not quite right about seeing them in captivity, although this was tastefully presented and indeed quite spectacular, but then I have seen the real thing in Africa, so perhaps my judgement is clouded. This zoo, perhaps because of its location or perhaps because of its layout, meandering down quite a substantial hill, certainly pressed our buttons. Each exhibit seemed to be quite naturally set out and had an educational section, whether it was for the big cats, elephants, giraffes, seals or a picture with a koala on the Wild Australia Walk.

The awesome big cats you can almost touch.

I can see the city, can you?

If you visit the zoo, take the Sky Safari cable car to the top of the hill and the main entrance and back down again to the bottom and the ferry wharf. Catering options at the zoo are very poor. To see and enjoy all the major attractions that are spread out, you would need a full day, so lack of food and beverages could be an issue.

In the evening, we again ended up at the Rocks, this time at Sailors Thai, the highly-regarded David Thompson inspired restaurant where there is a fine high-quality downstairs restaurant and a significantly cheaper option in the upstairs canteen where the food is, believe me, no less impressive. You must try the signature *som dtam*, nuggets of caramelised pork, with peanuts, dried tiny shrimps, cherry tomatoes and a particularly fiery sour salad of green mango. Exquisite authentic Thai dining.

My golfing day at Moore Park took place on Friday but more about that later. Saturday morning

The architecture at Cockle Wharf.

we spent leisurely strolling around the Rocks' weekend market, where you can pleasantly while away the hours looking at the quality arts and crafts, occasional antiques and collectables. Many stalls specialise in indigenous crafts and souvenirs. There was certainly a bargain or two to be found. There are many street entertainers, puppeteers, jazz singers and other musicians making this a most pleasant and relaxing morning. Matron found many cheap (so she assured me again) and unique clothing stalls. She will need another case soon. During the afternoon, we walked down to Darling Harbour after the obligatory bus ride around the city which, whilst interesting to a degree, was simply a good way to rest the tootsies after a morning's shopping.

The reclaimed dock front of Darling Harbour is a twenty-minute stroll from the Rocks or a ten-minute boat ride from the Circular Quay. It boasts much acclaimed architecture (courtesy of Philip Cox) and a huge retail complex (courtesy of global capitalism). This is very much a tourist area; there are many different attractions besides the bars, nightlife and top eateries. Besides the famous Sydney Aquarium, the main reason for our visit, there is the National Maritime Museum and the Chinese Garden of Friendship. The Sydney Entertainment Centre, with a large casino, is based here as well as the massive IMAX cinema. The harbour hosts regular free festivals, concerts etc., throughout the year and you may be lucky enough to catch some of Australia's finest performing in front of your very eyes. Indeed, had we come a day earlier, we would have seen Natalie Imbruglia; instead we got the new Rolf Harris, enjoyable anyway. The eastern side of the harbour is the splendidly titled Cockle Bay

Wharf, so named because historically it had such an abundance of shellfish, sadly no more. It does house an array of cafés, restaurants and clubs spread across quite a substantial space in, it has to be said, quite a tidy and attractive manner. The wharf and many of the surrounding areas have been quite tastefully designed by Eric Kuhne, possibly more famous for the massive Bluewater development in Kent, but the boy done well here, that's for sure.

Which is the TSG?

During the day, the bars and restaurants seem a haven for teenagers and families, but come the evening the area comes alive for the older generation and that included Karen and I. From here, walking north, you arrive at the Sydney Aquarium and what a splendid place this is. This most fantastic of all the many city aquariums I have visited, comprises a main exhibit hall, two floating oceanariums, one dedicated to the Great Barrier Reef and the other to a seal sanctuary. There are two touch pools and you can see the saltwater crocodiles and the elusive platypuses. The obligatory underwater tunnel takes you under a myriad of colourful fishes, majestic rays and

An aquarium resident ... glad the roof is reinforced.

magnificent, gigantic sharks. There is also an attached wildlife park with a bird and butterfly sanctuary, much native fauna on display with plenty of the nastier little creatures who also abide on this island continent. Sadly, time constraints and my lack of desire to see creepy crawlies stopped us doubling up the package. In Sydney, don't miss out on the aquarium.

Next along the wharf is the tranquil, beautiful and peaceful Chinese Garden of Friendship which was designed as a gift to celebrate the 1988 bicentenary from Sydney's sister city in China, Guangzhou. This oasis of serenity in the midst of such liveliness is a bit of a contrast, but with waterfalls, a lake full of colourful carp, weeping willows and ornate colourful flower displays, it really is quite a most pleasant and idyllic area. Carrying on from here along the harbour, you arrive at King's Wharf, more bars and restaurants and a fine shopping centre which is open until late,

The Maritime Museum.

Kings Wharf at night.

unfortunately! Finally along the wharf and you cannot miss it, is the splendid National Maritime Museum. You can't miss it because it features actual vessels as exhibits. You can walk amongst them, including the *Spirit of Australia*, then the world's fastest boat, designed by Aussie, Ken Warby, on his kitchen table and built in his backyard in 1974. This could only happen in Australia. The 1950s naval destroyer, HMAS *Vampire* is berthed here as well as a traditional Vietnamese junk, the delightfully named *Tu Dou*, meaning freedom, which sailed into Darwin in 1977 with thirty-nine refugees on board. You cannot imagine the ordeal those poor souls endured and wonder if it was worth it. What happened to them, was this truly the land of opportunity for them? It would not happen now of course, our colonial cousins are a lot stricter with regard to immigration and no doubt, the boat in today's age would not have been allowed to berth.

To end the evening, we revisited the Zaafran on the seafront at King's Wharf. Two years earlier, this had been one of the culinary high points of our antipodean adventure and, whilst we once again had an excellent meal at this superb example of Asian Australian fusion, they say things can never be as good second time and that was the case. Maybe our expectations were too high. Perhaps we were already in travel mode, ready for the short hop across the Tasman Sea to the Land of the Long White Cloud early the following morning but whatever, it was hard to criticise but the X-factor of our first visit was not quite there. Nevertheless, if you are partial to Indian cuisine with a twist, this is the place for you.

So early the next morning, we headed off to New Zealand for ten days and even I had to admit that Sydney had exceeded my expectations. We would be featuring two three-day spells at the majestic golf resorts of Kauri Cliff and Cape Kidnappers and then a long weekend in the capital, Auckland. Perhaps the idea of six days on a golf resort explained Karen's lack of enthusiasm for the trip compared to mine.

Sydney Golf

Compared to Melbourne, Sydney is a pauper in golfing terms. I had no real desire to go in

With gentleman, John Borden, at Moore Park, and this is not my only golfing attire!

Moore Park, the downhill Par 3 5th Hole at 173 yards. I hit a 4 iron to the heart and two putt
for an easy par, my first of the day.

search of much golf here as there is definitely a surfeit of outstanding courses available. Also I was equally aware the next part of the adventure featured six days in golfing resorts. So I gave way to a bit of tourist sight-seeing to keep Matron happy. I had played and reviewed the magnificent New South Wales Golf Course in the first book, which was designed by the mercurial Alistair Mackenzie in the early twentieth century. This should rank in any top twenty of the world's finest and should be any visitor to Sydney's first choice. Tee off just above Botany Bay and where Cook historically landed. It remains one of the best I have played. So shying away from that, it really left just three possibilities within easy commute of the city centre – Royal Sydney which was recommended, but I found dealing with them from the UK a nightmare. Bondi, where even golf was second citizen to the surf and Amazonian beauties. So I picked Moore Park because it was closest to us in the centre and because its location under the magnificent Sydney Cricket Ground is really unrivalled. Also, imagine a golf course in Hyde Park or Central Park, that's how close it is to the centre. It has hosted the NSW Open and obviously, the convenient location is a big draw but I have to say I found the course in exceptional condition. Fantastic quality fairways and greens, an interesting design without being arduous, it was a fair challenge. At just over 6,300 yards of the blues, it gives enough of a challenge to all handicaps. It has six par 3s, only one significantly further than 200 yards, so plenty of opportunity for finesse not crash bang wallop.

Karen joined me to take some photos and I was paired up with the first, but certainly not the last, Canadian I would meet on this adventure, an octogenarian from Ontario, the much-travelled John Borden, down under visiting his son. This sprightly chap walked the course whilst I buggied, I was

An idea of the central location of Moore Park Golf Course.

embarrassed, and Karen joined him down many holes. We had a splendid round, his desire simply to break 100, he so nearly did it. He was well on course until a disastrous eight on the par 4 last hole took him to 101. I played erratically to just break 90, thanks to a four-hole par finish. As would happen a lot on this trip, the scores seemed immaterial. Great company, fantastic course, 'Happy golf is good golf', Gary Player famously said and here, we played tremendous golf. The club has a splendid 19th with fine food available in the splendidly titled Long Apron Restaurant. An Aussie mixed grill and cold beer – the perfect end to a perfect day.

If you wish to play Moore Park in Sydney, go to www.mooreparkgolf.com.au or Tel: (02)96631064 or New South Wales go to nswgolfclub.com.au or Tel: (02)49281984. You can expect to pay about 100 A$ at NSW while Moore Park would cost about 65A$. Info for Bondi (9-hole): green Fees about 25 A$ go to www.bondigolf.com.au or Tel: (02) 9130 1981. If you wish to try your luck at Royal Sydney go to www.rsgc.com.au or Tel : (02) 93714333.

Aottearoa: 'The Land of the Long White Cloud'

A month into our journey and we arrive in Auckland for ten days, six to be spent at the country's two prestigious golfing resorts, Kauri Cliffs and Cape Kidnappers, then a long weekend back in Auckland before heading east to the Olympics, via Hawaii.

Now I don't mind admitting, we both fell in love with this quaint country from the moment we arrived. One of my favourite travel writers, Joe Bennett, a UK teacher who came over here for a twelve-month contract and stayed for twenty years, wrote a hilarious, compelling diary of a hitch-hiking trip he did around these isles which initially entranced me about this mystical small dot on the globe. Joe subsequently returned to the UK and did a similar trip around Britain and, like his peer, Bill Bryson, had particularly nice things to say about my home town of Wigan. Hence, my considerable appreciation for this guy who is likely to be quoted quite extensively in this section. The country is without doubt, as Joe says, a throwback to the UK in the 60s and 70s, my happy childhood years. The countryside is reminiscent of the Lake District, the unspoilt beaches like those of Cornwall before the M5 brought swathes of city dwellers down. The city is more like Chester or York than Birmingham or Manchester. House doors still remain unlocked and everyone is your neighbour. Please and thank you are the norm rather than exception. The type of place, where you know that youths are still likely to stand up for an older person on public transport. Definitely my type of country and they play rugby rather well, both codes!

Downtown Auckland.

Most great cities are set next to water whether it be rivers, seas or oceans. Auckland is particularly unique for its geographical location, it has harbours on two separate major bodies of water, the Tasman Sea and the Pacific Ocean. It is also surrounded by fifty or so mainly dormant volcanoes enhancing an already stunning location. The flight in is quite stunning as you land at the international airport. However, our first visit was to be a brief one as we were simply transferring for an internal flight up to Kerikeri. So far, our experiences at the major airports had been quite daunting. Not so here, as we met a different culture and a certain chill factor of the pleasant type. 'We want to leave two cases here', 'no problems. There is your ticket, they'll be waiting for you in ten days. No cost, transfer to domestic terminal, just follow that yellow line. Need a chair? No, a lift? No, oh sorry you fancy a walk, then let us at least take your hand luggage over'. It was so different, so laid back, a big airport with a corner shop attitude.

The flight north up the island took just over an hour. We could have gone by helicopter but not with the amount of luggage we had for a round the world trip, maybe next time. You appreciate the barrenness of the land literally from Auckland to Kerikeri, apart from hamlets and a few farms, there were just sheep and bloomin' loads of them. We did fly over Waitangi, where on 6 February 1840, the Maoris inexorably placed their trust in the Empress Victoria by signing the Treaty of Waitangi. That this treaty was necessary, I doubt not, but that it also produced an almighty difference in interpretation that still manifests today, cannot be disputed. In 1840, the whole country was really in a complete mess. Settlers were arriving in growing numbers, many from Australia, and there was no real authority to control what they did. A commercial operation called the New Zealand Company was planning to establish settlements, governing and taxing them, without any consideration or belief that the indigenous Maori population had any reasonable rights or claims. Also the magnificently titled Frenchman, Baron de Thierry (although he was born in England) decided to annexe the islands personally and appoint himself king. This may seem insane, but he had successfully appointed himself king of a small Pacific island, so this nutter felt he had established a precedent. Clearly, the situation demanded some sort of constitutional agreement and quickly. Ironically, the Baron did make it to New Zealand, not as a king but as a music teacher in Auckland. Only here!

London did not really want another colony as it already ran half the world, and what was to be gained, it was a poor man's Australia, small, at the edge of the world, not many resources and no strategic usefulness. The colonial office despatched Governor Hobson, mainly out of philanthropy, and it was out of a genuine concern for the Maoris that he was asked to sort out the mess. Perhaps the fairest deal would have been to leave the islands alone, but by 1840, it was already far too late for that. The grog sellers, musket traders and land grabbers were swarming all over both islands.

The treaty gave Victoria sovereignty over New Zealand, the Maori became full British subjects which guaranteed them 'full, exclusive and undisturbed possession of their lands, forestries and fisheries.' That's what it said in English and sounds clear enough, unequivocal and for its time, quite fair. However, the Maori translation was somewhat different. Victoria had governorship and the Maori, *Te tino rangatiratanga* which translated gave the chiefs unqualified exercise of over more than forty individual tribal chiefs and control over their particular tribal lands. Naturally, after signing the treaty, the chiefs left under a total misrepresentation of their rights and obligations. That Hobson was well-meaning and actually gave the Maori rights no other colonised people had ever been granted was probably the intention from the outset. The misinterpretation was a complete bungle, however the ramifications were immediate and are still being felt today. The Maori continued to lose lands to the Europeans and continued to suffer educationally, financially and socially as modern

The replica meeting house at Waitangi.

European capitalism ruled the roost. It can be said even with the best of intentions, Hobson really gave the Maori, a Hobson's choice of a future.

We arrived at Kerikeri, hardly an airport, more a bus depot, but Kiwi hospitality still continued. We were collected and transported in style by John, the local taxi driver, milkman, dairy farmer and part-time fireman. In these parts, it appears everybody multi tasks with a variety of occupations. He apparently also did some maintenance at the golf course. We arrived at the lodge at twilight and could only really tell that it was located on the edge of a cliff on a big rural farm. Yet the lodge was unbelievably luxurious. We arrived at 8 p.m. just in time for the evening meal. After booking in, we were taken to lodge room 1 and what a place! I was also given a blue blazer as gentlemen were obliged to wear a jacket at all times in the lodge area when dining or drinking. To say we were totally gobsmacked, overawed, taken aback, delighted would all be an understatement. This place was truly enchanting and charismatic, romantic yet exciting – we could not wait to dine.

There has been a lot written about this superb facility but again quite frankly, words do it little justice. In Matron's opinion (and that matters more than any golf review) it was the best and most romantic resort we have visited and this includes Cape Kidnappers and Pebble Beach where we stayed later on the trip. It is the one place I am sure I will have little difficulty getting her to re-visit at a later date. The facilities were first-class, spa, infinity pool, the food which was Michelin standard, superb location, gorgeous beaches and then, the golf. I cannot tell you what I scored as I found the views too mesmerising. Every tee shot was delayed whilst, Matron, Jason (a Canadian international banker based in New York who I had the pleasure of playing with), took copious pictures continually. They say every picture tells a story, well I will let these tell ours at Kauri, but trust me they don't really do it justice.

The lodge was tastefully decorated, in the style of the pre-war era I would suggest, but the rooms, spa and pool were twenty-first century, top-notch and as good as anything I have ever seen. The

Our room, cosy fire and wine to greet us – splendid.

The lodge reception area.

The view from our veranda that we awoke to.

A culinary delight every night, the best of local produce from sea or land. You could not fault the dining experience backed up with the finest local wines.

The pink beach, glorious unspoilt paradise, where Matron and I whiled away the afternoon with a lodge-prepared picnic. Idyllic, romantic, tranquil and a splendid way to idle the time away with your loved one. When I was in hospital, thinking my life was being dragged away from me, I could never in my wildest dreams have believed we would be at the end of the world enjoying God's splendour so much. I thanked the Lord many times that day.

dining was quite sublime and the views were to die for. We had lovely weather, not I gather always the case, but our three days were just one quite superb stay, we wanted for nothing. Of course, it was not cheap, but quality of this standard could not possibly be. A room equates to about £300 per night and I can assure you that for most it would definitely be the trip of a lifetime.

Occasionally, the most beautiful golf courses can be found in the most remote of places. This course is a perfect example, tucked away on the mountainous land that overlooks the Bay of Islands, this course is simply outstanding, from the clubhouse and pro shop, to the food and accommodation, the location and then the course. It is so perfectly maintained and manicured, you feel guilty if you take a divot and TSG does sadly take a few of these. The course is set up for visitors as if it was tournament play every day. All the fairways are striped and the greens perfectly cut and rolled. The money behind this place has to be monumental but then, I can assure you, so is the golfing experience. You can hold the US Open Trophy in the clubhouse to inspire you before you go on to play. Michael Campbell's replica is available, not behind some glass display cabinet, just on a table so you can pick it up, awesome!

The course can be enjoyed by all, from the very best professionals to the Sunday hack, such as the Social Golfer. It is tough but fair. The fairways are forgiving and so too is the rough, in places. Don't be misled, it can be a monster and long, particularly if the wind gets up, but it is certainly not as punishing or difficult as its sister course, Cape Kidnappers, but is the type of course you could play for the rest of your life and be happy. You could shoot great scores or bad scores but either way you would never tire of the views. It winds up and down hills, along cliff tops and even through marshes.

View from Kauri golf course. A portent of what was to come. Taking a photo was better than hitting your ball.

It has a terrific variety of environments and each hole is unique and challenging. I believe it always says something about a course when you cannot pick a particular favourite hole because it is the whole experience that comes to mind foremost. Fifteen holes on the course have sensational vistas over the Pacific Ocean and stunning Bay of Islands, which are so gorgeous they can actually be a distraction. Golf can take you to some stunning places, this is one of them and, in my humble opinion, possibly the best.

I have just realised that I have three balls in the Pacific Ocean, one each side, Kauri and Pebble and

Matron and I on the 7th tee.

Yes, the US Open Trophy.

Matron has a practice on the putting green.

With Jason Henderson on 1st tee.

Kauri – putting at the end of the world.

It doesn't matter what you score, 7th Green at Kauri.

Above left: The famous Kauri tree.

Above right & right: The Wednesday evening putting competition at Kauri, won by TSG with two hole in ones at 17 and 18, another title. The Freddie Tait Putting Champ does it again. It completed a title at golf of some sort or other on every continent. OK, not too much to really boast about, but I was delighted.

one in the middle in Hawaii. Once again, a ball in every ocean and a divot on every continent – love it!

From Kauri, we moved along with Jason and his wife, down to Cape Kidnappers, the sister resort where we both doubted the experience could be remotely as good as we had just encountered. The course is probably one of the most photographed in the world, always rated in the top fifty in any world list, so from that perspective, I was really excited. The Farm at Cape Kidnappers was the lodge here and in my opinion, not as luxurious as Kauri. The location, splendid as it is, is more rural, the Farm is still a working agricultural unit. The Lodge is top notch. The rooms again were superb, the food rather special but just lacked a certain *je ne sais quoi* that Kauri had. The weather was not quite as good, perhaps that affected our judgement, but if I had to choose one, it would always be Kauri, although the golf course at the cape is more demanding and a better golfing challenge. Again, the views although gorgeous, were not in my mind as good as Kauri.

I had been told that the cape was quite breathtaking but I was still not prepared and had no idea you could possibly build a championship course on such terrain. It certainly is one of the most dramatic courses in the world. Playing this course is truly some task, far too big for the Social Golfer. The front nine lull you into a false sense of security in that as it winds its way around the farm, the fairways are extremely generous and the greens, whilst undulating, are particularly large and very fair. The main trouble is the seemingly perfectly placed fairway bunkers that gobble up fairway-splitting drives when you least expect and miss the fairways – the long fescue rough will quickly punish you. The course is, by nature of its location, obviously influenced by the weather but, after the turn, becomes particularly difficult whatever the weather. The back nine take you to places golfers can rarely ever imagine. Greens on the side of 150-metre cliffs, tees isolated on slits of mountain tops. The ball carried over enormous valleys and gullies. The views on this back nine of the cliff faces and Hawkes Bay add to certainly one of the best golfing experiences of your life. Certainly don't come here expecting to shoot your best score. Come to appreciate and accept the challenge. You are in golfing heaven. Every passion-

Cape Kidnappers – tell me any golfer who would not want to play here.

ate golfer should at some time take the challenge that is Cape Kidnappers. The 16th tee shot is possibly the finest I have ever played. I stood on the tee for over a quarter of an hour experiencing the view, it was more appropriate for a picnic than a golf shot. I defy anyone not to be totally exhilarated and absorbed as you stand over 200 metres above the ocean, watching the gannets flying down to their colony and looking at this splendid 600-yard par 5. You just pull out your driver and want to whack it with gay abandon because I assure you that at this stage, you will feel totally alive and well and ecstatic that you are playing golf. You have to be straight, if you miss the fairway, your ball has gone, but as you leave the tee, look round, you will remember the view for the rest of your life.

The nearest town of note near the Cape is Napier which is about an hour's flight from Auckland. This place is unique and well worth a pleasant day's visit. On 3 February 1931, a massive 7.9 rated earthquake struck Hawkes Bay, virtually every building in Napier and Hastings, the next town on the way to the Cape, collapsed and subsequent fires laid waste to Napier's commercial centre and heart. When the quake lifted after ten days of aftershocks, the city was destroyed and over 250 people had died. However, Napier was also over fifteen square miles longer. An area of land was raised from the sea which facilitated the building of the city's new airport. The city was totally rebuilt in the styles fashionable at the time – Spanish mission, stripped classical and above all art deco, ensuring that in the twenty-first century, Napier has probably the highest concentration of art-deco architecture on the planet. A pedestrianised centre makes it a very easy place to get round. Fair play to the politicians of the day, you can imagine it: look, the bay has disappeared so OK, build a runway. We need an entire town rebuilding; OK, Los Angeles and Miami look nice, look at all those pastel-coloured buildings in the magazines. OK, let's do it. Clearly, the townsfolk of Hastings did not have as much foresight because as you leave the rebuilt city of Napier which oozes charm, to head off to the promentary called Cape Kidnappers, with the Pacific on one side and the mountainous vineyards on the other, you simply pass through village after village, just where was Hastings? Napier and wineries, yes there's not much else here. The Cape was so splendidly named by Captain Cook after his Tahitian cabin boy was kidnapped here by the local Maoris on first contact. I can't say I blame them. Imagine their fear as first they see a boat on the horizon, then several fair-coloured men with muskets land on their property. Imagine a space ship landing in your back yard, the aliens then disembark and promptly laser your dog; you probably would not have the friendliest of intentions and, if the tiniest of these invaders just happened to be on his own, perhaps having a jimmy riddle, I think we might kidnap him too.

Cape Kidnappers marks the end of Hawkes Bay at its southernmost point, twenty kilometres out of Napier and tall, jagged rock formations 100 metres high protrude from the ocean at the end of the eight-kilometre peninsula. The peninsula's European history started when Captain Cook first sailed the area in 1769. Cape Kidnappers is most famous for the world's largest and most accessible gannet colony. Tours run regularly to this plateau sanctuary, with close-up views of these incredible birds nesting. The plateau also showcases stunning panoramic views over the bay.

The coastline is formed by spectacular geological cliff formations, with rugged beaches below and

That walk was easy!

a world-famous golf course above. Take an enjoyable scenic walk or cycle ride along the remote coastline while the distinct cliffs tower above you. The Black Reef gannet colony can also be viewed from the beach.

And for those who are wondering about the cabin boy, when Captain Cook's crew opened fire at the Maori *waka* (canoes), he jumped overboard and swam back to the ship.

If you are not into golf, wine, fine food, bird-watching or walking, the Farm at the Cape is probably not for you. As a golf destination, it has few peers. The spa, Matron assures me, was again exceptional. From the Farm, there are several nature trails, all leading to the cliffs or the gannet colony. They are marked for guests, easy to hard. Trust me, these Kiwis are tough,

because the easiest walk was bloomin' hard. The weather turned here and the last day we could not see more than five yards from the patio of our lodge as the torrential rain and sea mist engulfed the peninsula. A party of golfers booked in for just the day, spent the afternoon wine tasting in the hope of some golf later. The wine must have dulled some of their senses as one or two wanted to risk the elements until it was pointed out there was a good chance they could walk off the cliff. The Cape is rated higher in golfing circles and I can accept that, the course is a championship challenge in a unparalleled setting which is pretty unique. However, as a social golfer, I preferred the location and set up at Kauri more. Would I care to visit both again? I sure would. It does not make sense to travel all the way round the world and not visit both. Thank you, Mr Robertson, the boy done good!

We then headed back to Auckland for a weekend break before heading onwards to Hawaii. The

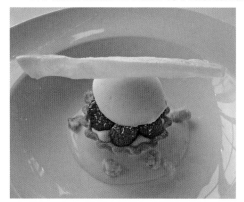

More fine food.

architect, Hugh Jacobson, said, 'when you look at a city, it's like reading the hopes, aspirations and pride of everyone who built it.' Nowhere is this truer than here in Auckland. European intertwined with Polynesian influences abound. It is clear that North American and Asian, particularly Chinese, influences are also now being clearly felt. There is an ancient Maori proverb, 'A house full of people is a house full of different points of view.' Auckland is the largest and most populous urban area in New Zealand, with over 1.5 million people it represents nearly $^1/_3$ of the entire population and is the world's largest Polynesian city.

In 2009, Auckland ranked fourth on the Mercer Quality of Life Survey. Summer weather has an average high of just under 24 degrees centigrade and winter weather is seldom cooler than 14.5. With a total of over 2,000 hours of sunshine a year, it is no wonder the city is so popular. Auckland was cosmopolitan before the word became trendy, because it has always attracted people from a variety of cultures and myriad walks of life. By the late 1800s, it was already a city with dozens of languages and differing cultures.

Auckland is New Zealand's only truly big city, and that said, it is still small when compared to most other countries' principal metropolis. Size however certainly does not diminish its charms as 'The City of Sail' and it is consistently included in any top ten cities listing for its cosmopolitan and eclectic lifestyle and exhilarating recreational opportunities. In Maori, Auckland is known as Tamaki Makau Rau, 'the spouse of a hundred lovers', not sure why, but again that mystique epitomises the city. Aucklanders have good reason for their patriotism. The city blends modern city living with an easily accessible outdoor playground. Mountain ranges, rain forests and the glistening Hauriki Gulf, with its myriad islands are all within reach and even the bustling downtown areas have countless parks that cover the city's dramatic volcanic landscape. Whilst the European heritage is never far away, as home to the world's largest concentration of Polynesian people with its wide mix of language and traditions, the city seems to pulsate to the rhythm of the Pacific. It is also the ideal gateway to the sub-tropical Northland and magnificent Bay of Islands or the rugged and romantic Coromandel peninsula.

Auckland's heart is naturally the waterfront, with its busy wharf, attractive marinas and an inviting nightlife through its cafe scene with many lively bars, bistros and restaurants.

Apparently one in five Aucklanders owns a boat, further reason why everything happens around the waterfront. The focal point of the city's waterfront is Viaduct Basin, home to the fishing fleet since the 1930s, but extensively rebuilt and substantially redeveloped for the country's defence of the Americas Cup in 2000. Located just a block from the Sky Tower, and yards from the historic ferry building and the cruise passenger terminal at Prince's Wharf, it really is the centre of Auckland's social scene.

Set in the Auckland Domain, one of the city's oldest volcanic cones, is the truly magnificent

The stylish waterfront.

Bagpipes at the America's Cup exhibit.

The imposing Auckland War Memorial Museum.

Auckland War Memorial Museum. In my opinion, this is one of the finest on the planet. This imposing landmark building has sensational vistas down to the waterfront of the city centre and houses probably the best collection of Maori treasures and ethnic crafts from the Pacific and provides a compelling introduction to the islands' history and culture. Here you can attend a live performance of the Haka, as well as follow the story of New Zealand's favourite son, Sir Edmund Hillary. It has a particularly unique section which chronicles New Zealand's involvement, usually at Britain's request, in global conflicts from the from the Crimean and Boer Wars to the two World Wars, the Asian conflicts in Korea and Vietnam, to the latest in Iraq and Afghanistan. The memorabilia and interactive exhibitions left a lasting impression. One of my long distant relatives, who left Wigan for New Zealand in the 1890s, lost his life in the First World War and I found his name on the memorial, a rather poignant moment. With a wildlife and fauna section, it was a memorable afternoon. No visit to Auckland should be made without a day set aside to visit this museum.

I had decided that we would spend our weekend break at the splendidly titled Great Ponsonby Bed & Breakfast. This restored 1898 villa lies down a quiet cul-de-sac in the lively chic district of Ponsonby, with easy access to Auckland Zoo, the waterfront and Eden Park. It has a quaint and unique charm. Its breakfasts are legendary, each cooked to order. Ponsonby is one of the oldest parts of Auckland and certainly one of the trendiest, with fine restaurants, lively wine and music bars to ensure the tourist has a great evening's entertainment within walking distance of this

Traditional Maori house.

The Haka.

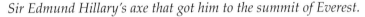

'It is the destiny of the British nation to spread good and just Government over a large portion of the earth's surface. Wherever her flag floats equal justice meted out to all . . . There is only one sentiment throughout the Empire – we must win regardless of the cost in man and treasure!'
– *The Waikato Argus*, 31 January 1900

Yep, our colonial friends actually believed this line.

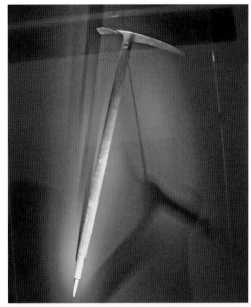

Sir Edmund Hillary's axe that got him to the summit of Everest.

Interactive experiences abound, totally enthralling experience for a civvy like me.

A particularly poignant moment, finding long-lost relatives who were true heroes.

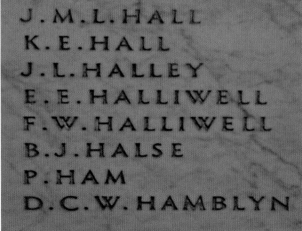

fine establishment. Sadly, Matron left her brand new size 6 leather boots here; I say this because this was to become an issue later in the trip. If you see a waitress at the Ponsonby with a pair of brown leather Louis Vuitton boots, they could well belong to Matron.

We spent one evening down at the harbour and I particularly enjoyed seeing the winning Americas Cup yacht, KZ1. The Americas Cup Story at the National Maritime Museum is particularly interesting. This is a splendid way to while away the evening, before imbiding in the local produce in a waterfront bar or restaurant.

Hawaii

We left Auckland on 2 February and arrived in Honolulu on the 1 February. Yes, we had crossed the international date line but I only realised this just before boarding in Auckland. I had booked the hotel in Waikiki from 2 February, so we would not have a room booked when we arrived. I hurriedly sent the hotel a begging e-mail explaining my cock-up and subsequent dilemma. I also realised, and I know it may sound daft, that we were entering the 'Good Ole US of A'. When applying for my ESTA visa, I had put our date of entry into California as 28 February after leaving Vancouver. So we boarded with no room booked and a possibility that we would be denied entry. Matron was none too impressed with me on this flight, I can tell you. Anyway, as it transpires both problems were sorted and we arrived safely in Honolulu and transferred quickly to our hotel in Waikiki. I must say I was disappointed at the airport, I had hoped and expected to be greeted by buxom Polynesian ladies with garlands of flowers. It did not happen at the hotel either.

I had booked Oahu Island because it remains the more famous island, it is home to the world-famous Waikiki Beach, the famous Banzai Pipeline Surf, Pearl Harbour, Koolau Golf Course which is rated the hardest in the world, and Ali Wai, the busiest municipal course. On reflection, I may have got it wrong, as it was always my intention at the half-way stage of the trip to have a truly romantic holiday here for two weeks, but sadly I have to admit Waikiki did not deliver. Our hotel was fine, but basic, overlooking the Ali Wai Golf Course and within easy reach of the nightlife and the beach.

Waikiki Beach, well we have all heard of it, but what a disappointment. A small strip of land between a myriad of hotels and the ocean, the beach at best was only twenty yards wide. It was harder to get a space than to get a sunlounger at a mediterranean resort where the hotel is full of Germans. I suppose it must have been different in the 1920s when Duke Kahanamoku, the 'father of surfing', now immortalised and daily adorned by surfers at Waikiki, first rode the waves. There was hardly any surf of note, great I am told for learning. The highlight was the periodic, impromptu,

Waikiki beach.   *The statue of Duke Kahanamoku.*

Hanuman Bay, Oahu.

acoustic music concerts on the promenade. The nightlife in Waikiki is similarly tacky, 'ladies of the night' roam the streets, there is an obvious drug problem and after two or three days, the urge to see the rest of the island was being fuelled by our obvious disappointment at this supposedly world-famous resort.

Chinese New Year celebrations, Honolulu.

Honolulu, the state capital, is a vibrant capital with an undeniable Oriental slant. Chinatown is a must visit, this unique section of town not only features exceptional cuisine but also has quite impressive gardens. We were extremely fortunate to see the New Year parade, a particularly lively, trouble-free spectacle. You may even see Duane 'Dog' Chapman, the reality television star of *Dog, the Bounty Hunter* – his office is here!

For most tourists, however, it is the beaches and surf that are a must see. You can encounter hundred-year-old turtles whilst sunbathing or re-enact that most famous of kisses on the *Here to Eternity* beach. Well I wanted to, but not Matron, explaining that a fifty-year-old northerner with a beer belly did not put her in mind of Burt Lancaster but I have got to say that in her bikini, I thought she looked better than Deborah Kerr. You can even learn to surf, better at Waikiki than the aptly titled Banzai Pipeline, although stunning, it was clearly the coastline where the experts played.

120-year-old turtle.

The Beaches of the Wai'anae coast are particularly stunning especially Makaha Beach where the big waves approaching ten metres can be found. Snorkel in Hanauma Bay and there is every chance you may be joined by a school of dolphins.

Another must visit is the Byodo-in Temple, a replica of a 900-year-old Japenese temple. It really is a hidden treasure, tranquil, beautiful and scenic. Ring the three ton bell and you will be assured a long life and receive the blessings of Buddha. We also visited the famous Dole Plantation, devoted to all things pineapple, very appropriate as Matron is allergic to them but again, after Waikiki, an interesting diversion. The island's

Sunset Beach.

Local Buddhist temple.

main attraction is the Polynesian Cultural Centre, the afternoon show, *Rainbows of Paradise,* is a stunning spectacle of singing, dancing and martial arts, all performed on double-hulled canoes. The best views of the island can be found at Wamea Bay where the original Polynesian human sacrifices took place and Kaena Point which has the world's largest waves, slamming into the cliffs – no surfers here.

The Nuuanu Pali Lookout is a perennial favourite stop among visitors to Oahu. The panoramic views of the windward side of the island from this expansive cliff will blow you away. Located at Nuuanu Pali State Park, the lookout overlooks the 985-foot cliffs of the Koolau mountain range. (Translated, *pali* means cliffs.) And yes, it is extremely windy. The trade winds blow through the valley between the high mountains on either side, forming a strong wind tunnel. On extra windy days, you can even lean into the wind and let the gusts hold you up. The Nuuanu Pali was the setting for one of the most significant battles in Hawaiian history. In 1795, Kamehameha I and his army invaded Oahu, arriving in an imposing fleet of war canoes at Waikiki Beach. The Oahu warriors were led by Kalanikupule, the *alii nui* (chief) of Maui and Oahu. Kamehameha's army marched to Nuuanu Valley to face Kalanikupule's troops. The ensuing battle was fierce, bloody and unrelenting. Gradually, Kamehameha's men gained an advantage, forcing Kalanikupule's forces to retreat further up the valley. The Oahuans attempted to make a final stand, but Kamehameha's army was too strong.

Pali Lookout.

Thousands of Kalanikupule's men were pursued and driven over the steep cliffs to their deaths. It is said that the victory was so complete that not a single Oahu warrior who entered the upper part of the valley escaped alive. An engineering firm was hired in 1897 to build what is now the Old Pali Road, a winding road used to carry traffic across the mountains. During construction, workers found an estimated 800 human skulls and other human bones at the foot of the cliffs – the century-old remains of Kalanikupule's slain warriors.

No visit however is complete without a visit to Pearl Harbour. Enjoy the free film and relive the Japanese attack. Stand on USS *Missouri* and envisage the final surrender of the empire back in 1945. It really is a most humbling place. The whole experience is currently undergoing a major facelift which should further enhance this historic, chilling monument. Do not miss it if in Oahu. I can say Matron and I were both moved by our visit in a way neither of us really envisaged.

List of the dead at Pearl Harbour, quite unbelievable numbers and ages.

TO THE MEMORY OF THE GALLANT MEN HERE ENTOMBED AND THEIR SHIPMATES WHO GAVE THEIR LIVES IN ACTION ON DECEMBER 7, 1941 ON THE U.S.S. ARIZONA

THIS MEMORIAL WALL WAS INSTALLED AND REDEDICATED BY AMVETS APRIL 4, 1984

Name	Rank		Name	Rank
C. A. IVEY. JR.	S2c		V. W. OGLE	S2c
R. "B" LA MAR	FC3c		L. H. OGLESBY	S2c
D. P. JACKSON. JR.	S1c		R. B. OLIVER	S1c
R. W. JACKSON	Y3c		E. K. OLSEN	ENS
J. B. JAMES	S1c		G. M. OLSON	S2c
E. E. JANTE	Y3c		R. E. O'NEALL	S1c
C. T. JANZ	LT		W. T. O'NEILL. JR.	ENS
E. C. JASTRZEMSKI	S1c		D. J. ORR	S1c
V. L. JEANS	WT2c		S. J. ORZECH	S2c
K. JEFFRIES	COX		M. E. OSBORNE	F1c
R. H. D. JENKINS	S2c		L. G. OSTRANDER	PHM3c
K. M. JENSEN	EM3c		P. D. OTT	S1c
P. F JOHANN	GM3c		F. H. OWEN	S2c
D. A. JOHNSON. JR.	OC2c		R. A. OWENS	SK2c
J. J. LAKIN	S1c		G. H. RIGGINS	S
G. S. LAMB	CSF		F. U. RIVERA	MATT
H. LANDMAN	AMM2c		D. F. ROBERTS	F
J. J. LANDRY. JR.	BKR2c		K. F. ROBERTS	BM2
E. W. LANE	COX		M. T. ROBERTS	CPH
M. C. LANE	S1c		W. C. ROBERTS	BKR3
R. C. LANGE	S1c		W. F. ROBERTS	S
O. J. LANGENWALTER	SK2c		W. S. ROBERTS. JR.	RM
H. J. LANOUETTE	COX		E. ROBERTSON. JR.	MATT3
L. C. LARSON	F3c		J. M. ROBERTSON	MM
W. D. LA SALLE	S1c		H. T. ROBINSON	S2
B. LATTIN	RM3c		J. J. ROBINSON	EM
C. V. LEE. JR.	S1c		J. W. ROBINSON	S2
J. C. McCLAFFERTY	BM2c		R. W. ROBINSON	PHM3
H. M. McCLUNG	ENS		R. A. ROBY	S1c
L. J. McFADDIN	Y2c		J. D. RODGERS	S1c
J. O. McGLASSON	GM3c		H. T. ROEHM	MM2c
S. W. G. McGRADY	MATT1c		T. S. ROGERS	CWT
F. R. McGUIRE	SK2c		S. ROMANO	OC1c
J. B. McHUGHES	CWT		D. R. ROMBALSKI	S2c
H. G. McINTOSH	S1c		V. M. ROMERO	S1c
R. McKINNIE	MATT2c		M. L. ROOT	S1c
M. M. McKOSKY	S1c		C. C. ROSE	BM1c
J. B. McPHERSON	S1c		O. A. ROSENBERY	SF2c
L. MEANS	MATT1c		D. L. ROSS	S2c
J. M. MEARES	S2c		W. F. ROSS	GM3c
J. A. MENEFEE	S1c		E. J. ROWE	S1c
			F. M. ROWELL	
			W. N. ROYALS	
			H. D. ROYER	
			J. F. ROZAR	
			J. S. ROZMUS	
			C. R. RUDDOCK	
			W. RUGGERIO	
			R. G. RUNCKEL	BU
			N. RUNIAK	
			R. P. RUSH	

Name	Rank		Name	Rank
E. R. JOHNSON	MM1c		T. L. OWSLEY	SC2c
J. R. JOHNSON	RM3c		A. P. PACE	BM1c
S. C. JOHNSON	COX		H. E. PARKES	BM1c
S. E. JOHNSON	CDR(MC)		P. J. PAROLI	BKR3c
B. S. JOLLEY	S2c		H. L. PATTERSON	S1c
D. P. JONES	S2c		R. PATTERSON. JR.	SF3c
E. E. JONES	S1c		H. PAULMAND	OS2c
F. B. JONES	MATT2c		B. PAVINI	S1c
H. C. JONES	GM3c		R. P. PAWLOWSKI	S1c
H. JONES. JR.	MATT		A. PEARCE. JR.	S1c
H. J. JONES			N. C. PEARSON	S2c
H. L. JONES			R. S. PEARSON	F2c
L. JONES				

Name	Rank		Name	Rank
H. L. LEE	S1c		V. G. MENO	MATT2c
D. A. LEEDY	FC3c		S. P. MENZENSKI	COX
J. G. ...ETT	BM2c		H. D. MERRILL	ENS
J. M. ...ROS	S1c		O. W. MILES	S1c
	GM3c		C. J. MILLER	F2c
	S2c		D. A. MILLER	COX
	ENS		F. N. MILLER	CEM
	EM3c		G. S. MILLER	S1c
F. LE...	CWT		J. D. MILLER	S1c
W. A... WIS	CM3c		J. Z. MILLER	S1c
N. S... VISON	FC3c		W. O. MILLER	SM3c
W. R...GHTFOOT	GM3c		W. H. MILLIGAN	S1c
G. E... BO	M1c		R. L. MIMS	S1c

Pearl Harbour, a Second World War submarine.

'I 'ave the big guns, I want that new dress.'

165

Another daiquiri for Matron.   *Vietnamese boat people celebration of arts at Waikiki.*

Waikiki Beach is a resort with a variety of budget to high-class hotels, motels and guest houses which are more like Benidorm than St Tropez. It is what you would expect – loud, brash and in your face. Ideal for a lads' trip, not so romantic for a vacation with your partner. The biggest disappointment was Waikiki Beach which was small and overpopulated, so go to Ewa, Laniakai or Waimanalo. All beaches on Oahu are open to the public, so enjoy.

Hawaiian golf

Anyone who truly loves golf will no doubt, at some time, have dreamed of a trip to Hawaii's renowned courses. Playing golf in these sensational sunshine isles is quite unlike anywhere else in the world. Whether next to the ocean, in a tropical rain forest or on the edge of high cliffs, you are sure to be playing through some of the most breathtaking scenery on the planet. It is a cliché often used by writers but where else can you play golf on the side of a volcano, in stark dark magnificent lava fields, dense jungle gardens or alongside the beach. You can putt and watch whales breaching in the Pacific Ocean, dolphins frolicking alongside the local fishermen in their colourful kayaks, hear and

see a myriad of different types of birdlife or lie on the beach next to the sleepy turtles. With waterfalls and sensational flora, you really are playing where the golf seems, at times, to be a sideshow of the wonderful natural habitat of the courses, so superbly designed that they seem to meander serenely through as if they were there from the dawn of civilisation. Whether you play golf here just the once or are a fortunate regular visitor, you are guaranteed an experience you will always remember. Be warned, once you have discovered Hawaii's best

Golf … think Maui.

golf, you will be spoiled. Nowhere else will ever seem quite the same.

The first problem the golfer faces is choosing where to visit. All of the inhabited islands with the exception of Nihau, boast golf courses you would love to discover. Time and cost will as with any vacation, dictate your eventual location, but most visitors and certainly first-time visitors will inevitably base themselves on OAHU, the most populated island, home of the largest city and state capital, Honolulu, and also of the state's number one resort, Waikiki. It also has the largest number of courses, featuring reputedly the hardest in the world – Koolau, to the busiest – Ali Wai Municipal. Professional tour courses such as Koolina and Turtle Bay are as easy to play as several fine municipals on the island. Golf is priced significantly cheaper than mainland USA, continental Europe and the UK, making a golfing vacation here very good value when compared to other destinations.

To book golf tee times, I would recommend the internet as the easiest method and I can vouch for the efficiency of www.TeeTimesHawaii.com. I would always phone the course the day before to check tee times, often these are changed at the last moment. Also always check the approximate travel time to your course because the roads are extremely busy on this small island, making journey times much longer than anticipated. Sole golfers can use the services of local travel companies who for a fixed fee arrange for the golfer to be collected from the hotel, which is definitely a plus, and taken with playing partners directly to the course and collected later. Clubs and balls can be hired. All leaflets are readily available at hotels and tourist information offices.

Koolau is considered to be the world's most challenging course and a memorable experience for golfers of all skill levels. It is carved out of a magnificent tropical rain forest under the historical Pali Lookout in the Koolau mountains, and the golfer faces a golfing challenge unlike any other. A pictorial delight with breathtaking views of cascading waterfalls, it is a spectacular setting which should inspire from beginning to end. The golf course matches this majestic setting. The mountains, at over 3,000 feet of ribbed rock and sheer ridges, form a stupendous backdrop. Impossibly beautiful tropical flowers burst open on vertical bluffs. The senses are driven and tested at every hole. The course hits you like a ten-ton truck from the first hole, where the starter recommends you have enough balls to

The challenge of Koolau – tropical forest …

... sheer mountains.

your handicap, drop zones are in front of the hazards. As well as the tropical rain forest, which starts as the narrow fairways end, there are also deep, twisting gullies and ravines to contend with. Forced carries are everywhere and the greens are like long, narrow, thin torpedoes or narrow shallow affairs, either way pinpoint accuracy is necessary to score well here. The course has no weak holes and several outstanding ones, but nothing compares to the final hole. The 18th is a beauty, with twenty-four bunkers and two forced carries. The drive is a peach, you can aim left (a carry of 230 yards) to a narrow fairway where, left and short, lie two massive sand traps; aiming right sees you in the ravine that splits the fairway from the green or you can take it right (a carry of nearly 300 yards) to a twenty-yard-wide plateau which if successful, would leave a little wedge in. A fantastic finish to a splendid course.

Turtle Bay, Koolina and Kapolei have all hosted PGA, LPGA or Champions Tour events. All are immaculate courses. Turtle Bay has two courses of which the Palmer is the must-play situated on the ocean, however don't expect ocean views. The Fazio, fine as it is, really does not compare. Koolina and Kapolei are very similar, pristine courses featuring

Koolau, the hardest drive of my life, no hope if you miss the fairway either side; an awesome test.

extensive water features, multi-tiered greens, landscaped floral gardens, manicured fairways and countless coconut palms. They are visual delights but are both eclipsed by the Royal Hawaiian, formerly known as Luana Hills. Near Koolau, it is probably more beautiful but not as difficult. Its feature hole, the 11th (the pond hole) is not always open but there is a substitute par 3 which sadly diminishes the pleasure of playing this magnificent course, if you are unlucky.

Ali Wai in the centre of Waikiki is the busiest course in the world. A fine flat, well-maintained course, tee times are six balls, and rounds take in excess of six hours. Clearly one for the keenest

Beautiful Kalopie.

golfer only. Hawaii Kai is a much more pleasant public alternative. It offers a fine cheap alternative with exceptional greens next to the coast. Also in the Koolau region is Olomana which is where Michelle Wie honed her game and she still holds the course record of 64 when she was only thirteen. Best of the rest include Ewa Beach, Coral Creek and Hawaii Prince.

Stunning Royal Hawaiian.

Always plenty of new friends to meet along TSG's journey.

Six of the other islands have courses of note and renown. Every island is different and has its own character but after speaking to my fellow travellers, the following represent the island's finest.

The Big Island naturally has the most courses and a bevy of beauts, the best of all and possibly the best in the whole of Hawaii, is the Robert Trent Jones Senior Classic Mauna Key. The *grande dame* opened in 1964 and this resort classic features narrow fairways and severe bunkering with knee- buckling ocean carries, is an uncompromising test but according to all, it is well worth the trip and cost. If you want to tee off on a live volcano, try the Volcano Golf and Country Club where you can watch whales basking, before heading off to Waikola where there are two fine coastal courses, the Kings and the Beach.

Lana'I or the Pineapple Isle has just two major courses set in two distinctly different resorts. The Challenge at Manela is a signature Nicklaus ocean design with a forced carry off every tee and the Experience at Koele is an enchanting tropical forest course, designed by Greg Norman. The signature downhill 17th is a must play. In an exhibition game in 1991 between Norman and Nicklaus, Jack took an amazing 17 at the 17th, bet you beat that!

Maui has several high-end resorts such as Kapalau and the Plantation course, home of the first event of the PGA Tour for the past ten years. Clearly, a must play. But on this exceptional golfing isle, Royal Kannapali, featured on *Big Break*, the Dunes at Maui Lani and the three courses at Wailea are all worth a mention. Many think Maui is the best place to play in Hawaii, who am I to argue?

Getting around the islands takes some serious planning but there are regular boats and planes between the isles. On most islands, it seems better to stay in a tailor-made resort.

Oahu golf directory and contacts:

Turtle Bay Resort   808 293 6000
www.turtlebayresort.com
Koolau   808 247 7088
www.koolaugolfclub.com
Kapolei   808 674 2227
www.kapoleigolf.com
Koolina   808 676 5300
www.koolinagolf.com
Luana Hills   808 262 2139
www.luanahills.com

Thanks guys, it was a pleasure.

Olomana Golf Links   808 259 7926
www.olomanagolflinks.com
Hawaii Kai   808 395 2358
www.hawaiikaigolf.com
Ali Wai Municipal   808 732 7741
www.honolulu.gov.des/aliwai.htm

Kaui'i or the Garden Isle possesses some of the world's most compelling natural features, including the wettest place on earth, Mount Wainaleale. Naturally, it has some absolutely stunning golf courses. The Prince course is a jungle golf experience like no other. The Kiele course boasts the kind of over the water shots that tend to induce drooling. Wailua Municipal is arguably the island's finest pay as you play course.

Vancouver – the Olympic city

So on 18 February, we left sunny Hawaii for the snow of British Columbia and the Olympic experience. What did we find when we got there, a glorious sunny afternoon, albeit a bit cooler than Hawaii, but no bloomin' snow anywhere.

Two years previously when planning this trip, it had been my PA, Nicola's, idea to visit Vancouver when the Winter Olympics were on. 'Where's the golf,' I ask. 'You will find somewhere and then you can say you played golf at the Olympics,' she replied. Quite right too, it had plenty of appeal and after all, every sporting *aficionado* would want to enjoy the Olympic experience if possible, because like most northerners, I certainly had not bought into the London Games at all. So, Vancouver for ten days, golf on the hoof, sightseeing and Olympics, the job's a good 'un.

Travel writer, Jan Morris, said '… the sort of town nearly everyone would want to live in.' In fact, since the year 2000, the annual survey by the Swiss-based Corporate Resources Group, has regularly ranked the city in the top three places to live.

As well-known author, Patrick Bourneville, put it, 'Every single study in the world about the quality of life, inevitably comes to the same conclusion, Vancouver is the place to live. The city is relatively safe, beautifully squeezed in between the Pacific Ocean and Rocky Mountains, with both an infrastructure and an economy to meet everyone needs.'

Why is Vancouver so popular, after all, the weather might not always be great, it rains here like in Manchester, and then rains some more, but the setting is sublime: the urban environment is clean and safe, the integrated multi-cultural population welcomes and encourages diversity. Where else could you ski in the morning, sunbathe on the beach over lunch and still have time for a round of golf in the afternoon. There are beaches literally just minutes from the city centre. You can watch whales breaching in the ocean just yards from the coast. Stanley Park is one of North America's biggest and wildest, again just minutes from downtown. The restaurants are widely acknowledged as second only to New York in quality and variety.

In short, Vancouver explodes Canada's image problem, that the country is stunningly beautiful but dull and boring, nice place, nice people but no fun, because in reality, this city is attractive, at times hedonistic, with a real zest for life, spectacular scenery, excellent nightlife, beaches, funky chic café scene, fashionable bars and a myriad of outdoor activities similar to west coast hot spots such as San Francisco and Los Angeles.

We stayed at the wonderful Ocean Breeze bed and breakfast in North Vancouver, where we were treated quite royally by mine host, Margaret. Like Auckland, there were copious amounts of tasty tucker for breakfast every morning which set you

The splendid Ocean Breeze, North Vancouver.

up for a glorious day in this most splendid of cities. Karen and I, despite having stayed in many of the planet's finest hotels still always enjoy the quintessentially quaint, quite British local B & B. Given that our colonial cousins always put a classy edge to the experience, that usually incorporates all that is best from a family-run business with the quality of food you would expect from larger, more renowned gastronomic hosts. It was no different here. We had a super clean, spacious and comfortable airy room

Our view of Grouse Mountain with not much snow about.

with fantastic, big, tasty, hearty breakfasts. North Vancouver was the hub for all fans heading north to Whistler for the alpine events, so that the ferry and market area, with its eclectic mix of café bars, pubs and restaurants was constantly busy throughout our visit. Many an enjoyable evening was had here. On a first visit to Vancouver, unless you were looking for cheaper Olympic accommodation and a vibrant social scene, most visitors would ignore North Vancouver, but the journey is memorable for two reasons. The views from the sea bus are unforgettable as are the views from Grouse Mountain, a high mountain eyrie which rises above North Vancouver and can only be reached by cable car. There are stupendous, unrivalled panoramic views of Vancouver and its surroundings.

From here, you head into the uniquely planned city, created in blocks, whereby the ocean can be seen from every angle. The sea bus crossing was cheap and quick, landing at Canada Place where the Olympic Flame proudly burned. From here, it was an easy walk to Stanley Park, Granville Island, Gastown and Downtown. It is rare to go to a major city where, quite frankly, it is so easy to get around on foot.

Gastown is the redeveloped heart of old Vancouver. Once a skid row, then an over-pretty tourist trap, it is now a more dynamic mix of shops, bars and restaurants and increasingly popular with the younger élite of Vancouver as a desirable residential area.

You will often see cameras rolling on these streets, and not only when the Olympics are in town. The X Files has a lot to answer for, as it was shot in and around the city for five seasons. Vancouver is now North America's largest film and TV production centre after New York and Los Angeles. Visit Vancouver and the likelihood is that you will see a film or TV show being filmed. The city's rise to prominence has occurred in just over thirty years. In the mid 70s, there was no industry as such. By 1978, the net worth was approx $12m per year and by 2008, it was estimated to be $1 billion in all revenues.

The famous Gastown clock.

Matron gets her boots.

Given the city's natural beauty, it is perhaps no wonder that the city was home to the world famous Greenpeace organisation formed in 1971 when twelve Vancouver members of the 'Don't make a wave' committee took a small boat out into a USA atomic test zone, setting the tone for subsequent eye-catching and often controversial, direct action that has characterised the organisation ever since.

Vancouver, despite having so many tourists, seems so well organised, it feels safe and secure and the famous Red Jacket was there on the street corner to reinforce this feeling of well-being.

The Canadian frontier, unlike its US counterpart, was more mild than wild west. Records show that there were just three gunfights in the nineteenth century, and pretty inept ones at that. But it was not all plain sailing, the west still had to be won and the men who won it were the world famous mounties. This is Canada's most potent symbol, the famous red coat of the North-West Mounted Police. The red coats came about because the government, in an urgent response to a drink-fuelled riot/massacre in Cypress Hills on the Alberta border, despatched a small troop of men dressed in a handful of old British army jackets to bring order to the unpoliced US/Canadian border. This was where many US adventurers often traded with the indigenous population, bringing with them the notorious consequences of gambling, prostitution and alcohol. The area had become known as 'Whoop Up Country'. The facts of the massacre were never fully established but it appears five Indian women were raped and twenty-one men killed, more than likely by US white hunters. None the less, the way the Mounties dealt with this episode helped lay the foundation for their long-standing reputation and respect for their probity and fairness. It may be Canada's best-known symbol

internationally: a police officer in a scarlet coat, sitting on a horse. It has been used to promote Canada abroad since 1880 – and was glamorized by Hollywood in the 1920s, '30s and '40s.

Hollywood took great liberties with the Royal Canadian Mounted Police, and is usually cited as the source of the saying that the Mounties 'always get their man.' However, the phrase can be traced to the Fort Benton [Montana] Record in April 1877,

The SG meets an unorthodox 'Mountie'.

four years after the formation of the North-West Mounted Police. The force was created after Prime Minister, John A. Macdonald, declared that the prairies needed a strong police force. The force's job would be to solidify Canada's claim to the west, improve relations with First Nations and wipe out the illegal whisky trade. This police force was initially only meant to be temporary; it was to see the west through its transition period and then be disbanded. Macdonald modelled the Mounties on the Royal Irish Constabulary, one of the world's first national police forces. The recruitment of officers for the new force started in September 1873. On 8 July 1874, 275 mounted police officers set out from Dufferin, Manitoba. They covered 1,500 kilometres over the next three months, arriving in what is now southern Alberta. They set up camp and started to build Fort Macleod – and began the work of enforcing Canadian law in the west.

In 1909, the city's enlightened civic leaders decided to put into service a motorised ambulance service. Within hours of being on the streets, it had its first casualty– a shopper at the corner of Glanville and Pender was run over by the ambulance itself … only in Vancouver!

Thieves who stole $56,000 in cash from the Bank of Montreal on the city's Prior Street in 1942 confessed to burying much of it 'in a clearing in a clump of trees bordering the cricket pitch in Stanley Park.' The pitch and trees are still there, but be warned, penalties for digging in the park start at $500.

Stanley Park is one of the world's greatest city parks. At over 980 acres, it rates among the continent's largest urban parks with beaches, formal gardens, miles of walks and bicycle trails and a remarkable semi-wilderness of forest. It is also home to the magnificent Vancouver Aquarium.

The Winter Olympics dominated – that and finding Matron some boots, as you may recall her other pair had been left in Auckland. Hence, I became the resident expert on economy shoe shops in Vancouver. What made matters worse, after two days traipsing around, the first pair bought lasted just twenty-four hours before the heel came off. My fault of course, I rushed her into making a decision. Still, all this mooching around the shopping centres did make us feel a big part of the Olympic experience and six days in a new pair of boots were required before Matron felt adequately dressed to watch some Olympians in action.

We watched the curling and great it was too. We are both crown green bowlers so we had some affinity with what we were watching. The Great Britain won, although without Matron's full-on vocal support, they were to fall at the next hurdle. That night, the whole country came to a standstill as the

The GB curling team in action.

USA beat Canada in the ice hockey group games. I suppose it was like England and Scotland, but with the Canadians all wearing the red top like the England soccer team in the World Cup, where the shirts are worn by everyone at home for the day of the match. Like Capello's and Erikson's boys, Canada played the part fully by being the 'Lennie Let Downs'. The city was in shock. Of course, it had a great ending, the hosts defeating their neighbours six days later to take the Gold Medal when I was in Pebble Beach. Good job perhaps because two years later, the rink became the focal point of a major riot and disturbance after the Vancouver National Hockey Team lost the Stanley Cup Final. An event I found hard to reconcile to the friendly city I had visited just two years earlier. This was not just Vancouver's games, the whole country had bought into it, it truly was Canada's Games and I can't help feeling we won't achieve the same sense of national pride and involvement in the London Olympics. It could be, of course, that Vancouver is not the capital or largest city in the country and Canada does not have a north/south divide like the UK; the national pride and fervour was a joy to behold from the moment that first gold medal was won. In the Summer Olympics in Montreal in 1976, the Canadians infamously failed to win a gold medal, something that clearly irked and grated in this great nation, but it was put right big time here in Vancouver.

We decided to end our vacation here by visiting the splendid State Capital of Victoria reached by an hour-long ferry ride where you can see whales basking, dolphins frolicking, mini glaciers forming and sensational vistas abound. It was so beautiful even Matron forgot she suffered from sea sickness.

Victoria is a small sedate city, perched on the end of Vancouver Island, a ferry ride from downtown Vancouver, it is British Columbia's capital, an historical anomaly given its respective size compared to Vancouver. Much of its charm is derived from its quaint English feel, the leafy old town, exquisite harbour, a world away from the hustle, bustle and noise of most North American cities.

To some extent, the city overplays its role as a last corner of the British Empire on which the sun has not quite set – the tea drinking and scone ritual is self-consciously indulged and bagpipers, union

The beautiful passage over to Vancouver Island.

The majestic state capital, Victoria, on Vancouver Island.

jacks, royal bunting, red pillar boxes, phone boxes and buses as well as imitation pubs are everywhere. Many I suspect would find this Anglophile effect a tad excessive but maybe it gives our North American cousins a taste of their lost heritage. However, little can detract from the city's overall prettiness and relaxed way of life, nor the appeal of some of its premier attractions, principally the Royal British Columbian Museum and the glorious Butchart Gardens. For most, the city will be remembered for the pedestrian-friendly appeal of its old fashioned streets and hidden historic corners or maybe the whale-watching, its temperate climate, its many fine cafes and restaurants and its fine golfing options too.

The lovely inner harbour is the heart of the city, a sweeping waterfront that contains many of the city's best known landmarks, principally the Parliament Buildings and the Museum. At night, it comes alive when the gardens and promenades are full of people and street entertainers. The museum is rated as one of the best in the world. Its displays embrace the myriad strands of British Columbia's social, cultural but also natural history, with particular emphasis on the indigenous peoples.
Butchart Gardens lie about thirteen miles north of Victoria and represent the single most impressive gardens in an isle of gardens. They are truly unmissable, even if like me, you have only a passing or little interest in all things horticultural.

I got my golf in at the splendid Northlands Golf Course. The course had re-opened early due to the unusually dry winter the city was having. Snow still had to be shipped into Whistler for the skiing events sixty miles north. The course was fantastic, one of the most underrated it has been my pleasure to play. My particular thanks to Eric, Martin and Gary, from the club who made the whole day truly enjoyable. Golf in the Rockies – I think that even this fair-weather golfer could be encouraged to play in the snow, cold and rain. Finally, thanks to the staff at the club, who again looked after me, getting me home etc., feeding me, lubricating me and supplying some wonderful pictures. Thank you.

With a little bit of a sad heart and realisation we may never visit again, we bade *adieu* to Margaret

Above & below: The Butchart Gardens, simply stunning, beautiful and a must visit.

The stunning 4th hole, with the waterfall in the distance.

and set off for the *piece de resistance* of the trip from a golfing perspective, six days at Pebble Beach. I had waited a lifetime for this, yet despite this, I have to admit leaving Vancouver whilst the Olympics was still going strong, was disappointing. *C'est la vie.*

'Sydney may disagree, Rio too, and San Francisco may demur, but it is hard to think of a city more beautiful than Vancouver, or one where it must be such a pleasure to live. The city is scenically unparalleled, set between ocean and mountain, the waters of the Pacific bounding the downtown core, the peaks of the coastal mountain ranges rearing majestically in the near distance.'

Last night in Vancouver, from top of Pier Head, Vancouver City skyline in the distance.

Pebble Beach.

Pebble Beach

When I was first approached about a round-the-world golf trip, it was inevitable that a stay at the prestigious Pebble Beach resort would be a major highlight. It could never really be described as the ultimate golf road-trip or really 'living the dream' unless the Social Golfer visited this golfing mecca on the Monterey peninsula, just outside Clint Eastwood's home in Carmel, sunny California.

Organising this would prove difficult as in our six-day stay, I wanted to play the three principal resort courses, hoped for an invitation to the prestigious Cypress Point Club and maybe a knock at Del Monte, Poppy or the municipal at Pacific Heights. I had also been given instructions by Matron to leave a day free to explore the peninsula properly and enjoy the stunning vistas along the seventeen-mile drive, culminating in an evening in Carmel.

I decided, after much review, to play the top-hundred rated Spyglass first. The second day I chose Spanish Links and my stay would be completed with a round at the daddy of them all, Pebble, home later in the year to the 2010 US Open. Ironically, after the sunshine in Vancouver, the weather was pretty inclement. Wednesday, Spyglass day, was chilly, grey, overcast but dry and still. On Thursday, it was sunny at the Links, gorgeous with a pleasant wind. Friday, my big day on the Pebble links, saw gale-force winds and a torrential storm came in when we were on the 5th. Three completely different successive days (good job the US Open is held in June not February) but it certainly demonstrated to me how difficult all the courses could be, depending on the weather. It also enhanced my appreciation of all three course designers as they had to consider the changing weather patterns and particularly the

Spyglass par 5 opening hole sweeps down to the ocean.

4th green, open to the elements.

The back 9 at Spyglass, water hazards and trees come into play.

winds coming in off the Pacific, to make them so unique, challenging but also interesting and beautiful.

It is a matter of literary debate whether the inspiration for Robert Louis Stevenson's *Treasure Island* came from May Island off the east coast of Scotland or here at the Monterey Peninsula. What is known is that Stevenson did live near what is the Pebble Beach Lodge and it seems inconceivable that this rugged terrain and glorious scenery should not have insinuated itself some way into this most classic of seafaring tales.

Spyglass Hill, the second course on the Pebble Resort, takes its name from the Stevenson connection. Annually rated as one of the toughest courses on the US PGA tour, the 6th, 8th and 16th holes are among the most difficult the professionals will play all year. Designed by Robert Trent Jones and opened in 1966, the course has subtly hidden water hazards which require an A-game mentality. When I visited, the area had been suffering quite a loss of trees due to some local fungi and this had affected the look of the course. Pictures in the clubhouse, particularly of the 18th, showed how the forest impinged on every fairway and was clearly a major defence on the back 9. Whole swathes had been lost and the beauty of the course was sadly diminished. I am reliably informed that by 2020, the original masterpiece, nature willing, will have been restored. Spyglass has a most wonderful opening five holes that take you downhill from the fine clubhouse, through sand dunes, to the ocean where any wayward drive or errant approach is severely punished. It is a super golfing test and experience after which you rise inland, through the forested plantations, away from the sea and it feels more like a Carolina course. Sadly, there has been quite a loss of both pine and oak trees which has affected the course somewhat. I am pleased to say that there is a major planting exercise underway which hopefully will bring the course back to its pristine set up and condition. As you would expect, the greens were in great condition, a bit slow but with some deceptive slopes and gradients.

The third course of golf Mecca's imposing trilogy is the Links at Spanish Bay, which is almost certainly going to be the last built on this particular stretch of Californian coastline because of complex planning and conservation issues, and the price of real estate. A joint collaboration between Sandy Tatum, Trent Jones and Tom Watson, the Links and its prestigious resort, the Inn at Spanish Bay, were opened in 1987. The intention was to design and create a course in the spirit of the traditional old Scottish links where, of course, Watson famously had so much success in the British Open. Its tumbling fairways, almost haphazard greens right on the coast,

You are never far from the Pacific Ocean at the Spanish Links.

with stunning views, make this course particularly vulnerable to changes in the wind, but on a glorious sunny spring day, there can hardly be a more pleasant or interesting golf course to play. This is a particularly environmentally sensitive site and the course was designed around these issues and carefully routed to avoid disturbing the many indigenous plants and creatures. There is a unique charm and beauty to this place and Matron, who accompanied me, would suddenly wander off into the dunes, camera in hand, and come back elated at some of the sights she had found.

I then visited the splendidly-titled Spanish Links – what a great experience that was. The weather was great, the course, despite being wet, was in fantastic condition, but did not play as a true links because of the previous week's rain but that did not distract at all from a fine experience. I started with a birdie 4 at the 1st by nailing a forty-footer and proceeded at last to find my putting touch which helped me put together a fine round. Apart from a loop from 8 to 12, all the holes are within a drive, even one of mine, from the ocean. So on a windy day, I believe it could be treacherous. The finish from hole 15 to 18 is as good as it gets, playing the par-4 15th, you are only sixty yards from the beach, but

The inland holes are spectacular too.

Nature abounds at the Spanish Links.

Stunning little par 3, I birdied this.

Sweeping 17th, open to the elements.

amazingly in that small acreage, is the par 3 16th (playing north) and stunning 17th (playing back south) before heading back north with a difficult final par 5. The wind gives an advantage then takes it straight back – super design.

The Pebble Beach Golf Links was established on central California's Monterey peninsula in 1919, spanning a spit of land famously described earlier by artist, Francis McComas, as 'the greatest meeting of land and water in the world.' Designed by Jack Neville and Douglas Grant, two local amateur golfers with no prior golf design experience, these two produced the masterpiece that many golf luminaries consider the finest in the world.

There are many fine holes but in my opinion, the tiny, much pictured 7th hole to a well-bunkered green flanked by the Pacific, which can play from a wedge to a 5 iron even for the pros, is the most mesmeric. Like the 17th at Sawgrass, it's an iconic tee shot; you really want to hit the green. When I played, despite the advice to just aim into the ocean, I under hit the club taking a 6 iron for the 130-yard carry, when my caddy advised my 5 wood. I did not reach the bunker short. However a chip and a thirty-foot putt will show I parred this hole, albeit not very impressively. The 8th plays back inland from the ocean and demands an approach, over an ocean chasm, to reach a precipitously sloping green. On a normal day for the average golfer, this 416-yard par 4 would be bail out left and treat as a par 5. When I played the howling gale of the ocean, which actually blew me over on the tee, it meant that my drive, my longest ever measuring at 339 yards, nearly ran into the chasm but left an approach across the widest part of just over a hundred yards. A sand wedge and 2 putts later ...

Majestic 7th at Pebble.

The 18th, the view from my veranda.

another par.

Stunning holes are in abundance here, indeed from the 4th, there is a fabulous sequence of seven consecutive ocean holes. Throughout the round, there are daunting drives and difficult approaches but it is the constantly changing wind directions that mean a 130-yard shot could be anything from a wedge to a 5 wood. A true golfer's test. As Billy Andrade said, 'It really is the Holy Grail for most Pros,' and that's why us hackers want to play it, just one hole played well here will live long with you. If there is one hole that defines the image of Pebble Beach, it's the 18th. I stayed at the Lodge and my room was behind the 18th green, looking back down the fairway, and for seven days in February 2010, I breakfasted on my patio with this stunning vista. This 543-yard par 5 tees off on a small headland in the ocean to a fairway that skirts Carmel Bay. Widely considered to be golf's finest finishing hole, you tee off aiming over the ocean to gain maximum advantage, then you walk up the misty fairway, accompanied by the sound of the crashing surf on the coastal rocks and the barking of the lapping seals. You play up your approach to the well-bunkered green and imagine you are G-Mac with thousands cheering you to US Open victory. Holing out on 18 is a unique, special feeling. Exhilaration, exultation and memories that will last a life time. Jack Nicklaus famously said that if he could only play one more round, he would choose here, it's not hard to see why.

Everything ever written about Pebble is true, an exceptional golfing test, spectacular backdrops; it does not get any better. Probably the best I have ever played.

On Friday, the big one here at Pebble, we had been told a major storm had been coming in which was due at 1 p.m., so it was going to be touch and go whether we would get round. We did get to the 7th before getting drenched, but the gale was with us all day. Despite this, I played superbly starting par and no doubles despite losing a ball on the first par 3, the 5th, when the wind of the ocean took my ball into some millionaire's garden. The par 5 6th up the hill took a drive and three 3-woods into the wind and I was still short. The famous 7th was just 100 yards downhill, but into the teeth of the gale. I was forty yards short with a 6 iron, but got up and down. The 8th, with the wind behind, was just a drive and a wedge, an

Matron wrapped up to protect her from the elements.

Greens fit for the US Open later that year.

I gave it everything ... as the rain poured down.

unbelievable experience. When the rain came down even harder on the 16th tee, I needed a 3 par finish for 80. A great drive set up the par at the 16th, but the famous dreaded finish was left. The 17th long par 3 was yet again into a massive left to right wind, so I needed a drive to reach the par 3 narrow green.

I gave it everything and just reached the front and two putts as the rain poured down which left me needing a last par at the famous par 5 as shoot 80. We were in the teeth of the storm, but the wind was with me and off the ocean here on 18. I launched a drive over the Pacific and watched expectantly that the ball would fade back into the fairway. It did go over the fairway and nearly into the bunkers at over 300 yards. Impossible. A lay up and a wedge to two feet, a birdie 4 on the 18th at Pebble for a sub 80 in horrific conditions. Awesome, if I say so myself.

I did receive my invitation to Cypress so sadly missed out on two of the peninsula's hidden gems

The fantastic Pacific Grove Municipal.

but I did visit both and had a walk around them. The Pacific Grove Municipal Golf Course lies just two miles north of probably the world's priciest golf real estate. Yet, despite its glamorous zip code, there is no elaborate clubhouse, no bag drop, no parking attendants – and the green fees won't buy you a lunch at its most prestigious neighbours. Yet this 'poor man's Pebble' was quite enchanting. There are two distinct and separate 9s. The front more benign inland 9 was laid out in 1932 by Chandler Egan, a former US Amateur Champion, the back 9 laid out in 1960 by Jack Neville of Pebble Beach fame. This is similar to Pebble as it becomes a fabulous links-style layout, weaving back and forth along the Pacific. The 16th and 17th form a splendid conclusion to probably the best value for money round in California. The 16th tee box is situated next to a lighthouse, whilst the 17th is a stunning par 3 carry over a freshwater pond, with cypress trees surrounding the green and the Pacific crashing against the bay on the left.

Finally, and I am grateful to mein host at Lefty Odouls in San Francisco, who alerted me to Poppy Hills Public Course, inland on the peninsula often used by the PGA for the A and T. He describes it as the hidden star, very pretty, long and tight, well-bunkered with lots of hail Mary go for glory holes. The best part, he says, is that it is half, about 130 bucks (one hundred quid) of normal Pebble Course prices.

Cypress Point, probably the most scenic and beautiful golf course in the world. The best … debatable.

The problem when travelling the globe in eighty days and competing at the same time, is that

Approach to the 18th at Cypress.

inevitably there have to be omissions from the golf itinerary which you would not normally consider. Similarly, as this is mainly a golf vacation, I was tied by the necessity to write about the problems the traveller would encounter and this reared its head in Monterey, California and to a lesser degree, in Vegas. Despite all the golf being arranged from the UK, I am pleased to say there would have been no difficulty in playing at any of the courses documented previously had you just arrived in Singapore, Australia, New Zealand and Hawaii.

Not so here in California. Anyone can play Pebble, but at a cost of over $500, it is prohibitive to many. Of the many other courses on this splendid headland, the grandaddy of them all is probably the prestigious, exclusive, private enclave of Cypress Point. Of course, in any top hundred, this course will feature in the top three, more often than not this Alister Mackenzie masterpiece will head the list. Is it as magnificent and sensational as they all say? Well yes, without doubt it is visually stunning, immaculately manicured and set up, but number one – never, in the Social Golfer's opinion. Let me justify that. If you had the Mona Lisa in your house, would you cover it up or open it up so your neighbours could enjoy its beauty. Would you stop visitors taking photos, I doubt it. Part of the mystique of Cypress is its total exclusivity. Ask any social golfer to describe the course and, apart from the well-documented and photographed coastal holes, they would struggle because they cannot play it, nor have they seen it played on TV by our peers. Tiger, Big Phil, Rory *et al* would now likely eat it up and the allure as a

course could be lost for good. Secondly, a course which features two successive par 3s at 15 and 16 is at best unique but at worst simply a distraction in that the terrain takes precedence over the golf hole. Spectacular they are, I kid you not, possibly the most sensational views you can encounter on a golf course. Better than New South Wales (another Mackenzie classic) or Kauri and the Cape in New Zealand? They are good, but no way significantly superior. The 18th is certainly not a hole befitting such a quality course, a simple short par 4 dog leg, which even this mid-handicapper played as a 4 iron and 8 iron. Mackenzie's greens did me in three putts. My main criticism is its exclusivity, I had to pull favours to get a round and I cannot name the

The sensational closing par 3s.

member I played with; I even had to smuggle my camera in. I love beautiful courses which this certainly is and play it if you have the opportunity. I, however, like to walk in the footsteps of my heroes, not Monterey's wealthiest. On this day, the fact that the only other group we saw included Clint Eastwood and his wife, says it all really. The Social Golfer represents all golfers and supports opportunities to play. I could understand limiting opportunity due sometimes to ability, but not to have any reciprocal playing arrangements to even courses such as St Andrews is pomposity at its

View from the 16th tee.

highest. The best – not in my opinion; one of the best – certainly.

Pebble Resort principally consists of the Lodge and Spa at the Pebble Links and the Inn at Spanish Bay on the Spanish Links. Both are what you would expect top-notch resorts to be, with high quality restaurants and amenities. We stayed at the Lodge overlooking the magnificent 18th, and I breakfasted for a whole week on a veranda, watching the waves crash on the beach and the early starters weaving their way down this magical hole. I had a spa bath one evening and my mobile rang. It was my son phoning from home. 'Where are you, Dad?' 'Well, I am having a bath in the very same bath that Tiger may have bathed in'. 'Oh and where's Mum?' 'Having a lie down in bed …' Paul quickly retorted 'Who knows what Tiger did in there'.

The peninsula is quite stunning. From the pleasant little town of Pacific Grove in the north of the bay, to Carmel in the south, is a spectacular seventeen-mile drive, which for any visitor should be treated as being as essential on the itinerary as a round is on the famous links. Well, nearly, but not quite! Pacific Grove is a mellow town, known for its Victorian houses and lovely bayside coves, among them the splendidly titled Lovers Point Park Beach. The seventeen-mile drive is a private

road and involves a toll (unless you are staying at the resort), but it would be a mistake to miss out on this splendid stretch of eye-catching coastline, particularly the peculiar phenomenon known as the restless sea, where opposing ocean currents crash into each other and the waves appear to break in two different directions. Bird Rock is a granite outcrop populated by seals and sea lions, gulls, cormorants and other wildlife, and the magnificent 200-

The lone cypress.

year old, Lone Cypress, sculpted over the years by the mighty winds of the ocean.

Carmel is annoyingly quaint, flooded with boutiques, cafés, galleries and, at weekends, the culture is more of a yuppie type. However, the location is beautiful and the beach typically clean, safe and quite sensational. Locals tell me we should have also made time to head further south to the Big Sur, a land of fierce beauty much photographed, but we simply ran out of time. Next time, perhaps …

And so we left this golfing paradise and hired a car to head north to San Francisco, not with flowers in our hair but plenty of joy in our hearts and great memories as well.

Pleasant, quiet, beautiful Pacific Grove.

San Francisco

If you're going to San Francisco, make sure to take some tablets for vertigo! Karen drove the car up from Monterey to San Francisco for two reasons – she is the better driver and I am certainly the better navigator. Our journey up was not without incident as the bad weather closed in with fog banks around San José, turning what should have been an enjoyable scenic route into a turgid hard afternoon until we hit the outskirts of San Francisco and the weather cleared somewhat.

I had booked us into the highly recommended White Swan Inn on Bush Street, which meant Karen had to drive all the way up to the top of the city and turn at California Street before heading back down to Bush – rather complicated. At California Street, the lights changed to red and Karen stopped the car on a 45 degree slope, giving us a feeling of vertigo. When the lights changed, she accelerated hard and the car took off like a rocket, landing with a bang on the street. She negotiated her way through the trams and we headed down towards Bush when the lights changed again. This time it was like the Tower of Terror as we slipped down the ramp. Karen had had enough. She pulled over, gave me the keys and said she would see me at the hotel. I finally parked in front of the inn and the concierge took the keys to park the car up outside the city. 'Will you need the car, Sir, to see the sights?' he asks. 'No, we bloody well won't,' shouted Matron. San Francisco has so many iconic sights that even golf has to take a secondary role. No visit here would be complete without a trip to Fisherman's Wharf and then on to Alcatraz.

The car is secondary in this hilly city and getting around is easier by cable car, taxi or bike tandems. In such a big city, there are many accommodation options to suit all budgets, but location is important. I can recommend the elegant White Swan Inn on Bush Street, just five minutes from Union Square. A bed & breakfast with

No wonder the locals here are fit.

Evening snacks at the splendid White Swan Inn.

Cosy bedrooms with real fires, needed whilst we were in town.

Imposing Alcatraz, Matron now has no fear of water.

Magical without being over the top, the Golden Gate Park is a botanical heaven featuring the gorgeous Japanese tea gardens. Great museums, outdoor venues, another fine city-centre park. I am now more convinced than ever that to be a truly great city, you need a public park of some magnitude, as in New York, Vancouver and here in San Francisco.

Matron far happier with this mode of transport.

Golden Gate Park

a unique English feel, with fireplaces and four-poster beds which is superbly located for Chinatown and an excellent selection of restaurants and bars.

A day in Golden Gate Park at the Botanical Gardens is a different type of city experience, but one I would not have missed.

No visit to San Francisco would be complete without a day on the world famous wharf from which you have spectacular views of both bay bridges and, of course, Alcatraz. Splendid restaurants and bars, trendy shops, old funfair for the kid in us all and the seals (albeit a reduced number each year) make this a unique place to spend a day. It is also where Matron discovered why, when we had a meal and I ordered the wine, she only ever had one glass to my three. I always told her it was the food affecting her taste buds. She drank slower than me, but in a splendid wine bar we whiled away an afternoon with a wine tasting session when it was proved beyond any doubt, that I preferred the more acidic tastes of the Sauvignon Blanc whilst Karen preferred the smoother Chardonnay. As a result, we now order glasses not bottles, unless it's Chablis, the only one we both like …

This city truly represents all that a social golfer wants from a golf break. Some affordable golf, iconic sights and attractions and a lively social scene. Go and enjoy!

Stunning, vibrant Fishermans Wharf.

Yes, this is the one for me, need some help with yours, darling?

The must visit whilst in San Fran has to be Alcatraz. You will remember this place as long as you live. Sit where Al Capone did. The interactive tape as you go round is a must. It really brings home the ferocity of the penitentiary; you feel you are actually incarcerated.

Alcatraz was seen as an ideal prison from the very beginning. In 1859, eleven soldiers scheduled for confinement arrived with the Fort Alcatraz First Garrison and became the first inmates. During the Civil War era, soldiers convicted of

Lombard Street, the world's most crooked street and San Francisco's must photographed.

Some swim, once thought to be impossible.

Was this Al Capone's cell?

I'm a celebrity get me out of here!

desertion, theft, assault, rape and murder, together with citizens convicted of treason and Confederate prisoners of war were all confined here. In the First World War, conscientious objectors joined the inmate population. During the Great Depression, the Bureau of Prisons wanted to create a maximum security facility and it was transferred from the War Department to the Department of Justice in 1934. Of the 1,545 men who did time on Alcatraz, only a handful were notorious – among them, Al Capone,

Machine Gun Kelly and Robert Stroud, the Birdman of Alcatraz (although he actually conducted his famous studies at Leavenworth prison, his real nickname being the Bird Doctor of Leavenworth). Hollywood, with Burt Lancaster in the title role, took the story and changed the facts. Most prisoners here were men who had caused problems in other prisons, trouble-makers who were escape risks, but of course Hollywood again refused to let

In 1964 and 1969, local activists claimed the island for all Native Americans. The occupation lasted over nineteen months.

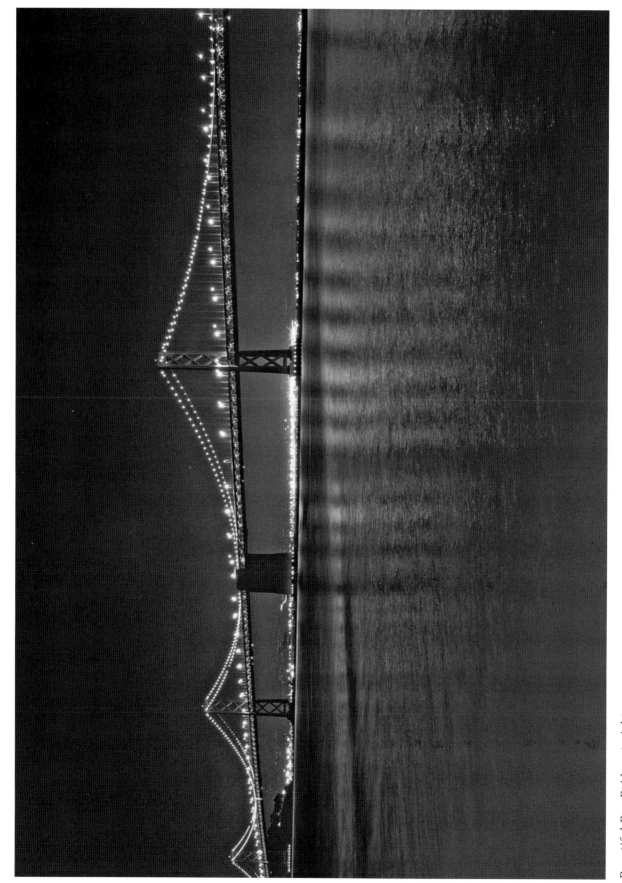

Beautiful Bay Bridge at night.

the facts spoil a good story. There were fourteen attempted escapes and all are known to have failed except attempt thirteen, on 11 June 1962, carried out by Frank Morris and brothers, John and Clarence Anglin. Using raincoats as floating devices, they slipped into the water, never to be seen again. To maintain the allure, the authorities assumed, and stated as such, that they had drowned, but nobody knows for sure.

Increasing maintenance and operating costs, and a nearly successful escape (the fourteenth) on 4 December 1962, by John Paul Scott and Carl Parker, resulted in the US Attorney General, Bobby Kennedy, closing the prison. Scott and Parker, who sawed through bars in a basement room under the kitchen and used inflated gloves to give extra buoyancy, jumped in and swam to freedom. Parker soon gave up against the prevailing currents and turned back, but Scott actually reached land under the Golden Gate Bridge, but was too exhausted to walk away. He had however destroyed the myth that the swim was impossible.

You really do get a feel for the place, its history, and its formidable reputation.

You are entitled to FOOD, SHELTER, CLOTHING and MEDICAL ATTENTION anything else you get is a Privilege.

Rule 5, Alcatraz Prison Rules & Regulations

Golden Gate from a helicopter – sensational.

The lighthouse on the island has been in operation since 1854, predating the Fort, and was the first on the Pacific Coast. The exact location of Al Capone's cell is unknown and a large part of his $4^{1}/_{2}$ years here was spent in a hospital isolation cell. There were no executions on Alcatraz, although there were five suicides and eight murders. The average stay on Alcatraz was between eight and ten years and had nothing to do with the term of sentence, only whether they were considered to be disruptive or incorrigible. The sharks that swim in the San Francisco Bay are not man eaters, but every effort was made to ensure the prison population believed that they were. In 1926, when rumours of a mass breakout were surfacing, Commandant-Colonel G. Maury Cralle's response was simple, 'Go ahead, swim.' The belief that no-one escaped cannot be proven or disproved and, apart from Morris and the Anglins, Ralph Roe and Theodore Cole escaped in 1937 (attempt 2), never to be seen again.

San Francisco has two of the most beautiful bridges and one of them is possibly the most famous bridge in the world, the Golden Gate is stunning, sensational and a really special way of viewing this most awe-inspiring vista is via a helicopter trip.

If it was on its own, the fabulous Bay Bridge would be highly rated anywhere else. In 2013, the Americas Cup will be fought out in the bay; one can imagine now how this event will fit nicely into the San Francisco mind set

San Francisco street cars.

and the pictures of the boats under both magnificent bridges, or with Alcatraz as a back drop, are sure to impress the world.

San Francisco, despite the weather, did not disappoint – Chinatown was fabulous and Union Square, where Lefty Odoul's bar enticed us in several times. Plenty of wine, beer and top food, just no golf. But after Pebble perhaps I, and certainly Matron, needed a break and we headed back to our Florida home via the party city of Las Vegas, with a burning desire to return one day.

Golf

The cosmopolitan city of San Francisco offers a unique opportunity to party in one of America's most dynamic and interesting cities, at the same time as playing some of the country's outstanding tracks and some less well-known, but nevertheless, fine courses within the city's boundaries at some very reasonable green fees. Good food, carefree living and an active cultural scene have been San Fran's trademarks since the gold rush. Add to that fine golf and you have a city golfing destination which has it all.

The quite stunning Presidio Municipal which was closed during my stay due to thunderstorms.

Assuming the visitor stays in the city (and to properly enjoy the San Fran experience you really should), you have two of the classic public courses on your doorstep in Harding Park and Presidio. These truly are must-play courses. The Presidio meanders through the park of that name, which is heavily wooded with cypress and eucalyptus, and green fees are a real bargain at less than $90. A renovated Palmer design, with great greens that offer a tremendous challenge. Even better is Harding Park. This sprawling tree-lined course around Lake Merced is probably the finest in the area and fees again are likely to be less than $90. If you have the connections, Olympic and the San Francisco are the city's opulent tracks, both rated in any world top 100. If you wish to stay in a purpose-built resort then the luxurious new Ritz-Carlton at Half Moon Bay is well recommended. The whole bay area hosts a number of impressive public courses and has a fine mixture of classical designs as well as many new courses that have opened further east as the city spreads its wings. In a city of many surprises, the quality of golf available may well be a surprise.

As mentioned previously, I was very much tied by travel details as well as the golf and San Francisco proved to be the most difficult to arrange. During our three days there, I had considered as usual the two main criteria for a social golfer – close-

Harding Park, a superb President's Cup venue and great value for money.

ness to the city, which in this case led me to the Presidio.

Walking in the footsteps of heroes, you are a bit spoiled for choice here, with Harding's Park, a public course that hosted the last President's Cup, or the Olympic, a regular US Open destination and the top-twenty rated San Francisco Golf Club.

A mixture of atrocious weather (it hardly stopped raining) and once again private non-reciprocal arrangements (members only), made it impossible to get in a round in the small window of opportunity I had.

The Presidio, redesigned by Arnold Palmer and open to the public since 1995,

Harding Park.

meanders through the hills overlooking the city, the Golden Gate and Alcatraz. For less than $90, George Fuller in *California Golf* places it in the top thirty in the state and describes it as a must play. I tried, but the weather beat us. A rolling thunderstorm in the bay put paid to that.

According to all the information I collected on San Francisco, the three finest courses were all located on a small stretch of land in south San Francisco, along the Pacific Coast. This terrain is clearly similar to the sandbelt in Melbourne and hosts the Olympic, Hardings Park and the San Francisco golf courses. It is also San Francisco's most affluent residential area. They are both private courses and I was simply unable to arrange a tee time in the timescale we had. Hardings, a public course, was sadly another victim of the terrible weather. Hardings Park was available at the amazing price of $88 for

US Open venue, the Olympic.

a round, what value. The Olympic has two courses – the Lakeside, which hosted the US Open in 1955, '67, '87 and '98, and the shorter, tighter and still highly rated Ocean Course. Guests can only play with a member.

San Francisco Golf Course was rated the best of the three in all ratings that I examined prior to the trip. Tom Doak renovated the course in 2002 and it is now accepted as a true great. It hosted the 1974 Curtis Cup Match where no doubt the USA again thrashed GB. Unfortunately, guests can only play with a member. Again, disappointingly, there is no reciprocal club policy in place. It is a place I must re-visit in good weather and tie in with a trip up north to Oregon and Bandon Dunes perhaps. Don't tell Matron.

The Majestic San Francisco Golf Club.

Golf directory – all these courses are within ten miles and twenty minutes from Union Square and the White Swan Inn

Presidio Golf Course, 300 Finley Road, Sf 94129.
Tel: 415/561/4661.
www.presidiogolf.com

Harding Park Golf Course, Skyline Boulevard, SF 94132.
Tel: 415/661/1865.
www.harding-park.com

San Francisco Golf Club,
Junipera Serra Boulevard, SF 94132.
Tel: 415/469/4122

Olympic Club, 524 Post Street, Sf 94102.
Tel: 415/587/8338
www.olyclub.com

Other city centre courses:

Golden Gate 9-hole Course,
Fulton Street, SF 94117.
Tel: 415/751/8987
www.goldengateparkgolf.com

Lake Merced Golf & Country Club,
2300 Junipera Serra Boulevard, SF 94015.
Tel: 650/755/2239

Gleneagles International 9-hole Course,
2100 Sunnydale Avenue, SF 94014.
Tel: 415/587/2425

Cypress Golf Club 9-hole Course,
2001 Hillside boulevard, SF 94014.
Tel: 650/992/5155 www.cypressgc.com

California Golf Club, (next to airport)
844 West Orange Ave, SF 94080.
Tel: 650/589/0144

Las Vegas

This was not our first trip to Vegas, we had visited in the summer of 2006, just a few months before my stroke, and so in many ways it would be a poignant reminder of the 'old Ian' and an opportunity to reflect on how far I had really come in my ongoing recovery. It would be an opportunity to also get to know Vegas as our first visit did not quite go as anticipated. In July of 2006, we were in our Florida home for the summer and Matron, a red-head naturally, was quite literally feeling the heat of a Floridian summer. With our anniversary on 10 July, I booked a surprise three-day vacation in Vegas, being the true romantic that I am. Karen was not completely enthusiastic as we had been airborne quite a lot that year. When she asked how long the flight was, I replied, 'Leave Orlando at noon, arrive Vegas 3 p.m., you can manage three hours to Vegas, darling.' Of course when we got to Orlando airport, we soon realised that the flight was three hours to Houston, change and then another three hours to Vegas as we were going through three time zones. Easy mistake for a Brit to make. It was touch and go whether Matron got on the plane. No-one told me that Vegas in July was unnaturally hot, over 115 degrees during the day. Karen was melting, we could only sunbathe at 7 a.m. for an hour. We could not walk outside at all so I was not a popular bunny.

The entertainment capital of the world offers just about everything: the world's largest hotels, the brightest stars in show business, shops and restaurants to rival any on earth. It's true too, that the lights really are brighter in Vegas. Yet not far from the glitter and glamour is a world of beautiful lakes and the solitude of the desert as well.

Until 1855 Las Vegas was just home to the native Americans until a settlement was agreed by Brigham Young and a group of Mormons established a trading post here. Quite what they would make of it all now, is not hard to imagine. In 1931, gambling was legalised in Nevada, an acceptance that it might be easier to control legally rather than continue to allow the widespread betting and gambling of

The lights really do shine brighter in Vegas.

the depression era. The invention of air-conditioning and irrigation following the completion of the Hoover Dam were the main constituents that allowed Las Vegas to flourish post- war. Los Angeles hotelier, Tom Hull, built the first motel, El Rancho, establishing the concept of motels aimed at the car market. It was mobster, Bugsy Siegel, who set Vegas on the glamour and glitz road when, on Christmas Day 1946, he opened the Flamingo Hotel. As vividly portrayed by Robert de Niro in the 1995 film, *Casino*, organised crime and Vegas quickly became natural bedfellows from the 1940s. Gangsters were drawn like magnets to the glittering cons piling up so effortlessly in the slot machines. Mid-west crime don, Moe Dalitz, followed Siegel and opened the Desert Inn in 1950. These days, it is big corporate money that controls Vegas and improved regulation and policing does appear to have virtually eliminated mob involvement, but rumours always abound in this cosmopolitan metropolis.

The next big boom came in the late 1950s and early 60s with the establishment of the 'Rat Pack' as entertainment became an important part of the casinos continued appeal. Frank Sinatra, Sammy Davis Jnr, Dean Martin, Peter Lawford, Joey Bishop, *et al*, opened the doors in later years for Elvis, Tom Jones, Engelbert Humperdinck and latterly, Elton John, Rod Stewart and Billy Joel. Indeed you had not really arrived unless you had played in Vegas. Vegas has always moved with the times or set its own agenda. The 1990s and the new millennium have seen the development of the theme hotels and latterly, the mega resort. Sport too has been drawn inexorably into the Vegas web, particularly boxing. Caesar's Palace, the MGM and the Mandalay host nearly every world championship of any note or renown.

And so we arrived at the Luxor, the majestic pyramid-shaped themed hotel at the bottom of the

The Excalibur, first of the theme resorts.

strip. Why the Luxor? Although it is at the bottom, there is a walk-through to the magnificent more expensive Mandalay and a free monorail to MGM, with New York, New York just higher up the street. Who am I kidding? Trust me, it probably offers the best and the cheapest deals. It offered superb value for money on all web searches for both visits. I would not say it is any better than any other, but on two visits to Vegas the room only cost was absolute value for money at less than 60 bucks (£40 per night). Great bars, great food, a casino and live shows. We have nothing but positive vibes about this place.

Shopping malls, Vegas-style.

My only complaint about Vegas is the blooming clickers, guys and gals who click business cards and give them to you as you walk the strip. It really cheesed me off when given cards for strip clubs and ladies of the night when I was walking with the wife, how ignorant. Apart from that, Vegas has so much to offer. The themed hotels, particularly the Venetian, not quite Venice, but my word as close as it comes. New York, New York – the bars here are far more friendly than those in Soho and Chelsea in the Big Apple itself. The Forum and shopping at Caesar's are simply mesmeric. Anyone not impressed by the fountains at the Bellagio is, I think, really sad. It is Disney for adults and if you do not gamble, it's a safe, enjoyable week. We did see families in turmoil where people had lost fortunes. In a billion-dollar hotel, it is unrealistic to think you will clean up, but obviously some people think they can. A worrying but lasting memory for both of us was walking through for an early breakfast and we saw an old lady at a slot machine with a chain round her neck linked to a credit card that was placed in the slot machine. When we returned for lunch, she was still there with the card still in place.

I think Vegas is the type of place everyone should visit at least once, but you might need a

Is it Paris …

... or Venice? No, it's Vegas.

The real lions at the MGM.

The Bellagio Fountains.

Matron to control the purse strings. For the record, I did gamble $10. I went to put it on a roulette table, number 24, my birthday, to be told by the lovely lady it was a minimum $1,000 bet. I thought I was a VIP! So I put it in a slot machine but little did I realise how complex they were. They have nine pay lines, which means that you have to pay for nine lines if you wish to try and hit the top, mega prize, it is usually $4.50 a spin. I was playing at 50 cents a spin and thought I was winning. When I pressed 'collect' after investing my $10, all I came away with was 27 cents – never again. There is, however, never a dull moment from the white lions in the MGM, the toga-wearing waitresses in Caesar's, the street entertainers ... you are transfixed at every corner, but you sure need your wits with you at every turn.

Everyone who visits Vegas says you must visit the Hoover Dam and the Grand Canyon. I really fancied a helicopter ride, but both Karen and I chickened out and made excuses – cost, time, rather watch a show, even go shopping. Now that we are back home, we both regret it.

The opulent Forum shopping at Caesar's Palace.

At least from Vegas I do have some golf to report. Once again, choosing the course closest to the city, led me to the Bali Hai which was a fantastic experience, with two great German guys, Jens and Manfred, and Jim from Wisconsin, a fine 2-handicap golfer. Joined by our caddy, Mike, we had a wonderful day, some magic golf mixed with mediocrity – such is social golf. Firm friendships were established and in Mike's case, some exceptional green reading gave me my best putting of the trip. Many thanks!

The course was in the shadow of the strip and, despite being directly under the airport flight paths, was quite visually stunning. Some sensational holes and course conditions were exceptional, despite unseasonable weather for Nevada. Like everywhere on this trip, we found that course bookings were down, leading to some sensational offers being available.

The guys at Bali Hai.

There are a plethora of courses around Vegas, but I have to say costs are relatively high in comparison to what I think most social golfers would consider acceptable. The other problem being that most top-notch, highly-rated courses would require a hire car or the cost of a taxi to get there, most being a substantial distance from the city.

Oh, another green missed!

Vegas Golf Directory

This list is not exhaustive, there are over forty courses in any local directory but it comes from the Vegas Top Ten, so hopefully that should be so …

Reflection Bay Country Club – nominated frequently as one of the top ten courses in the USA, designed by the great Jack Nicklaus and is superbly located on the Lake Las Vegas shoreline.
75 Monte Lago Blvd, Henderson. Tel: 702 740 4653

The Legacy Golf Course – host to a US Open qualifier, it combines a Scottish links feel with a dramatic backdrop of desert vegetation. Holes 11 to 13 are known as the Devil's Triangle.
130 Par Excellence Drive, Henderson. Tel: 702 897 2187

Dragon Ridge Golf Course – Manicured fairways, superb greens and dramatic elevation changes, it offers some spectacular views. The bad news is that it is private with limited public play.
552 Stephanie Street, Henderson. Tel: 702 614 4444

Bali Hai, 5160 Las Vegas Blvd. Tel: 702 450 8000

Angel Park Golf Clubs – hosts two courses, the Palm and the Mountain, both designed by Arnold Palmer, self-styled as 'the world's most complete golf experience.'
100 South Rampart Blvd. Tel: 702 254 4653

Las Vegas Paiute Resort – with two famous Pete Dye courses, the Snow and Sun Mountain. Sadly these masterpieces are over twenty-five miles from the Strip.
Highway 95 (exit 95). Tel: 702 658 1400

Desert Willow – this challenging course, highly rated by my caddy, Mike, is carved in the foothills of

the Black Mountains and is surrounded by natural hazards and very hilly terrain.
2020 West Horizon Ridge Parkway. Tel: 702 270 7008

Las Vegas National – established in 1961 and where a young, innocent Tiger Woods won his first title back in 1996 – just when I was having my brain tumour removed, coincidentally.
1911 East Desert Inn Road. Tel: 702 734 1796

Royal Links Golf Club – this course features replica holes inspired by the famous holes back in the UK, the road hole for example, quirky for sure but immaculately maintained.
5595 East Vegas Valley Blvd. Tel: 02 450 8000

The Revere at Anthem – winding through three desert canyons, this course features natural changes in elevation and spectacular views of the Vegas skyline. Many golfers I spoke to rated this their number one.
2600 Hampton Road, Henderson. Tel: 702 259 4653

Rates do vary dependent on the time of year. I would use the www.GolfNow.com (Vegas site for offers available and updated daily). Beware, all Vegas courses require soft spikes and some state no spikes at all, so always check before booking.

So we leave Vegas, our epic trip about to come to an end as we head to our second home in Florida. We were not disappointed, saw so much more than our first visit in a lovely temperature. Can you Adam 'n Eve it, we did not see any snow in Vancouver, yet we did in Vegas.

Bali Hai.

Back to Florida

The last leg of our 30,000 mile trip saw us return to our Florida villa for a fortnight. To all intents and purposes, both Karen and I felt our journey was over, even though we still had the Atlantic to cross before we can officially say we have traversed the globe. So, whilst it was a good chance to have some R and R and to see what damage the Floridian frost had done to the garden (which was not a pretty sight), there were some important golfing matters to be attended to before concluding the golfing odyssey. Firstly, I was to play in the season opener at Black Bear on the Edwin Watts Tour. In view of my restricted schedule this year, this was far more important than a normal event as it would be imperative I finished up the field to gain vital points towards the end-of-season nationals. I only intended to play both majors on tour, so had my work cut out. Secondly, and on a personal note, very importantly, my final commitment was to meet up with my great buddy, Brew, to celebrate a milestone date in his ongoing recovery. As it turned out, I also had the opportunity to meet up with two great old golfing buddies, my Toys for Tots winning team partner, Scott Ramey, and Rich Poore from Oxford, whom I first met twelve months ago at Championsgate.

Big Scott and the guys.

As the Social Golfer it gives me particular pleasure to meet up with fellow SGs. As part of important practice, I also added to my Orlando resume by playing Kissimmee Oaks and Solvita Stonegate. I have now played virtually every public or semi-private course in the Orlando area, giving me an unrivalled tourist position from which to comment. So, plenty of golf in this last fortnight but also a bit of touring around our beloved Florida, in particular trips to our favourite resorts of Mount Dora and St Augustine. I also planned one last trip down the Gulf coast from Tarpon Springs to Naples, via Clearwater and Venice, then down Alligator Alley to the Keys and a few days partying to celebrate our journey at Key West. We would then go back up the Atlantic seaboard via Miami, Delray Beach and finally Melbourne Beach. We would have been around the world then doing Venice, Naples and Melbourne in one state. This final journey would allow Matron and me to enjoy one of the favourite aspects of Floridian getaways, the quintessential bed and breakfast experience.

My first golf on Florida would be the Golf Week Tour event at Black Bear. This is a fine links-style course just south of Eustis, not too far from Mount Dora, with undulating fairways and fast, hard, quick-breaking greens. A fine clubhouse enhances an enjoyable experience. My four ball featured some of the best in our class on tour, my good mate, James Rearden (third on last year's standings and still waxing lyrical about our sessions at Hilton Head), big-hitting Alberto Esperon and Steady Eddie, Jerry Harris. To be in the running, I clearly needed to win this particular four ball.

The Casablanca Inn, St Augustine, a fine example of a Florida bed and breakfast.

James in particular started like a house on fire. Then, on the 12th, when five ahead of me, he put his approach out of bounds and from then on imploded. Alberto led me all the way to the 15th where I got up and down from a 130-yard bunker for a par 5 and he three putts from three feet for an eight. Not without some trouble and the water on the fantastic 18th contributing to a six, I came home one clear of both James and Alberto and two clear of Jerry, which enabled me to finish second in the class, pick up 250 ranking points and my fist cheque of the year. I can now go on to defend the first major of the year at Grande Pines in May in good heart and looking forward to locking horns with these great guys again. I am also well on track to return to Hilton Head Island.

I played two new courses leading up to the tour event, in Kissimmee Oaks and Stonegate, Solvita. Both were fine tracks but had clearly suffered from the bad Florida winter; I would return in the summer when both would be in fine nick and very good value for money at $30 each. The bird life around Solvita literally had me salivating with pleasure. A final point, there was no sign of economic recovery on either estate, nor Legends or Ridgewood which I also played, with the number of foreclosures growing from my last visit the previous October. As I stated earlier, whilst in Orlando I was contacted by two fellow social golfers down in the area for a bit of sun. Scott, with whom I won the Annual Toys for Tots at Mystic Dunes back in December 2008, invited me to Clermont for my second go at the Legends and with two business mates of his down from the North, Ted and Mike, two damn fine SGs, we had a great day. I was also contacted by my Oxford pal, Richard Poore, in Orlando for a break with his good lady and we had a fine day at Ridgewood Lakes where we were joined by John and Carol, snow birding

Fabulous Mission Inn.

down from North America. This day ended with Karen and me joining Rich and his party at Bergamo's, to have a great Italian meal and listen to the singing waiters. Social golf at its best.

Whilst playing Black Bear, it offered the opportunity to spend a couple of days at the magnificent Magnolia Inn in Mount Dora (hardly a mountain, more a little hill), a quaint old town where I would love to retire to. Many nice restaurants mingle with fine wine bars, an Icelandic bar, the Frosty Mug and the Viking Bar with live music, and a great range and variety of beers which has become a particular favourite. The city hosts a major art festival in February and a crafts festival in October with over 200 stallholders filling all the city's streets and both have over a quarter of a million visitors over the weekend. Matron would shop, I would eat and drink. Matron would shop some more, I

The craft fayre, Matron's favourite weekend.

would eat and drink. Then Matron would eat and drink and I would join her. All this after a typical hearty breakfast at the Magnolia.

No Mickey in sight, this is the true Florida from the 1950s and '60s, before Disney. It may seem sacriligious to some, but not everyone who visits central Florida wants to cavort with Mickey, Donald and Shamu … there is so much to see which I hope our little trip round the coast will do justice to. However, good golf certainly is not restricted to the Orlando Triangle. Around Mount Dora, besides Black Bear, there are a handful of fantastic courses. Lake county is only a forty-five minute drive north from the city centre and is an engaging mix of rolling hillsides and lakes, over a thousand of them. This rolling terrain has proved to be an excellent location for golf. The green fees are usually substantially lower than those closer to Orlando. The best two in my opinion are Bella Collina, a fantastic Nick Faldo design near Sorrento, with an amazing Tuscany style clubhouse, and the best resort course is, without doubt, the family-owned Mission Inn. In the day of major corporate resorts, this superbly run resort with two fine courses offers an impersonal corporate mind set which is quite frankly refreshing. Add to this, the fantastic Diamond Players Club, environmentally outstanding Deer Island, a walk through a nature reserve as well as golf and it's easy to see why it has so much appeal to both Matron and me.

After my tour event, we set off on our little excursion heading initially for that little bit of the Med on the Gulf coast, the Greek sponge-fishing village of Tarpon Springs. This quite charming, enchanting village with a little harbour aquarium and a row of harbour-side Greek restaurants and pastry shops, is totally out of sync with the rest of Florida …

We stay at Ashleys Victorian B&B, which doubles up as an antique shop. It is unique and full of character. The town also boasts, at the appropriately titled Sunset Cove, probably the best sunset we saw on our travels. Locals enjoy a picnic or ice cream as the sun sets over the Gulf of Mexico.

Kites flutter, sail-boarders take to the sky and you may even see a young couple getting married – a perfect end to a wonderful day in paradise. And if you have got your sticks, there are two exceptional resorts on the doorstep, Firstly there is Innisbrook (the site for years of the PGA Tampa Bay Classic) is five minutes from Tarpon centre and the Copperhead (actually more North Carolina than Florida), with its rolling fairways and large pines. There are four courses here which are all splendid. The Island course is generally acknowledged to be the second course on the resort, just as

Tarpon Springs.

challenging, but probably more appealing to the eye. Less heralded, but in no way less rewarding, are the Highlands South and North Courses. Secondly, there is the World Woods Golf Club which is about twenty minutes from Tarpon, near Brooksville, a sleepy small-town backwater which is definitely Old South and not new Florida and is the home of two highly-rated Tom Fazio courses. The Pine Barrens course has often been rightly compared to the top three world-rated Pine Valley in New Jersey. Despite having generously wide fairways, the course sculpted from an expansive Pine forest with dramatic elevation changes and massive waste bunkers and slick greens, disaster seems to lurk behind nearly every shot. The second course, Rolling Oaks, has a reputation for being somewhat easier than its sister course but don't be fooled, it is no easy picking. Despite being built next to pine, everything about this course offers a totally different golfing experience. Soil content means there are giant oaks, Spanish moss, glorious fauna and in places, it is reminiscent of Augusta National with its azalea bushes. The 16th, a massive 234-yard par 3 from an elevated tee to a green guarded by bunkers, framed with oaks is possibly the pick of what many regard the hardest back 9 in the state.

From here, we headed south on the lovely coast road through beautiful little hamlets like Dunedin to Clearwater Beach for an afternoon of sunbathing on possibly the best stretch of beach in the state. With a wide choice of small motels, lively bars, good food, a wonderful pier, it is no wonder that this place is so popular. There is plenty of good golf in and around Clearwater and its sister town of St Petersburg, but frankly I did not want to get off the beach, the bikini-clad ladies were the

Sunset Beach.

Relaxing at Clearwater.

only birdies I was interested in that afternoon. My transition spectacles did their job and Matron could not see where I was looking, but often it's just at her as she looks splendid in her leopard-skin bikini too.

We then head over St Pete's bay and the awesome seven-mile bridge, spanning St Pete's to Sarasota and Bradenton, and head further south to another of our favourite spots – Venice, home of the shark teeth, another quaint old-fashioned town. With its boutiques, café bars, antique shops, annual craft and art shows, wild beaches and lazy river, it has a laid back feel, far away from the razzmatazz of the Florida hinterland.

We stayed again at a superb example of Southern hospitality, the Horse and Chaisse Inn, with individually styled and named rooms, such as the Yellow Room or the Carriage Room, offering a distinct and different flavour to each visit. What never changes is the massive Southern-styled breakfast every morning. Karen went shopping as usual and I played the local municipal at Lake Venice Golf Club, a quite splendid 27-hole track that meanders through the sandbanks with a pleasant summer breeze blowing in off the ocean, making the round even more pleasant.

Within twenty minutes' drive there are many fine courses including Long Marsh, where I played in the 2011 Florida Open and finished runner-up. It was here, whilst shopping, that I found this poem by the famous painter and poet, Suzy Toronto, who leaves the faces blank in all her paintings. Matron bought this for me because she says it summed me up and also TSG philosophy to golf.

Horse and Chaisse.

Some golf for exercise
Some for the thrill of competition
Others for social or business contacts
BUT NOT YOU

You play simply for the love of the game
Doesn't matter where or with whom
Golf is in your blood

You don't even care
who kicks the ball out the rough
or fudges the score card
because it's all about being on the course
only in competition with yourself

Perfecting your swing
and sinking the putt
Playing the game it was meant to be
Yes, golf is in your blood
You are 'HE WHO LOVES TO GOLF'

We continued to head south down the Gulf coast to Naples, self-styled and named golf capital of the world. A bit pretentious perhaps, but who am I to pass comment, the best damned Social Golfer on the planet? We stayed in the magnificent boutique hotel, the Escalante, superbly located on 5th South and 3rd in Old Naples, simply the best location in town. Spend a day down at the old fishing harbour (now romantically called Tin City as it is completely housed in tin buildings) with fine bars, restaurants and a plethora of shops – a nice way to chill on a hot summer's day. Got to say it was far too hot to golf, never less than 110° during the day. No wonder it was quiet; the holiday seasons runs from November to Easter, then it becomes a ghost town as the snow birds head back home, but it is a truly, quaint, beautiful city, sensational beaches, great shopping and quite outstanding restaurants.

L'Escalante.

The golf would have been sensational and so cheap. PGA-recognised courses for less than twenty bucks, including compulsory buggy. Golf here is not for the squeamish though as alligators abound. On the news the other day, a local was explaining why so many alligators are on the move – they are all on the tap, it's the mating season. Subsequently, I have revisited two of the many splendid resort complexes in the south west around Naples. Marco Island, just south of the city, is one of about only eighty nationwide which is a fully certified member of the Audubon Cooperative Sanctuary programme, meaning a round here is as much of an eco adventure as it is a golf experience. Weaving through forests of pine or palm trees with lagoons, marshes and swamps, the golf course is a habitat to a variety of wildlife, like the gopher tortoise, brown bat, randy alligators and even the odd black bear. Water is in play on fifteen holes and this is a course where your game will have to be scored well because as well as the Ocean winds, the architect, Joe Lee, placed seventy-four bunkers in nasty positions and made the greens slick and undulating. Fortunately, golf is not the only adventure here.

Key West.

For those wanting the full Floridian beach and golf experience, the Naples Beach Hotel and Golf Club provides it; the resort and the course are but a pitching wedge from the shoreline. The course is particularly player friendly, in good condition and, like Mission Inn, is family-run.

From here, we headed to the southern-most point in Florida, the party town of Key West. The journey takes you across the Everglades and gives plenty of opportunity down Alligator Alley, the nickname given to the road from Naples to the start of the Keys. A journey by car along the Keys, through Marathon, Key Largo and down to Key West is one of the ultimate and iconic car journeys you can make. For any party animal, Key West is surely the ultimate destination. Duval Street, with its famous bars and restaurants, has a magnetism that attracts every age group. Twenty to sixty-year-olds can party here, no problem. The social golfer will feel really at home. You can play golf on the splendid little municipal just north of the town too, that's if you are sober enough to see the ball. Naturally, there are a wide range of accommodation possibilities but Matron and I stick to the tried and tested bed and breakfast, and again dropped lucky at the Island Oasis just off Duvall street, right on the beach – highly recommended.

Three days is ample here (the liver probably couldn't take any longer) so we headed back north via Delray Beach to Melbourne. We by-pass Miami, having visited earlier last year for Matron's birthday, but no-one should ever, ever avoid Miami if you have never been. We stayed at the splendid Avalon on South Beach, Miami. I ask you 'South Beach you all, swimming pools and movie stars and us …'

Above & left: Matron in Key West.

We went on Memorial Day, a national holiday here in the USA, which had little significance for me. For us Brits, it would be like Remembrance Day; imagine it in July when, instead of parading and wearing poppies, everyone celebrates in a party atmosphere the memory of their loved ones lost in conflict. South Beach was packed and one of the most haunting images I have seen was thousands of cardboard headstones on the boardwalk gardens in memory of lost servicemen. The significance to me was the average age of the deceased service men, the vast majority under twenty-five, my son's age.

Cardboard headstones at South Beach.

Whatever your political beliefs or the rights and wrongs of particular conflicts, I defy anyone on seeing this not to feel humbled, sad and touched by the simple serenity and poignancy of the scene. It will live long in my memory. On a visit to New York in 2004, I was similarly moved by thousands of yellow ribbons representing the victims of 9/11, simply tied to church railings in Manhattan.

Miami Beach was as I expected, chic, classy, expensive and full of beautiful people. All day long, and long into the night, the bars were full of bikini-clad lovelies of all shapes, sizes, ethnicity and ages (the dark glasses were a must to hide the stares that could not be avoided when looking at such a bevy of beauties!). Flesh City it was for all three days of the visit (there were plenty of six packs on display to similarly enthral Matron.)

We partied long and well, enjoyed some excellent food and wine in Lincoln Street, a must-walk if in South Beach. A half-mile pedestrian street with numerous top quality restaurants bars and shops. A wonderful place to while away the evening people-watching. The beach is as you will have seen on TV, brilliant white, punctuated by glowing, tanned Amazonian bodies. Despite my new trim look (who am I kidding!), I did not feel comfortable on the beach despite its attractions … too old and out of shape sadly!

We had a memorable time; golf despite being just a few miles from some of the most notable courses on the planet never entered my head. It was far too hot (nearly 100° every day). But Doral and Palm Beach will be played on my next visit as we will definitely return.

Rane Resort, Delray Beach.

Heading north takes you past Fort Lauderdale, Boco Raton, Palm Beach and Port St Lucie and near to some of the most highly-rated golf courses in the Americas. Try the Bear Trap, the infamous 15th, 16th and 17th at the PGA National, the Blue Monster at Doral, visit the PGA Museum at the PGA Village at Port St Lucie, where I capitulated in the heat in my 2010 defence of the Florida Open on the Fazio Course, one of three excellent courses. We arrived at Delray Beach, staying at the Crane, a

pleasant seaside beach resort on the Atlantic Seaboard. Noted as an artists' retreat, it does have a beautiful beach, many fine art shops as one would expect, as well as fine restaurants and bars. A smaller Naples in many ways. It was a nice break, but perhaps by now, it all seemed a little similar.

From here, we finished our trip at the luxurious, romantic, idyllic hideaway called the Port D'Hiver, right on Melbourne beach, and not to be confused with the pleasant town of Melbourne five miles inland. This small beach community is the start of the Space Coast and is simply charming, peaceful, relaxing and quite beautiful and the Port D'hiver fits in superbly with its *al fresco* breakfasts, large, colonial-style bedrooms, afternoon wine and cakes and lovely pool – a fine way to end our trip before we headed back through Kissimmee on the 417, passing more great golf courses like Harmony, Royal St Cloud and Kissimmee Bay, where I won the 2009 Florida Open and will return to in 2012. The beach has a fine municipal golf course and a couple of good bars, including a great piano bar; fabulous retreat really.

South Beach, Miami – chic, avant garde, art deco, you would be hard pressed to beat it!

*

'And so the end is near and so I reach the final curtain', and what a journey it was, memorable in so many ways – fantastic golf and sensational vistas. But for both Karen and I, our long abiding memory will be of the wonderful people we met along our travels, some of whom I now consider much more than passing acquaintances. They all touched us deeply and I sincerely hope that the feeling was reciprocated. To each and every one of them, a big thank you! In times of economic and social turmoil, this trip gave me considerable optimism for the long-term well-being of our planet.

I have learned a lot about myself, a lot about my golf and a great deal about this majestic green and blue globe we call home.

> I have swam in every ocean
> Watched the sun set from east to west
> Walked the lush green fairways
> Where my heroes have took the test.
> Put a ball in every ocean
> And took a divot on every continent
> Seen man's greatest achievements
> And gasped at God's great design
> It truly is a WONDERFUL WORLD.

My final golf was a magical day up at Orange County near Jacksonville. My good mate, Brew, had kept in regular contact during the RTW trip and it had always been my intention to try and see him. He is, for those not fully aware of his story, a remarkable forty-five-year-old who had a near fatal automobile accident from which he is still recovering. A remarkable chap, he pointed out it was exactly twenty years since that fateful day. He sent me the following:

Twenty years later, the SG, Brew and Charles make that tee time.

Friday, 12 March 2010
Greetings my friend!
I pray this note finds you and your loved ones eager in spirit and full in health. I have a few thoughts I wish to convey. I'm hopeful you find words of much interest.

'… when your new box of balls begins to disappear at a rate of knots; when the weather is as bad as your game, golf can seem both an aimless and costly game. No other sport has such a disparity in talent between the successful practitioner and the social golfer. However, when you're faced with the realistic possibility that you have played your last round, then your worst round is better than no round at all …' (Ian Halliwell, *The Social Golfer*)

My near-fatal, life-altering motor vehicle accident occurred on 21 March 1990 (the first day of spring that year). I'm told I had a tee time scheduled the next day (22 March 1990). Instead of spending a glorious spring day in Florida, leisurely hacking my way through 18 holes of golf, I would spend that day comatose in the Critical Care Unit tenuously clinging to life. In fact, I would spend two comatose weeks fighting for my life.

At the time of my automobile accident, I was an invincible 25-year-old aspiring Naval Aviator and full-time student. I was also working full-time. What precious free time I had was usually spent at the beach or on a golf course. When putting out that last hole, I never dreamed I may have just played the last round of golf in my life, '… When you're faced with the realistic possibility that you have played your last round, then your worst round is better than no round at all.' Ian, truer words have never been spoken!

I've spent two decades of prolonged, painful rehabilitation desperately rebuilding and recovering 'me'. I'm reclaiming my physical, intellectual, and spiritual self neuron-by-neuron, synapse-by-synapse. My goal has always been to not merely learn to live with traumatic brain injury (TBI), but to conquer traumatic brain injury. It has never been easy. It is still not easy.

If your schedule allows, I would consider it a great honour to golf with you and my golfing instructor, former PGA TOUR Professional, Charles Raulerson, at the Country Club of Orange Park on Monday, 22 March 2010. Albeit 20 years late, I will finally make that tee time I had scheduled two decades prior.

I cannot think of a more fitting way to mark an anniversary of my near demise than to celebrate life on the links with my good friends, Ian and Charles!
Your pal,
Brugh

He had a tee time booked for 12.15 p.m. on the day after his accident which, of course, he never made. Exactly twenty years to the day, he did make that tee time and I was privileged to join him and a wonderful PGA Pro, Charles Raulerson, Head Pro and General Manager at the magnificent Orange Park Country Club, to celebrate his recovery by playing this long-awaited round. In a trip of many highlights, this was up there with them all. A truly memorable and a sensational ending to my once-in-a-lifetime global golfing extravaganza.

And so, some eighty-nine days after leaving Manchester, we boarded one of Mr Branson's finest and headed back to Wigan and the UK. A lot had happened in that period, mother had been nearly, fatally taken and would never live in our old family home again. Our son had split from his long-standing girlfriend of five years. Our eldest daughter was getting engaged, the youngest had returned home with a new boyfriend in tow. Our middle daughter and partner bought a house. Very soon, it was back to normal, work, bit of golf, more work. Within a few weeks, our epic journey would seem light years away. Every so often though, even two years on, I may see something, Sydney Opera House, the Golden Gate, the US Open at Pebble, and the memories come flooding back.

4. Friends Along the Way

You will have come across my mucker, Charles M. Brugh (Brew), several times in this book. He is my mucker (a Lancashire term of male endearment meaning a good, well-respected mate). Its origins are probably from the pit face, where the miner on the face axing the coal, needed a partner who would shovel the valuable coal onto the rail barrow, bring food and drinks to the face and look after the miners' safety. Years ago, a successful miner's health and financial well-being would to some degree be dependent on how good his 'mucker' was. In the USA, it is strange watching the reaction, when meeting someone at a car park or a putting green, and all you hear is 'Hey up mi Muckaaa …'

From his first letter to me to our extraordinary round twenty years after his accident, I have remained in awe of the guy's strength of character.

The following was taken from *Florida Golf Magazine* 2011 which I hope emphasises and explains our extraordinary friendship:

While competing in the open tournament, stroke survivor Ian Halliwell (from UK) simultaneously coaches his friend. Ian is seen here acting as caddie and mentor to his 'mucker' (best chum), Charles Brugh from Orange Park, Florida, who is a Traumatic Brain Injury survivor.

Charles Manning Brugh, aka 'Brew'

All the participants got along very wonderfully, and since there were voluntary early tee times provided, (a full hour before the normal 8:00 am shotgun start) for any foursome who thought they might be a wee bit slow, 'Pace of Play' was not an issue either this year. At the open tournament back in 2010, we learned that some players very deservedly needed a little more time. In particular the tournament's only TBI (Traumatic Brain Injury) survivor, Charles Manning Brugh, also known as 'Brew'.

Brew, who is more than just the open tournament's token TBI survivor, is thought by many to be one of the most noteworthy golfers at the tournament. You see, although Brew walks and talks slow and methodically due to his TBI, he is really a very articulate writer and has previously written very moving and informative articles that were published in *Florida Golf Magazine* about what the open tournament has meant to him.

Since playing and counting every stroke was so important to Brew, his foursome teed off at 7 a.m. Ian Halliwell, the winner of the 2009 open tournament, who had once again come all the way from the UK just to play in the open tournament, had also taken it upon himself, just as he had done in the 2009 & 2010 tournaments, to be Brew's playing partner, mentor, coach and personal English caddy. Therefore, Brew gets better and a little faster every year.

Brew has written two inspirational articles which convey how this extraordinary human being has coped through all his adversity. I have pleasure in reproducing these here in full.

While competing in the open tournament, stroke survivor, Ian Halliwell, simultaneously acts as caddie and mentor to his 'mucker' (best chum) Traumatic Brain Injury survivor, Charles Brugh.

Looking for a place to happen: making stops along the way

I'm asked often: 'What does coma feel like?', 'Do you remember anything?', 'Did you see any deceased relatives or friends?', 'Could you hear people around you?'; 'Did you go through a white tunnel'? 'Did you see heaven?'

Such questions are difficult to answer. How does one convey existence in which nothing is concrete – no discernment of distance, no pull of gravity, no awareness of mass, no sensations of movement, no feelings of pain, no hunger, no thirst, and no perception of time?

The simple answers to these questions are surreal translucence; Yes; Not that I recall; Maybe – my father says my eyes tracked sounds of his voice beneath closed eyelids; Not that I recall; Not that I recall. These are the simple, straightforward answers. Of course, my experience with severe brain trauma is neither straightforward nor simple. I've spent over two decades of my life divining answers to these and other problematic questions inherent in this obtuse realm we call life. Some questions remain unanswerable. For example, I often wonder what my soul was doing for the two weeks I spent teetering on the brink of death.

My familiarity with coma is vaguely similar to what I imagine existence in a parallel universe would be – without the universe – and completely different. Words fail me – and I consider myself an individual with, at times, decent communication skills. No matter how articulate I may wax, mere words do my experience grave injustice.

The first five years post-coma, I struggled to re-enter tangible realms of the living – and when I say struggled, I mean really struggled. My arduous labors required extensive incremental, clinical and self-prescribed cognitive, physical, and spiritual rehabilitative efforts to convince myself I had, beyond doubt, returned as a living, breathing, thinking member of the human race. When man cannot choose, he ceases to be a man.

Kept alive in a Critical Care Unit for two comatose weeks, I'm told physical therapy and neurologic stimulation initiated while still deep in coma. Unbeknownst to anyone (including myself), I would spend the next two decades of my life obsessively engaged in varying modalities of spiritual, cognitive and physical labors – pushing personal limits of drive, talent, intelligence, and strengths of character. Our bodies and brains are designed to be pushed, and we were put on this earth to help others.

Discovering bloody socks after gruelling all-night bike rides became a peculiar source of joy – for the bloodied fibers were indisputable proof I was, in fact alive. Strange, I know, however, there was no denying my ankles (or shoulders, or elbows, or fingers, or knees) were glimmering with coagulating crimson fluids possessing sweet metallic properties that tickled my palate. Good for the body is good for the brain.

Caused by significant damage to my hippocampus, prefrontal cortex, endorhinal cortex, limbic system, neocortex and amygdala, resulting in severe memory and learning deficits, this bizarre ritual repeated itself many times, over many years. I am fortunate God blessed me with a high tolerance for physical and mental pain, accompanying an exceedingly strong will to survive and excel.

There are no manuals guiding my determined efforts. No how-to books. No crib notes. No 'Brain Damage for Dummies' – nothing telling me what to do – when to do it – or how often to do it – and nothing telling me when to cease physical and cognitive efforts for that matter. (Everything in moderation – including moderation?). Relying on a severely damaged brain, I write my working handbook of 'Dain Bramage' on the fly – a constantly morphing challenge.

Other than figuring it out on your own, through much trial, and much painful error, sometimes the best and least distressing way to gather new 'tricks of the trade' is by observing how others challenged by disability deal with impairment. Again, my learning and memory deficits greatly impeded this practice. I have an unfortunate knack for learning lessons of recovery, and life, the hard way. Chronic pain changes everything.

Similar in organization and structure, everyone's brain is exceptional in capacity and efficiency. As such, brain injury survivors' insults are unique in severity and scope. By definition, traumatic brain injury (TBI) means damage to brain tissue is caused by rapid accelerating or decelerating forces. Specifically, by a moving object striking the stationary head (assaults using baseball bats, crowbars, etc.) or by a moving head striking a relatively stationary object (automobile accidents, falls, etc).

Signature Injury
Rocket Propelled Grenades (RPGs), Improvised Explosive Devices (IEDs), mines, and other weapons have caused hundreds of thousands of casualities among US Troops in the wars of Iraq and Afghanistan. So prevalent are the incidents, Traumatic Brain Injury is considered the signature injury of these wars.

An example; enemy insurgents remotely detonate a roadside IED. The explosion produces a pair of powerful shockwaves. Lasting several milliseconds, the first is a high-pressure wave. A countervailing negative-pressure wave follows immediately. Even though there has been no direct blow to the skull, these shockwaves can have devastating effects on the soldier's cognition and neurophysiology.

Brain trauma challenges my entire neural network. Effectively decimated in a life-altering motor vehicle accident on a treacherous corner in Ponte Vedra Beach, Florida, Traumatic Brain Injury necessitates relearning all that is human.

Other causes of brain injury
Brain injury can also be the result of stroke, drug abuse (alcohol is a drug!), tumors, poisoning, infection and disease, near drowning, hemorrhage, AIDS, and a number of other disorders such as Parkinson's disease, Multiple Sclerosis, and Alzheimer's disease.

No matter how articulate I may wax, mere words do my experience grave injustice. I am hopeful a large part of what makes my diverse life-challenges significant are prolonged struggles to regain my humanity – persistent efforts to create, through much trial and much painful error, an enduring person of substance and worth. In so doing, I asked myself; 'what does it mean to be a 'person of worth'? 'What qualities define a person of substance?' Most answers are subjective – beauty is in the eye of the beholder. Surviving near-death trauma taught me what a person of substance and worth is not; qualities embodied in a person of worth and substance have nothing to do with money. Money cannot buy health. Money cannot buy family. Money cannot buy friendship. Money cannot buy integrity. Money cannot buy respect. Money cannot buy happiness. Money cannot buy love. Money cannot buy heaven.

Initially embarrassed by my new status as an individual with massive neurologic and cognitive impairment, my embarrassment soon turned to shame – and my shame turned to anger. I got pissed – really pissed. Talk about misplaced anger and enraged frustration! For years, I wondered why God would allow such major tragedies befall one as astute and talented as me – a diamond in the rough with so much promise. After all, I was destined to become 'the world's greatest Naval Aviator' – or so I thought. God has other plans.

God resisteth the proud, but giveth Grace unto the humble. [James 4:6]

Basing life-saving efforts on, what then (1991), was an unproven, emergent theory called neuroplasticity, after two decades+ of focused efforts, I have constructed new 'wetware', using greatly corrupted 'hardware' and 'software'. Me. Just me – with no formal training in neurology, neurophysiology, neuroscience, neuropsychology, neuroanatomy, exercise physiology, computer science or cognitive science. I am humbly proud of this formidable achievement.

Among others, my significant deficits involve motor-sensory areas of my brain – the cerebellum, the motor cortex, the sensory cortex, the basal ganglia, and the hippocampus. I've used regular strength training, moderate-to-intense aerobic exercise, copious independent study on diverse topics, purposeful outdoor endeavors, and multiple adaptive athletics, for over two decades to promote and enhance neurogenesis and neuroplasticity. The concept of using an enriched environment (i.e. adaptive athletics, copious independent study and/or vigorous exercise) to rebuild my damaged brain is a central focus of my restorative efforts, and is a core theme of this book.

After over two decades of focused efforts promoting and enhancing neuroplasticity and neurogenesis, I now do this 'on-the-fly', with little conscious thought. Often, I have great difficulty expressing how, or why, I do what I do. I attempt to rectify my linguistic shortcomings with this book. Akin to relying on corrupted parallel central processing units to diagnose and repair crashed computer networks; employing damaged software and hardware to repair broken 'wetware' can easily yield marginal results. One motivation for writing this book: To most, I appear an individual with only mild physical impairments – farther from the truth they could not be! Employing self-taught, self-directed neurogenesis and neuroplasticity to reconstruct intricate networks of damaged grey and white matter mandates continual improvisation of methods and techniques to rewire and reconstruct my 'new' brain.

In direct contradiction to the Scientific Method, 'intelligent intuition' largely guides my protracted labors. Not very scientific, I know. However, I always do the best I can with what I have – physical, cognitive, and neurologic deficits be damned! Through many years' sustained efforts, much repetition, variation, abundant tenacity, and focused attention, I am overcoming seemingly impossible odds. Am I all better? Hardly. Yet, I continually improve – with limitless potential!

After much contemplation, prolonged agony, and prayers said by me and on my behalf by family and friends throughout the world, I chose to embrace my near-death trauma for the benefit of others. I concluded my horrific neurologic challenges are a unique and fantastic gift of enormous potential – an opportunity to influence positively the lives of many – if (if and only if) I could do the seemingly impossible: restore my brain to its prior genius self.

Even in my 'dain bramaged fog', I knew I had my work cut out for me. Repairing massive brain damage is a mammoth undertaking of daunting complexity. Where do I start? They say the Lord never gives you more than you can handle. This challenge damn sure pushed me to near breaking point! Requiring more strengths of character than I knew I possessed, Traumatic Brain Injury (TBI) continues to challenge in ways I never knew possible. Tangible and non-tangible, by any metric, I assure you, TBI is a living hell.

He who refuses to embrace a unique opportunity loses the prize as surely as if he had tried and failed. [William James]

Greatly abridged in both content and scope, 'Dain Bramage: Cognition and Experience of a Traumatic Brain Injury survivor' represents extended efforts to convey the life-changing enormity of my experience following near-fatal brain trauma. Emerging from a two-week coma is, by definition, a near-death experience. In that context, my life experience post-coma is somewhat unique. However, I must emphasize – I do not feel inherently 'special' (though I am a very unique individual – just like everyone else). I am human – subject to the same impulsive desires, mistakes, foibles, irrational insecurities, errors in judgment, and nonsensical, self-destructive behaviors as any other pod.

An ongoing battle, prevailing over Traumatic Brain Injury involves combating overwhelming clinical depression (clinical depression is a biological disorder; very different from merely feeling overwhelmed, disappointed or sad). Mental health is dependent on a delicate molecular balance. Altered electro-chemical interactions among damaged neurons and synapses make maintaining optimistic dispositions especially difficult for survivors of Traumatic Brain Injury. Frequent, vigorous exercise and prescribed neurochemical supplements are but two of several effective tools for fighting clinical depression. I know, first hand, of what I speak.

 I have the utmost respect for individuals who, like me, confront the many challenges associated with disability – especially those who muster the will to soldier on with a happy heart and a smiling face. There are many foundational keys to overcoming physical and psychological adversity. One noteworthy key to success is this; for you, and those around you, a happy heart and a smiling face make life much more tolerable. Far from being 'the answer' to life's many tribulations, one's attitude is damn important. You really do catch more flies with honey than vinegar – really. That heuristic (rule-of-thumb), stems from a universal psychological truth called the Pleasure Principle:

The Pleasure Principle; people gravitate toward pleasure and away from pain.

A positive mental attitude is but one of many crucial elements in my quest for rehabilitative excellence. Through experience not always positive in nature, I have learned overcoming severe Traumatic Brain Injury requires numerous focused efforts on multiple, disparate fronts – simultaneously. Faith in God, personal honesty, focused attention, iron-clad determination, frequent prayer, abundant inner-strength, strict adherence to intellect over emotion, suitable nutritional and neurochemical supplements, much humility (It is my humility that makes me great!), a high tolerance for physical and mental anguish, ample hydration, much academic study, true friendship, physical and psychological fitness, applied knowledge of methods and techniques promoting and enhancing neurogenesis and neuroplasticity, a passion for knowledge, loving parents (my parents are my heroes!), vigorous exercise, and relentless pursuit of truth are all requisite components in my pervasive rehabilitative journey. This partial listing of attributes is what work for me. Individual methods, techniques, and results vary.

Whether confronting life-threatening disability, living with physical or mental disease, surviving unexpected tragedy, struggling with addiction, or just coping with the tedious minutia of daily existence, life is often an overwhelming bitch. Oh well. Suck it up. My father taught me a long time ago – you have a choice: 'You can roll over and die, or stand up and fight.' I am a FIGHTER (pilot) at heart.

When you're done wallowing in your misery – when you're sick and tired of being sick and tired – when the pity party is over and all your so-called 'friends' have gone home, leaving you to pick up pieces of shattered life and broken dreams, the fight is yours, and yours alone. The sooner you accept this basic truth, the greater your chance to prevail over adversity, both large and small. No one can battle personal demons for you. Ultimate responsibility for overcoming life's challenges is up to you. Deal with it.

I wish I could state unequivocally this work is a how-to manual for overcoming hardship. It is not. Though I make many mistakes, and experience much failure, through the Grace of God, I achieve more substantive victories than defeats (In conflicts crucial moments always be defined as victor). One objective of my life's work is to inspire others to push personal boundaries while assisting those less able. Another objective is to demonstrate to myself and millions of Traumatic Brain Injury survivors that massive brain damage can be overcome.

No one intends disability, overwhelming adversity, or near-fatal trauma. Familial bonds and social relationships are invariably strained. When individuals incur life-altering events, these tragedies have enormous impacts not only on their own lives, but also on those closest to them.

Disabilities' sphere of influence is considerable. Whether you are the individual challenged by disability, are a family member, therapist, close friend, or loved one, I am hopeful my regenerative struggles serve as conduit by which positive difference in others' lives are made.

Most of our obstacles would melt away if, instead of cowering before them, we should make up our minds to walk boldly through them. [Orison Swett Marden]

Many life-lessons contained within these pages are by inference. There are no simple answers to negotiating life's unexpected challenges. I ask you digest this book in its entirety. By taking the work as a whole, readers are better equipped to draw conclusions relevant to individual circumstance. Inductions, deductions, and conclusions drawn from my words will vary greatly. This is a good thing. I am hopeful much good comes from my struggles to reacquire humanity, and my influence on society is positive and significant. I can only pray to achieve these lofty goals.

Life-lesson #1: If you are going to be stupid, you have to be tough!

'Patience and persistence win out over superstition and ignorance every time.'

Golf as Therapeutic Modality is Positive and Meaningful

Effectively decimated in a life-altering automobile accident on a treacherous corner in Ponte Vedra Beach Florida, severe Traumatic Brain Injury (TBI) necessitates relearning all that is human. Kept alive in a Critical Care Unit for two comatose weeks, I'm told physical therapy and neurologic stimulation initiated while still deep in coma. Unbeknownst to anyone (including myself), I would spend the next two decades obsessively engaged in varying modalities of spiritual, cognitive and physical labors – pushing personal limits of Faith, drive, talent, intelligence and strengths of character.

I spent two weeks in a critical care unit, an additional week in an intensive care unit and then transferred to a rehabilitation hospital as an inpatient where I embarked on a demanding six months of physical and cognitive therapies. I was in outpatient therapy for an additional $1^1/2$ years. Though I could not really 'learn' much of anything (I had severe memory and learning deficits), I made concerted efforts to comprehend underlying principles of my numerous therapies. Two fundamentals of note garnered during my six months as an inpatient;

1. Always push yourself beyond your preconceived limits.

2. Never give up! (It is to the one who endures that final victory comes).

Through much independent study, I determined the only way to successfully rehabilitate was to expose my broken brain to widely diverse and challenging environments. To that end I engaged in multiple adaptive athletics and purposeful outdoor endeavors. The first adaptive sport I attempted was golf. An avid golfer prior to my near-fatal tragedy, I quickly realized the golf swing requires far more mind-body co-ordination than my severely damaged brain could grasp at this early stage. The fact that the golf swing requires so much mind-body integration is precisely why GOLF is such fantastic therapy for many survivors of brain injury. I channeled my rehabilitative efforts to other athletic endeavors in which I felt I could have more success. Bear in mind, I was an unco-ordinated buffoon at all athletic efforts … at first.

I never gave up – persevering with the ultimate goal of returning to the sport I am passionate for – GOLF! To date, I have twenty-one (and counting) distinct adaptive sports and purposeful outdoor endeavors under my belt. A sampling of my diverse rehabilitative backgrounds include: white water rafting trips (multi-day), rock climbing (Breckenridge, Colorado), adaptive water skiing/knee boarding, several multi-day bicycling tours, adaptive surfing, parasailing, adaptive alpine skiing, wheelchair rugby – I was a corporate-sponsored athlete for two years on a travelling quad rugby team (Brooks Bandits – United States Quad Rugby Association, Atlantic South Division), adaptive rowing – won gold and silver medals in the 2010 Southern Sprints held in Melbourne Florida and competed in the 2010 World Cup Indoor Rowing Championships in Boston where I missed 6th place by 6/100th of a second – for that weekend my world ranking was seventh (top ten in the world!), which sounds impressive until you learn there were only eleven adaptive athletes (from around the globe) competing in my division.

These varied rehabilitative activities fall under the broad umbrellas of cognitive and physical fitness, adaptive sport, experiential learning, outdoor education and purposeful recreation. I have used these tools extensively in my rehabilitative repertoire with significant positive result. In fact, to most I appear an individual with only mild physical impairment – farther from the truth they could not be! After many years of focused efforts I have finally returned to the great sport of golf, and I couldn't be more thrilled!

Like all my other rehabilitative efforts, I'm not very good – yet. It does not matter to me how long it will take, I will continue to push myself beyond my preconceived limits, and I will never give up – period. At this point, how far I can go is a matter of speculation. I will tell you this; I would love to be the first Traumatic Brain Injury survivor to represent America on the Paralympic golf team in Rio de Janeiro in 2016. Stranger things have happened.

The neurological, psychological and physical benefits of golf are precisely why GOLF is a cornerstone of my extended efforts to conquer Traumatic Brain Injury (TBI). I consider GOLF the equivalent of graduate study at a prestigious university for neurologic rehabilitation – it's just that good. I implore my fellow survivors of brain injury to pick up a club and smack that little white ball around. From much personal experience, it is with absolute certainty that I tell you: Golf as therapeutic modality is positive and meaningful! Done consistently, as part of an overall therapeutic regime, GOLF will greatly enhance both your rehabilitation and your life.

The only variable in golf is the person playing it. You are not trying to work on your game; you are working on yourself. [Geoff Ogilvy]

Another guy who has featured strongly in my story is 'Peg Leg' Roger Hurcombe, an amputee golfer and great guy who, with his wife 'Chardonnay Chablis' Chrissy Hurcombe, has become a close personal friend. I first met Roger and Tony Lloyd, another disadvantaged golfer whom I really admire, at the Show AM Celebrity Classic. Since then, Roger has become a focal member of Team TSG. Tony has invited me to play under his stewardship for Team England but more than anything, both these guys have proved that golf of a very high standard can be played despite a considerable physical handicap. The fact they always play with a smile says so much about both of them.

Peg always wanted to look like me! LOL.

Disabled golf is a fast-growing sport in the UK and was given an additional boost in 2010 with news that golf will become an Olympic and para-lympic sport from 2016 in Brazil. Tony's long-term aims are to represent the UK in Brazil but, in the meantime, he will be concentrating on matters closer to home.

Tony has been a keen sportsman for as long as he can remember and has never let his disability stop him having a go at any sport he wants. Before focusing on golf, he was also a successful cricketer playing for Shropshire and England and was undefeated as the England Captain.

The amount of time Tony can dedicate to golf is limited by his other commitments, including working full-time as a sales co-ordinator for a Telford-based manufacturer and spending time with his son, Taylor.

Peg, TSG and Tony. The latter is a leading UK disabled golfer and captain of the (winning!) England Disabled Golf Team.

Roger's Story

In 1992, I had a life-changing experience. I lost my right leg in a dramatic car accident. I spent days on a life-support machine but through sheer determination, I now live life to the full. My road to recovery was full of many challenges from learning how to walk again at the age of twenty-eight, to adapting to my life as a disabled person. The year 2002 was a milestone; I started playing golf on a Sunday morning with a group of friends. Determined to play the game I now love, I walked 18 holes at my local golf course. This was a challenge in itself as I was left in pain, however my passion for golf and improving my game had begun. A few weeks later, I bought myself a 3-wheel golf buggy and ever since then I try and play at least three times a week. Together with my two sons, we joined our local golf club and have enjoyed eight years playing in both competitive and social golf. My handicap has come down dramatically in the last few years with the help of coaching professionals and the support of friends and family. A big help has been playing in tournamnets around the country and in Europe. In some of these, I play alongside my partner and son, Tom, who plays off 5. Although he is an able-bodied golfer, I find myself being able to watch and learn from not only the way he plays but also the way he prepares and practises, as well as taking money off him on the odd occassion.

After eight years of participating in various disabled and amputee specfic golf organisation tournaments, I have made it my goal to practise, practise, practise so that I can keep improving and reach my overall target of representing Great Britain in the 2016 Paralympic Games as a member of the golf team.

On my travels, I have met so many different, interesting, great people but these three take some beating in the respect they have for the game of golf in particular. I try as TSG to bring a joviality and enjoyment to each and every round I play and it is a great joy to me when people keep in touch, maybe through Facebook or Twitter, or go to the great trouble of writing and personally thanking me for the day's golf we have had. That feeling has been totally reciprocated. Golf on its own without this great social interaction, humour and friendships now hopefully formed for life, would be woefully insufficient. It has allowed me to develop and continue my Stroke Awareness campaign and the importance of blood pressure issues but has now developed into promoting disadvantaged and disabilities golf worldwide.

5. The Next Chapter

I had anticipated this being the end of another chapter of my life and *Living the Dream* book and experience, then, cor blimey, I only go and win the British Par 3 Pro Am and a holiday to Mauritius. Then my mate, Steve Lanigan, gives me the use of his villa in Portugal, so 2011 had two more major destinations for TSG to visit and pass comment on. In 2011, the golf triumphs continued – Bunkerfest, G Tour Order of Merit, Show AM Title, Studley Wood and British Par 3 Team Titles. In 2012, I will have a real go again in the USA, playing on the Golf Channel Tour as well as the Golf Week … team TSG has qualified for the De Vere Loch Lomond event … the inaugural Facebook Open at St Andrews. Should I delay further, no I think that's another chapter in another book.

Another title at Lindrick at the Dave Edwards event with partner Ralph Harwood and my mate Dave.

Portugal

This is England's oldest ally and the home of the Algarve, a long-time favourite for north-European golfers which vies with the Costa Del Sol for the title of Europe's premier golf destination.

Portugal has many faces; under-developed and unspoilt regions co-exist with sophisticated resorts that have been firmly on the tourist map for over forty years. Lisbon, the capital, happily combines the modern developments required of the new millennium, with the historic, old-fashioned idiosyncratic charm of its long and ancient past. Each of the region's capitals, Porto, Cormbra and Evera, has its own particular distinctive personality and charm but to see the real Portugal, you need to head to the fantastic Atlantic coastline and the ocean, which has defined this nation both physically and historically.

For such a small country of just over 34,400 square miles, Portugal enjoys immense geographical diversity. The north is green, verdant, lush and rich in fertile woodlands, vines and olives. The south is sun-drenched and is the country's granary. Rugged hillsides are a constant feature throughout the hinterland and a spectacular 1,100 mile coastline of fantastic, beaches, dramatic cliffs, headlands, hidden coves with ancient castles, fantastic golf and some of Europe's finest surfing, offers a fantastic backdrop to this unique country.

Glorious Silver Coast beaches, Portugal.

Obidus Castle.   *Nazare Beach.*

Portugal's modern-day success story can be traced to joining the European Union in 1986 since when enormous strides have been taken. It is now the world's largest cork producer and its wines are now equal to any in the world. Tourism and golf are now a major part of the economy. Sadly, the budget and Euro problems affecting Mediterranean countries is also a worry here and no-one can confidently predict the future for this historic land.

The Algarve is the country's holiday playground. To the east of Faro, the splendid coast is fringed by long, sandy, offshore islands. To the west, bays and coves predominate. Since the 1960s , principally due to golf, the ancient old towns of Faro, Portimao and Lagos, rich in their Moorish heritage, have been joined by purpose-built stylish, chic resorts such as Albufeira, Carvoneira, Vilamoura and also the sporting enclaves of Vale de Lobo and Quinta do Lago. Most golfers head in this direction.

It had been a major black spot on my golfing resume that I had never played here. Madeira, although Portuguese, does not really qualify. Much of the Algarve has been written about and photographed by much more qualified scribes than I, so I never really felt the urge to visit. However, when my good friend, Steve Lanigan, offered us his villa for a few weeks on the Silver Coast, north of Lisbon, relatively unknown in golfing terms but rich in historic, ancient towns such as Obidus, it offered a unique opportunity to satisfy the golfing urge with a holiday destination of some note and great weather. So for my birthday, Matron and I, together with our great travelling buddies, Echo and Ledge, set off to this sunshine paradise.

Within twenty minutes of the villa are four golf courses of considerable note and renown. The

Rugged cliffs battered by Atlantic gales.   *Picturesque seaside villages.*

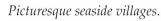

Obidus.

highly rated links-style course at Praia d'el Rey, joined by the new courses of Bom Successo and Royal Obidus, and a fine inland, parkland track, well-established and in fantastic condition called the Golden Eagle. So clearly, Ledge and I would get in some serious golf. The main attractions are however the splendid medieval town of Obidus and the spectacular enchanting coastline and its quaint old fishing villages.

Obidus really is stunning, the old castle standing proudly on top of the hill. In medieval times, this was a sea port and all the land for about fourteen miles, as far as Peniche on the coast, has only surfaced in the past hundred years. Walking through the quaint brick alleyways, whivh have at times a rustic charm, you are taken back to a time and place long ago. Smart wine bars, glorious smelling pastry and chocolate vendors vie with artisans and potters, making this a splendid place to visit far away from the razzmatazz of the Algarve. A long central street cuts through the town, from where steep alleyways, flights of steps and tiny cobbled squares open up, all dripping with flowers and lined with brilliant white-washed buildings. It really is a pleasure to explore this netwok of streets and squares. Obidus really is postcard pretty.

If Obidus is special, the coastline is even more so. The best beach is probably at the splendid hilltop

Nazare.

town of Nazare which somehow manages to hang on to its original role of a picturesque fishing village, yet in summer turns into a major resort with big crowds flocking for the superb beaches and bustling fish restaurants.

The main town beach is backed by a wide esplanade which opens up into a couple of laid-back squares, lined with bars and scattered with outdoor cafés. You can take a furnicular up to the old town on the headland from where the views are sensational.

But there are many delights inland as well. The small town of Mafra, with its wonderful palace, and Sintra, the summer residences of the kings of Portugal and of the Moors before them, are architecturally magnificent and should not be missed.

Palace at Mafra.

The Golf

In my opinion, the Praia d'el Rey experience is up there with the best. This seaside links commences with a few holes running through the hillside forests before exploding down to the beach and coast. A true links with fast, hard greens, glorious views, open to changeable elements, it offers hard, fair, dramatic challenges. The 18-hole golf course was designed by the renowned American golf architect, Cabell B. Robinson, and was inaugurated on 14 June 1997. Deep bunkers, sloping greens and sandy dunes contrast sharply with the lush fairways, making it the complete golfing challenge. Praia d'el Rey is rated amongst the top golf courses in Europe by *Golf World Magazine* and is one of Portugal's major golfing destinations for both private and sponsored events. The course is a mixture of seaside links and parkland holes with a par of 73, offering the golfer a unique experience.

Bom Successo and Royal Obidus, overlooking the Obidus Lagoon, are new courses still in the

Del Rey.

Stunning Del Rey.

process of settling in and with the ongoing continued resort development that has followed the usual pattern – course first, then houses, then infrastructure. Both are great designs and in immaculate condition, but I suggest will be much more enjoyable in about ten years' time. Opened in 2008, Bom Sucesso offers everything you would expect of a golf holiday resort with bars, restaurants, leisure activities and of course, a fantastic Donald Steel designed, 6,200 metre 18-hole championship golf course.

The golf course was designed as two distinct loops of nine holes leading back to the clubhouse and incorporates the natural landscape to produce a course which blends with its surroundings. With winding fairways and huge, well-protected greens, the first nine holes are played on reasonably level terrain whilst the back nine are laid out on more undulating terrain (and offer some spectacular views of the surrounding countryside, Obidos Lagoon and the coast). A fantastic course, it is always maintained to a high standard and offers an excellent and enjoyable challenge.

The late great Seve Ballesteros, designer of the golf course at Royal Óbidos Spa & Golf Resort, promised golfers 'a great and wonderful place' here on Portugal's Silver Coast. The course layout spanning 6,400m (+ 7,100 yards), will represent a

Bom Successo.

true test for players of all levels. The first hole, a difficult right-handed dogleg, heads north, setting up a spectacular combination of holes overlooking the lagoon (Lagoa de Óbidos). The feature hole of the front nine is the 5th, an exciting 520m par 5, with a final approach into a large undulating green, surrounded on three sides by water.

The second nine holes lie in the central and southern section of the development. Six of the holes meander between an intricate eco system of lakes which are inter-connected by cascading streams. The highlight of the back nine is the 12th, a 420 metre par 4, where the golfer has to negotiate both the drive and the second shot between and over two lakes and the curving stream. The clubhouse, sumptuously appointed with restaurant, spike bar and pro shop, is ideally located and overlooks no fewer than 9 of the 18 holes. Sitting out on the generous terrace, owners and visitors to Royal Óbidos will enjoy spectacular views of the golf course and the cascading lakes and streams, with the Atlantic Ocean 'and some truly wonderful sunsets' in the background.

Bom Successo.

Situated near Rio Maior, some sixty kilometres from Lisbon, the Golden Eagle Golf and Country Club is one of the newest jewels of Portuguese golf. Formerly, access was restricted to members and their guests, but since August 1997, it is open to visitors.

Designed by the US architect, Rocky Roquemore, the course covers ninety hectares, and is framed by a landscape in which beautiful local flora and gentle pines, decorative eucalyptuses and acacias all stand out. Its design is typical of the modern US school, which means target golf is the most important point. The course totals 6,200 metres of championship tees for a Par 72 (37+35).

On the first round, look out for hole 6, a par 4 of 354 metres, in which the golfer has to hit the second shot over trees strategically placed in front of the fairway. On the second round, pay attention at hole number 10 (354 metres) where, in order to get a par 4, the player has to make a second shot over the water onto a not very deep green.

Visit the Silver Coast; you won't regret it, fine golf but even better, a stunning location.

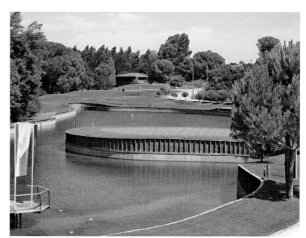

Golden Eagle.

Mauritius

This trip started in August when I curled in 8 footer or so on the 17th to send Simon Lilly and me to the top of the leader board in the British Par 3 Pro Am. The prize was a vacation in the idyllic holiday paradise of Mauritius. Far better, according to Matron, than a bit of glassware. And so for her birthday in 2011, we headed off, business-class by Emirates, to the Indian Ocean holiday of our dreams. It did not disappoint.

Emirates offer all business-class flyers, a complimentary limousine service to and from the airport. That sounds OK, but not so good if they turn up in a C-class Mercedes, lovely but small, and you have to sit in the back with your clubs on your knees. The new Airbus A380 is really something else, with unbelievable seats and of course, the bar area at the rear. If this is the face of future flying, count me in. I can put up with long-haul in this opulence. The Sunday we flew out was also 'Survival Sunday', the last day of the Premiership season, whereby my home town team, perennial strugglers, had to win at Stoke to have any chance of survival. So perhaps in view of the twists and turns that happened that afternoon, it was a good job for my blood pressure that I was at 35,000 feet somewhere above continental Europe. Fear not, this modern-day technological wonder had regular updates and a phone system that let me speak to my son back in Wigan. Quite what my fellow passengers made of, 'We are staying up, say we are staying up,' or 'Who put the ball in the Potters net? Hugo, Hugo?' from the front of the plane, I am not sure. Matron was not amused when the final whistle blew at Stoke,

Literally sunbathing all day.

Heritage Awali, Mauritius.

Coastal Mauritian fishing village.

that even the pilot knew that Wigan had stayed up. I was sent off by Matron down to the bar where there was a complimentary glass of champers waiting for me, poured by the stewardess who was a fellow Wiganer and had been following the game from my reactions.

After the stopover in Dubai, we were relegated to an older plane, so the journey on was much more sedate and to Matron's liking. Arriving in Mauritius, we were again chauffeured in a vehicle where this time, Matron had the clubs on her knees. Object lesson number one, always tell the limo firms that you have golf clubs.

Mauritius has beaches that defy all superlatives; wild landscapes that will be forever etched into your memory, loads of adventure options as well as some of the finest golf on the planet. You may get a rare glimpse into the history of this former trading post. A country with several different eco systems. Paradise found? Maybe …

Mauritius is cast in the warm azure waters of the Indian Ocean and what can be better than splashing about in glinting turquoise seas, sampling gourmet fare in a top-notch restaurant and sipping a cocktail on your private terrace? What became immediately apparent was that the island has certainly more of a French feel, despite Britain being the last colonial power to dominate the island. It is really this French influence that permeates this Mauritian experience as, although independent, the island retains so much of its French past, mixed with an equally beguiling Afro-Asian cultural influence, that will impress even the most cosmopolitan of travellers.

Mauritius had been squaring up to be one of the Indian Ocean's most progressive and dynamic nations, with an increasingly impressive and malleable economic model and a liberal democratic political culture that was once the envy of its African neighbours. Unfortunately, this millennium has seen a change with several serious examples of government corruption and a marked increase in crime, culminating in the sad murder of a newly-wed Irish tourist just weeks before we visited. Paradise on the wane? Perhaps! An important thing to realise is that all prices, certainly in the hotel resorts, are often quoted in Euros, so the impact of the global problem has certainly been felt here, even though it is thousands of miles from Europe.

The island has no indigenous native population, unless you count the ill-fated dodo. The initial colonial presence in the early 1500s was Portuguese, followed by the Dutch, the French and finally the British. The Dutch introduced slaves from Africa and killed off the dodo, so certainly left their mark. Traders from Asia, particularly India and China, made up the melting pot of ethnicity that still flourishes today. This cosmopolitan mix helps with the tolerance or multi-cultural well-being in the isle as no race can claim any sort of historic pre-eminence.

Sadly, British imperialism, despite giving the islanders independence in 1968, is not very well respected, primarily due to the British government's treatment of the Chagos islanders. It was described by John Pilger in 2004 in a superb TV documentary as 'the most prolonged betrayal in Britain's colonial history.' In the 1960s and '70s, our government uprooted and exiled the entire population so we could lease the island of Diego Garcia to the USA as an airbase. Between 1965 and 1973, they were resettled in Mauritius and the Seychelles with over 5,000 now living in abject poverty in the Mauritian capital of Port Louis. In 1982, the islanders won a derisory compensation of £4 million from the UK government, which was paid to the poverty stricken islanders who signed away their rights to return. Most islanders were totally unaware of and too desperate to realise just what they were agreeing to. In 2000, at the High Court in London, it was ruled that they had been evicted illegally and their rights to be repatriated were upheld, but nothing happened. In 2003, a further claim for compensation was rejected although the judge did accept that the British government had acted shamefully. In 2007, a further legal battle saw the islanders win another case where the government's behaviour was condemned as unlawful and an abuse of power. In 2008, this was, to the surprise of many legal scribes, overturned and the island archipelago is still ceded to the military until 2016. The islanders, many of whom have never set foot on their homeland, must wait and hope that in the future both the UK and the USA fail to see the need for a base here in the Indian Ocean.

Mauritius is naturally famed for its sapphire waters, powder-white beaches and large swathes of tropical forests, with most tourism centred on purpose-built 5-star resorts. The island is clearly a crucible of wildly dynamic and diverse peoples and is so much more complex and intriguing than a

The Awali promotes a strong African flavour.

simple dichotomy between tourist and non-tourist bubbles. The fact is that there is no need to leave the comfort and respective safety of these fabulous resorts yet, ultimately, this island is the kind of place that rewards even the smallest attempts at exploration. So, if your biggest discovery is the beach butler service at your hotel, you will be missing out.

Our prize took us to the award-winning Heritage Awali development on the south coast at Bel Ombre about forty-five minutes from the airport, but a good two hours from the capital. Despite being relatively isolated, Bel Ombre has quickly developed into a cosy tourist destination along the wild southern shores. The main attraction in the area is the Domaine de Bel Ombre, an open nature reserve set in an old sugar plantation. There are two hotels here, the Le Telfair (which captures the luxury and grandeur of the island's colonial heritage) and the Awali (which reflects the African heritage).

I can understand and fully realise the economic drive that will inevitably lead to further development on the island, but I am unsure as to the significance of enhancing an already fine reputation. The advantages of a vacation here are well known: natural beauty, the unspoilt and often slow pace of life, 5-star superior resorts and manicured golfing heaven.

The relative smallness of the island puts everything within easy reach, do they need more when there is so much spare capacity? I think not.

The current economic climate could I believe be a godsend to the island's tourist industry if it concentrates its future developments on more eco friendly ideals and revenue streams. I certainly would have liked to see the real Mauritius, the sugar plantations, small indigenous fishing villages, the colonial history, but staying as we did in a well-pampered all-inclusive spa/golf resort meant of course more time on the beach, taking up my two free rounds of golf, enjoying the superb wine and food. I can't complain about that.

Indeed, we had no complaints at all about the Awali, gorgeous, superb staff, everything about the place oozed opulence. A fantastic resort from its infinity pool to the choice of four fine restaurants, free beach activities, romantic secluded spa, the list just goes on and on … then the magnificent Golf du Chateau.

The Golf

My good mate, Mark Mouland, former Mauritius Open Champion, waxes lyrical about the courses here and he is a pretty good judge. Courses were well manicured, greens were slick and quite difficult to read, with a kaleidoscope of local fauna and colours. Play one and I suspect you may feel like you will have played all the others. That should not put the discerning golfer off a visit here. Your round will be a fine experience, of that you can be assured. Vistas will be sensational, quality and good value for money.

The seven superbly designed 18-hole courses have ensured that the island has quickly established itself as a most prestigious golfing destination. Diverse, all the courses have been set in outstanding locations and seem in perfect harmony with the environment. I recommend the visitor to Ludovic Albert's pictorial homage to Mauritian golf, whose images encapsulate brilliantly the beauty of golf in this sunshine paradise.

Golf du Chateau.

The Golf du Chateau is located among sugar cane plantations and takes its name from the imposing colonial chateau that houses the resorts most prestigious restaurant overlooking the entire course. The course manages to mix a blend of several outstanding parkland holes with several of a more Scottish links feel. Overlooking the ocean, the course seduces you with a contrast of colours, lush green verdant fairways, the yellow hues of long prairie grass, the azure sea and dazzling colours from the local plants and foliage. It is beautiful. Unique to this course is a 9-hole par 3 course which is enclosed by the main course. With lengths ranging from 50m to 120m , it is a great beginner's course, as well as offering a seasoned British par-3 champion, a worthy challenge with which to hone his game.

Other courses of note include:

THE CONSTANCE BELLE MARE PLAGE LEGEND, the championship course which has hosted may European Tour PGA Events.

On this resort is also the Links, designed by Peter Alliss.

THE FOUR SEASONS at Anahita is the newest course on the island.

LE TOUESSROK, designed by Langer on the Ile aux Cerfs, is the picture postcard course that most want to play if visiting Mauritius.

PARADIS GOLF CLUB, nearest to Golf du Chateaux, is considered a superb, exotic and technical course set between the emblematic Morne Brabant Mountain and its sumptuous lagoon.

TAMARINA GOLF, facing the bay, again offers stunning views as it is set in a luxurious estate surrounded by a wild environment resembling the African savannah.

Cambodia

New destinations are appearing in the most unlikely of settings. Next year I have been invited to visit the ancient kingdom of Cambodia, formerly 'the killing fields' it is now a vibrant Asian economy with a burgeoning golfing environment.

Anthony Langlois is a forty-one-year-old Englishman who has been travelling to Asia to play golf for the past ten years. He first arrived in Cambodia in 2006 and was impressed with the friendliness he received from the Khmer people and the diversity of the country's beauty, history and culture. Keen to promote Cambodia as a golfing destination to international travellers, he now works closely with the golf courses and the Ministry of Tourism to ensure the country develops a greater awareness as a viable destination for overseas travellers to play golf and experience the historic temples. Anthony can be contacted by email at: anthonylanglois@hotmail.com

Historic Temples ... Modern Golf
What does Cambodia conjure up in your mind? Magical temples or remote island beaches? Or maybe less attractive images, thankfully from a distant past, such as those portrayed in the Oscar-winning film *The Killing Fields*?

A more accurate picture of present day Cambodia is a peaceful and welcoming country that has retained the style of its former French colonial heritage and mixed it with indigenous cultural charm to completely redevelop itself and regain its proud title as the 'Pearl of Asia'. Indeed, the past decade has seen a flourishing tourist industry with some three million visitors each year enjoying a full range of cultural and luxury travel experiences – and golf is proving to be an increasingly important part of that package.

Sir Nick Faldo, Jack Nicklaus, Arnold Palmer and David McLay Kidd have all contributed in designing a range of courses to suit golfers of all abilities and budgets that are truly as beautiful to play as they are to see. Some of these courses are now open for play, whilst others are at a later stage of completion.

The catalyst of developments was the Phokeethra Country Club, which opened in Siem Reap in 2007 and soon became widely accepted as a world-class facility. Managed by the Sofitel Hotel Group, and home to the Asian PGA Tour's Johnnie Walker Cambodian Open, this challenging course, with sweeping fairways and water features on almost every hole, created the benchmark for Cambodian golf.

Sir Nick Faldo maintained that level of quality with his Angkor Golf Resort development as reflected by its 2009 rating as one of the top three new courses in Asia. The award was made by *Asian Golf Monthly*. The former world number one golfer is quoted as saying,

I am certain that this site and this golf course will become world renowned. We have designed and built a golf course that challenges all standards of golfers, from the casual weekender through to the seasoned professional. It is a golf course that will offer enjoyment to everyone and will hopefully have them coming back to be challenged by this strategic layout time after time. … Overall, I believe that we have created a course that offers great variety through all 18 holes and the fact that we have been working alongside such remarkable surroundings has been a real inspiration, the result is a strategically testing and very engaging round of golf. I also believe that our course at the Angkor Golf Resort will help to put this part of South East Asia firmly on the golfing map.

In 2010, a third international course, Angkor Lake Resort Golf Club (formerly named Siem Reap Lake Resort Golf Club), opened and added a new dimension in *aprés golf* with its opulent clubhouse and spa facilities. Similarly, Bellus Angkor Golf Club, scheduled to open in 2012, will include a water park and casino. Designed by David McLay Kidd, described by *Golf World* as the 'hottest architect in golf', you can certainly bet on the course being a winner too.

In the next five years, it is anticipated that a further ten new courses will be built in Cambodia. More developments at Siem Reap are expected and the beach resort of Sihanoukville (no courses at present) and the surrounding islands also have plans in place. The 36-hole layout at Bokor Mountain, an Arnold Palmer design, is expected to be ready to play by 2014. In fact, hardly a month goes by without whispers of new and even more elaborate golf developments.

In contrast, golf has been played in Phnom Penh since 1996 when two facilities, the Cambodian Golf and Country Club and the Royal Cambodia Phnom Penh Golf Club, were constructed to satisfy the needs of the local dignitaries. It is fair to say that they are not to the same standard (or fees) as the courses in Siem Reap but, as demand for golf has increased in the locality, the maintenance and presentation of these courses has steadily improved.

At the other end of the scale, Grand Phnom Penh, a Jack Nicklaus designed course, opened recently, catering for members only with a current joining fee of $40,000. You will need to befriend a member to secure a game here. Thankfully, Vattanac Golf Resort, a new development to international standard, is expected to open within the next twelve months in Phnom Penh and available for play to the general public, and again, Sir Nick Faldo, is the driving force behind the 36-hole development. In the meantime City Golf Phnom Penh, a 9-hole par 3 course with driving range and practice greens, offers a low-budget alternative.

Whatever the course designers come up with in their quest to make Cambodia a sun-kissed haven of golf, they will always be in the shadow of the main historic attraction, Angkor Wat, the world's largest religious building. It was built for King Suryavanam II in the early twelfth century and is the only one to have remained a significant religious centre since its foundation, first Hindu then Buddhist.

Another famous attraction is the Tonlé Sap, which is the largest freshwater lake in south-east Asia. The Tonlé Sap is unusual for two reasons, its flow changes direction twice a year, and the portion that forms the lake expands and shrinks dramatically with the seasons. From November to May,

Cambodia's dry season, the Tonlé Sap drains into the Mekong River at Phnom Penh. However, when the year's heavy rains begin in June, the Tonlé Sap backs up to form an enormous lake.

For the more adventurous visitor, there is so much more to see. Choices range from the relaxing city of Battambang to the bustling capital Phnom Penh and the quiet coastal towns of Kep and Kampot to the commanding Cardamom Mountains and the beach resort and islands of Sihanoukville. Cambodia is certainly a mixed bag of delights and whatever treasures you seek you will not be disappointed.

Facts and Figures:

Flights available to Siem Reap from the major Asian hub airports – Bangkok, Singapore, Kuala Lumpur, Hong Kong and Saigon.

Direct flight to Phnom Penh from Paris with Air France (via Bangkok).

Visa upon arrival, one passport-sized photograph and $20 required.

Currency: US dollar accepted at all major business outlets, Cambodian Riel for small purchases ($1 = 4,000 Riel).

Green fees: (with caddie) approximately $120 at the international standard courses, $70 at the long established Phnom Penh courses.

Hotel prices: 3 star from $40 rising to over $100 for luxury 5 star.

Cuisine: a great variety ranging from traditional khmer dishes to readily-available western food.

For further information, visit:

www.GolfCambodia.com
www.facebook.com/GolfCambodia
www.youtube.com/GolfCambodia

6. What the Future Holds

It has been five years since my stroke, and nearly sixteen years since my brain tumour. Looking back at both my books, I think you will agree I have achieved a lot despite my misfortunes. After a stroke, one small problem is how one should be referred to. 'Stroke victim' has quite an ominous ring even though, trust me, I really did feel a victim and still do on odd occasions. 'Stroke sufferer' is I think even worse, it portrays a life in constant pain or suffering, plus it suggests negative thoughts where a positive outlook is required to enhance any recovery. 'Stroke patient' is technically only true whilst you are in hospital, in rehab or under medical care. And, although patience is a virtue essential to anyone attempting a full, or even partial recovery, I have never met anyone who was prepared to be patient in their recovery. 'Stroke recoverer' is again not plausible as few people ever achieve complete recovery; after all, the stroke has killed part of your brain. 'Stroke survivor' is starting to get more realistic, we have all survived if we are still here, no matter what collateral damage we carry forward. Yes, I am a stroke survivor but I also think this book shows I am a stroke thriver as well. It is that of which I am particularly proud. I do not see myself as disabled, just disadvantaged. I have been unfortunate to have suffered both a tumour and a stroke, but fortunate enough to have survived both relatively intact. I am sure this positive approach has been my biggest strength in the continued struggle which, despite everything, it still is at times.

With both my tumour and stroke, I have had some unexpected and unwelcome experiences after these illnesses. You have to try not to let them get to you. They are inevitable; the only thing you can do is put on your emotional overcoat and weather the storm. A positive attitude is the essence of any recovery from a major illness and it is essential that you have the support from family and friends to identify problems, and offer help and support at traumatic times. On Facebook of all things, there is a fantastic wealth of stroke support groups led by *Strokes Suck*. This network has been of considerable support, encouragement and in particular, understanding of problems, more than any book you may read.

I have been involved with support groups and I hope my positive attitude throughout my recovery and ongoing life, gives some solace and shows that it is possible to lead a near normal, different or even a better life, no matter how dark the problems may seem. Setbacks to recovery are not necessarily inevitable, but they do happen and it is always better to be prepared for them. They can be physical as well as emotional and you should be gentle on yourself. Most of the time, they are not of your making and, just because I have been lucky, do not mean others will be as fortunate, but it is important that if there are setbacks, you need to hang on in there until you turn that corner into a happier place.

Thomas Gillespie wrote, 'An attitude not only of defence but defiance' (*The Mountain Storm*) and that is the attitude that I carry with me throughout life. I do not want sympathy or even respect, I want people to recognise there are others more unfortunate who do need help. I find my golf a therapeutic aid to my well-being. I never realised how truly therapeutic golf could be until I had my stroke and this is by far the most effective occupational therapy I underwent. To some, it may be music, to others art or literature, but it is essential that a stroke survivor finds this trigger if they are to thrive. I really can relate to Kylie Tennants, 'To be born is to be lucky, later, life may prove a failure or success, depending on the outlook of whoever is living it: but that there is life should be a matter of congratulation daily renewed. So many find life a slender chance ...' Sometimes I consider my greatest achievement is staying alive and it sure ain't been easy. I'm a lucky man.

It is difficult, perhaps impossible, to encapsulate an illness like a stroke in a book. Each stroke is different, pertinent to that specific individual, and how we deal with it is likely to be as individuals. There are however certain sureties that may provide a foundation for aiding a recovery, and life thereafter. I am sure that a positive mental approach, patience with the recovery and time are actually your best friends. Goals are also singularly important – first step, first swing of a golf club, first walk round a course, first flight, anything that enables, then empowers. Its important that you look at life for what it can bring, not for what it may have been.

And so I look to the future with continued optimism, further trips, maybe further successes on the golf course ... who knows but as long as I keep waking up, then I will be happy.

7. Just a Little Bit Extra

A picture by Goddard, that fine Vegas-based impressionist painter, is one of three originals I am fortunate to own. It is on our landing, outside the bedroom, and makes me chuckle each morning.

The sartorial Social Golfer tees off at Pebble Beach.

Like most golfers, I am enthralled when the top list of courses is published by such luminaries as *Golf Digest* and *Golf World* which is a combination of votes cast by the chosen select few. I have now played over 1,000 courses worldwide, left a divot on every continent and a ball in every ocean and so, whilst on nobody's list of select invitees, I do believe my top ten has validity in that I have played each and every one of these courses. My list has been compiled on one over-riding premise – the enjoyment factor – not on how hard the course is, how many majors it has held, who designed it, but simply which did I enjoy playing the most. My enjoyment is based on three principal considerations – firstly, value for money; secondly, the beauty and location of the course and finally, the course as a golf challenge.

Why pick twelve and not ten? To be honest, for two reasons – it will be easier to put on my 2012 calender and I was struggling to narrow it down to ten. On this basis, I commend the following:

1. Royal Melbourne

Number one in my humble opinion by a country mile. Two autonomous quality courses, the east and the west, that for competitions such as the President's Cup, become one by taking twelve holes from the west and six from the east. This does not suggest that the east is the weaker course; this amalgamation was done simply as a beneficial expedient in 1959 for the Canada Cup (and now for the World Cup) simply to avoid the busy roads that cross both courses and facilitate arrangements for spectators.

These courses are simply one of the most fantastic designs on the planet, something outstanding and exceptional was inevitable given that many of the earliest members had their origins in St Andrews and the outstanding natural terrain of the course was so similar to the Scottish duneland links. Given the principal architect was the peerless, Dr Alister Mackenzie (Cypress Point and Augusta National would follow for this doyen of the inter-war period), backed up by Alex Russell and green-keeper supreme, Claude Crockford, these three wise men produced two masterpieces. In the first book, I comment principally on the greens, definitely the best I have encountered, why even Ernie Eels (2002) agrees, 'You won't putt on better greens than these all year' and the bunkers, and I found plenty with strategic placing and careful design. The contest of man against nature on this course is just so enjoyable. It is a 1920s design and does need lengthening, which would be difficult in view of the original design, but I watched the 2011 President's Cup with interest, when even the best struggled on these magnificent greens. They were trying to make it Tiger-proof when I visited in 2008 – how times have changed. A full detailed review can be found in the first *Social Golfer* book.

2. Pebble Beach

Jack Nicklaus famously said if he had but one round left to play it would be at Pebble. Yes, it is that good – historic, spectacular, difficult and unique. The coast holes in particular are mesmeric. And anyone can play it, it is a municipal – a bit costly, but far easier to get on than St Andrews for example.

3. Kauri Cliffs

This is the last course I would want to play. Why? Well, Karen and I found the experience to be the most romantic, idyllic, special golfing week of our lives. The Lodge has everything – Michelin dining, fine wines, super spa, stunning location overlooking the Bay of Islands with sensational views, and the course is a bit tasty too. We found the experience here better than its sister course at the Farm at Cape Kidnappers which was also absolutely fabulous.

4. Gary Player Country Club

Located in the Sun City Complex, it is simply the best place on the planet for a group of guys or couples to visit. This course, home of the twelve-man annual million dollar challenge has it all. It is always in immaculate condition. Its Gary Player design has stood the test of time – holes 9, 17 and 18 are sublimely outstanding and stay in the memory. Its sister course, the Lost City, with the famous crocodile pit, ain't no slouch either. Sun City is a resort every discerning golfer should visit some time.

5. The Emirates Golf Club, Dubai

Today, the Emirates may not be considered the best in Dubai by some, with the Els, Montgomery, the Creek, *et al*, some quite exceptional courses, but when I visited Dubai, I only wanted to play the original, the one, the iconic Emirates, with two equally exceptional tracks. Building this course in these conditions in the desert is a modern-day wonder, now much replicated across the Middle East, but this first real desert course may have been imitated, but rarely bettered in my opinion. It is pricey, but then everything in Dubai is at the top end of anyone's budget.

6. Tecina Golf, La Gomera, Canary Islands

I doubt if this will appear in any top ten list, so why does it deserve to be in mine? Those who have the first book will know that on the front cover is the 4th at Tecina, one of 18 spectacular holes on a hillside cliff falling down to the beach. The club house is at the 18th, it is a two-mile journey up the hill to the first tee. Quirky, unique, a fair challenge, in fine condition with sensational vistas, anyone who has ever played here will want to return. It is detailed in the first book.

7. Flamingo Golf, Monastir, Tunisia

Again, I doubt this would appear in any classics listing, but this place is special to me. Allow me a bit of indulgence, it is where I played my first ever over-seas round and won my first ever overseas compet-ition, so the memories are rather special. Tunisia is, in my mind, a very much neglected golfing oasis on the African Med. The courses are well-maintained, superbly designed and, compared with the rest of the Med, unbelievable value for money, often less than £20 per round. Golf in the sun does not get any better.

8. The Jockey Club, Hong Kong

This three-course complex on two islands in Hong Kong Bay is rather special. You can only get there by ferry, a rather daunting, intimidating twenty-minute ride which does give sensational vistas, weather permitting. A splendid clubhouse and three championship courses await. Great value for money, a unique oriental experience, but the golf is challenging and absorbing. It was reviewed in my first book.

9. Golf du Chateau, Mauritius

Once again, this may not be considered the best out of nine or ten very special courses in these islands. Le Touessrok, for instance, but I have not played them, so this course will pass muster representing them all. It is a superb coastal course that is designed around plantations and on a hillside. The natural beauty of the location is consolidated into each of the 18 holes. Add to that a course that was in as good a condition as any I played this year. It was a wonderful prize for winning the British Par 3.

10. Praia d'el Rey, Obidus, Portugal

I have found golf in Spain and Portugal to be often very Americanised and there's nothing really wrong with that, but it can be extremely costly, especially the best courses like Vilamoura and Valderama. I also had, until my visit to Obidus, never really found a true links on the Iberian peninsula. The D'el Rey is a links similar to Pebble and Royal St George's but, in respect of the latter, it certainly has far more sensational vistas. It may only have two really magnificent holes, but is great value for money when compared to other more highly-rated courses on the Algarve.

11. Koolau Golf Club Oahu, Hawaii

If you played the course which is reputed to be the hardest in the world, how can you not include it in your list. Is it that difficult? Yes, most certainly, but it is as spectacular as it is difficult. They say you need as many balls as your handicap … yes you do, you won't ever forget a round here. To be reviewed in the next book.

12. Nailcote Hall, Berkswell, Coventry

Home of the British Par 3 Championship, this 9-hole course is included because it is that good as a stand-alone challenge. I do not know any of my peers who have not loved this place, its intricate pin placements, its natural beauty and, in my opinion, the number-one social golf competition in the world. Tony Jacklin said it was like playing a major championship around a country manor whilst a tea party was on. Maybe, different and certainly unique, but as the professional scores reflect, it is also a considerable challenge.

Extracts from *Today's Thoughts*

On facebook, TSG has a daily thought, often a famous quote, sometimes a laconic view of life, rarely something deep and meaningful.

Happy golf is good golf and therefore we are all capable of good golf. (Gary Player)
Hit it hard, find it, hit it hard again. (Arnold Palmer)

You are going to lose more than you win, you miss more than you hole out … it's life, it's as inevitable as the sunset, deal with it and learn from it. (TSG)

The average social golfer does not look for professional advice; this has two differing results … the bad faults are not corrected but good habits and techniques aren't being tinkered with, sadly the former probably outweighs the latter, don't be afraid to seek help to gain improvement … (TSG)

The great thing about golf (like life) is that it's not a fair game, at one point or other it's unfair to everybody, but you know what, there's nothing wrong with that, indeed there's something quite fair (Ben Wright)

Do your best, be seen to do your best, but more than anything know yourself that you gave it your best. (TSG)

Golf is not a game of great shots; it's a game of most accurate misses. (Gene Littler)

Always keep a sense of humour out on the course, for sure you have enough to worry about with normal life, than let a few bad shots get to you. Never, ever, take your bad rounds home with you … and as Bernard Hunt told me, 'there's only one bad round you will ever play, and that is the last one that you will never play'. When faced with that difficult shot, that big challenge, hope is not enough. You need faith in your ability to succeed. The knowledge that you have worked hard enough to justify that belief but above all, the temperament to accept and deal with the consequences of the end result. Always keep learning and be willing to learn, it will keep you young … (Patty Berg)

Be decisive, a wrong decision is generally less disastrous than indecision. (Bernhard Langer)

Always try to think where you want the ball to go, not where you don't want it to go. (Billy Casper)

The most important shot in golf is the next one. (Bobby Jones)

Yesterday is history, tomorrow is a mystery, and today is a gift, that's why it's called the present … (*Time waits for no man*, origin unknown, statement so relevant)

Success depends almost entirely on how effectively you learn to manage the game's two great adversaries, the course and yourself … (Jack Nicklaus)

Play the shot you can play not the one you hope to play … (Tommy Armour)

Drive for show, putt for dough, of course, but that bit in between, getting to the green is important too. (TSG)

You might putt better if you hit the ball closer. (Mrs Marianne Mouland to Mark)

The old saying 'it's a bad craftsman who blames his tools', is pretty accurate to most golfers with a putting problem. Putting is 90 per cent up top, if you think you can't putt, you won't. (Gay Brewer)

Never look for excuses to lose, look for reasons to win. (TSG)

If you are smart, you learn something from every round you play … (Sam Snead)

In golf as in life, you will get out of it what you put into it … (Sam Snead)

You are meant to play the ball as it lies, a fact that may help a touch on your own objective approach to life. (Grantland Rice)

Life consists of a lot of minor annoyances and only a few matters of real consequences. I can sum it up like this: thank the good Lord for the game of golf. (Arnold Palmer)

I'm missing a few putts Ian,
Marianne says hit the approaches closer.

The following is an extract from the Social Golfer's blog www.thesocialgolfer.blogspot.com:

I have become a golf aficionado – anorak you might say – and my love and passion for golf now involves reading as many articles and opinions as I can, and collecting as many glorious pictures of the stunning golf holes as I am able, but a particular interest is the collection of the many superb comments, quotes and paraphrases regarding golf which I bring into my business life. Every day, I end each email with a *Today's Thought* and this is usually a comment or opinion I have read and then believe particularly pertinent to the way I feel that day. The following are some of my phrases and their relevance to me:

My two favourites, which following my illness is the way I now try to look at life. This particular week tragically I learned that a business colleague had lost a young child just short of his first birthday. The poignancy of these comments is particularly relevant now as I wonder about God's grand design.

As you walk down the fairway of life, you must smell the roses; you only get to play one round.

[Ben Hogan]

Health, not wealth, should be man's primary concern. [TSG]

I believe that golf can bring out the best and worst in a person. I have met some truly wonderful people on my travels and had I not had my stroke, without doubt this would not have been possible.

Golf enables us to advance in the great business of being a human being. [Charles Macdonald]

Golf reflects the cycle of life. No matter what you shoot … the next day you have to go back to the first tee and begin all over again and make yourself into something. [Peter Jacobson]

In golf character is laid bare to character. This is why so many friendships and some enmities are formed on the links. [A. Haultain]

Golf requires an individual to use virtues which, perhaps as in my case, are particularly alien in the normal daily routine, in particular, patience, the ability to acknowledge failure, honesty, integrity and humour …

Golf is the infallible test … the man who can go into a patch of rough alone, with the knowledge that only God is watching him, and play his ball where it lies, is the man who will serve you faithfully. The only way of finding out a man's true character is to play golf with him. In no other walk of life does the cloven hoof so quickly display itself. [P. G. Wodehouse]

18 holes of match play will tell you more about your foe than 19 years of business dealings. [G.Rice]

The struggle of the game, that's a big part of my life, a big part of the fun of my life. [Arnold Palmer]

Golf without mistakes is like a dinner without wine. [Jim Murray]

One minute you're bleeding, the next minute you're haemorrhaging, the next minute you're painting the Mona Lisa. [Mac O'Grady]

Playing the game, I have learned the meaning of humility. It has given me a better understanding of the futility of the human effort. [Abba Eban]

Adages I often use in business dealings …

It's all a matter of getting out of bad situations with the least amount of damage. [Rick Rhoden]

Winners listen to people. They are always trying to learn. They respect other people's opinions. Losers just want to talk. [Doug Sanders]

There is no such luck as bad luck. Fate has nothing to do with success or failure, because that is a negative philosophy that indicates one's confidence, and I'll have no part in it. [Greg Norman]

Golf puts a man's character on the anvil and his richest qualities, patience, poise, restraint … to the flame. [Billy Casper]

If you wish to hide your character, don't play golf. [Percy Boomer]

I have had the opportunity, following my illness, to play with many professionals and I remain in awe of their talent when compared to my golf which could be described as:

An endless series of tragedies obscured by the occasional miracle.

Or as Bing Crosby put it, 'my Golf is woeful but I will never surrender.'

But golf despite my limitations in playing it gives a perverse pleasure in failure and unrivalled expectations of anticipated success.

Obviously, yet mysteriously, golf, furnishes its devotees (me) with an intense, many-sided, and abiding pleasure unlike which any other recreation affords. [Herbert Wind]

I cannot explain the feeling when a masterful shot comes off. Every shot I play, I imagine a great result but inevitably because of my talent, mediocrity results.

The occasional great stroke of the poor golfer remains a joy forever.

The Great Bobby Jones probably had a round of mine in mind when he is attributed with saying:

On the golf course, he may be the dogged victim of inexorable fate, struck down by an appalling stroke of tragedy become the hero of unbelievable melodrama, or the clown in a side-splitting comedy.

Don Quixote would understand golf. It is the impossible dream. [Jim Murray]

Golf is a simple game, made difficult by man. [Tom Haliburton]

Golf beats us all, and that is the chief reason we shall never cease loving her. [Robert Hunter]

Golf is the pursuit of the infinite. [Jim Murray]

It is one of golf's greatest ironies and merits that the poorer player derives more pleasure from the pastime than the experienced practitioner.

Golf is so popular simply because it is the best game in the world at which to be bad. [A. A. Milne]

A golfer traverses broad acres of the green earth rejoicing in the fact he sees the end from their beginning. He has escaped from macadam and asphalt and the madding crowd. [R. S. Weir]

I love the fairways with such lovely turf that can put a little spring in the most leaden and depressed foot. [Bernard Darwin]

Golf brings us consolation as we walk its open spaces and it offers us a subtle balance of companionship and solitude. [L. Rubinstein]

Golf … satisfies the spirit. You are out in the grass and the trees. You are out there with nature. You're not really competing with each other, you're competing against yourself, the course and the elements.

Golf is a game which the player's true opponent is the golf course. That is why the game can be enjoyed in solitude or with other golfers of every calibre and age. [Rees Jones]

A Little Bit of Light Humour

It was a sunny Sunday morning on the first hole and I was beginning my preshot routine, visualising my upcoming shot, when a piercing voice came over the clubhouse loudspeaker, 'Would the gentleman on the women's tee back up to the men's tee please!' I could feel every eye on the course looking at me. I was still deep in my routine, seemingly impervious to the interruption. Again, the announcement, 'Would that man on the women's tee kindly back up to the men's tee. I simply ignored the announcement and kept concentrating, when once more, the man yelled, 'Would the MAN on the WOMEN'S tee back up to the MEN'S tee, PLEASE!' Finally, I stopped, turned and looked through the window directly at the person with the mike. I cupped my hands and shouted back, 'Would the c*** in the clubhouse kindly shut the f*** up and let me play my second shot?'

A businessman was attending a conference in Africa. He had a free day and wanted to play a round of golf and was directed to a golf course in the nearby jungle. After a short journey, he arrived at the course and asked the pro if he could get on. 'Sure,' said the Pro, 'What's your handicap?' Not wanting to admit that he had an 18 handicap, he decided to cut it a bit. 'Well, it's 16,' said the businessman, 'But what's the relevance since I'll be playing alone?' 'It's important for us to know,' said the pro, who then called a caddy. 'Go out with this gentleman,' said the pro. The businessman was very surprised at this constant reference to his handicap. The caddy picked up the businessman's bag and a large rifle; again the businessman was surprised but decided to ask no questions. They arrived on the first hole, a par 4. 'Please avoid those trees on the left,' said the caddy. Needless to say, the businessman duck-hooked his ball into the trees. He found his ball and was about to punch it out when he heard the loud crack of the rifle and a large snake fell dead from a tree above his head. The caddy stood next to him with the rifle smoking in his hand. 'That's the mamba, the most poisonous snake in all Africa. You're lucky I was here with you.' After taking a bogey, they moved to the second hole, a par 5. 'Avoid those bushes on the right,' says the caddy. Of course, the businessman's ball went straight into the bushes. As he went to pick up his ball, he heard the loud crack of the caddy's rifle once more, and a huge lion fell dead at his feet. 'I've saved your life again,' said the caddy. The third hole was a par 3 with a lake in front of the green. The businessman's ball came up just short of the green and rolled back to the edge of the water. To take a shot, he had to stand with one foot in the lake. As he was about to swing, a large crocodile emerged from the water and bit off much of his right leg. As he fell to the ground bleeding and in great pain, he saw the caddy with the rifle propped at his side, looking on unconcernedly. 'Why didn't you kill it?' asked the man incredulously. 'I'm sorry, sir,' said the caddy, 'this is the 17th handicap hole. You don't get a shot here. 'That's why you never lie about your handicap.'

A retired corporate executive, now a widower, decided to take a vacation. He booked himself on a Caribbean cruise and proceeded to have the time of his life, that is, until the ship sank. He soon found himself on an island with no other people, no supplies, nothing, only bananas and coconuts. After about four months, he was lying on the beach one day when the most gorgeous woman he has ever seen rows up to the shore. In disbelief, he asks, 'Where did you come from? How did you get here?' She replies, 'I rowed over from the other side of the island where I had landed when my cruise ship sank.' 'Amazing,' he notes. 'You were really lucky to have a row boat wash up with you.' 'Oh, this thing?' explains the woman. 'I made the boat out of some raw material I found on the island. The oars were whittled from gum tree branches. I wove the bottom from palm tree branches, and the sides and stern came from a Eucalyptus tree.' 'But, where did you get the tools?' 'Oh, that was no problem,' replied the woman. 'On the south side of the island, a very unusual stratum of alluvial rock is exposed. I found that if I fired it to a certain temperature in my kiln, it melted into ductile iron, I used that to make tools and used the tools to make the hardware.' The guy was stunned. 'Let's row over to my place,' she says. So, after a short time of rowing, she soon docks the boat at a small wharf. As the man looks to shore, he nearly falls off the boat. Before him is a long stone walk leading to an exquisite bungalow painted in blue and white. While the woman ties up the rowboat with an expertly woven hemp rope, the man can only stare ahead, dumb struck. As they walk into the house, she says casually, 'It's not much, but I call it home. Sit down, please.' 'Would you like a drink?' 'No! No thank you,' the man blurts out, still dazed. 'I can't take another drop of coconut juice.' 'It's not coconut juice,' winks the woman. 'I have a still. How would you like a Pina Colada?' Trying to hide his continued amazement, the man accepts, and they sit down on her couch to talk. After they exchange their individual stories, the woman announces, 'I'm going to slip into something more comfortable. Would you like to take a shower and shave? There's a razor in the bathroom cabinet upstairs.' No longer questioning anything, the man goes upstairs into the bathroom. There, in the cabinet is a razor made from a piece of tortoise bone. Two shells honed to a hollow ground edge are fastened on to its end inside a swivel mechanism. 'This woman is amazing,' he muses. What's next? When he returns, she greets him wearing nothing but some small flowers on tiny vines, each strategically positioned, she smelled faintly of gardenias. She then beckons him to sit down next to her. 'Tell me,' she begins suggestively, slithering closer to him, 'We've both been out here for many months. You must have been lonely. There's something I'm certain you feel like doing right now, something you've been longing for, right?' She stares into his eyes. He can't believe what he's hearing. 'You mean …' he swallows excitedly as tears start to form in his eyes, '… You've built a golf course?

GOLF – Grow old living fine … can't beat it!

Whilst travelling to Hilton Head, it was my great pleasure to come across a fellow golfer, Mr Vincent Lawler. Vinnie was travelling to the island for an annual reunion with his brothers. On the hour long flight, we exchanged many golf tales and it transpired that he was a budding poet having penned the following missive for his favorite club, that is till I cured his slice by simply suggesting dropping the right foot back a bit. Perhaps this most durable of clubs in his bag will now have a bit of a rest now the big boy has come to the aid of the party.

The Three-Wood

Whether fine-crafted persimmon or tempered metal, the Three-Wood is always prepared to play. Perhaps, not the biggest club in the bag, but others never fail to acknowledge its durable presence.

The Three-Wood sails the straight and consistent route. Strong and versatile. Soaring just a little bit higher than most, providing a balanced perspective.
What a game!

Its mark is true whether in the fairway or in the low-rough. Adjusting to the conditions. Never complaining about the lie.
It's a match with any 'big stick' when things are teed up, but it has no equal when the ground is level.

No need to impress while there's yardage unmet. The "click" of a true, clean strike, its sole proclamation of lofty performance. Deferring always to the strokes played by the other clubs in the bag.

A unified vision for the round. Passion for the game.

Over the years, the Three-Wood has hoisted its many spheres like delicate progeny. Respectfully. Occasionally, dimpled by discipline, but always better prepared for the journey ahead. A legacy without par.

The Three-Wood's essence has remained unchanged over the years (though the times have brought some minor expansion on all).

It has always anticipated and adapted, though never yielding to the fads nor the clamor for excess. That's not how the game was meant to be played.

Semper fidelis.

And, now the turn has been taken back to the clubhouse. Still, plenty of fairways left to play. But, time, nonetheless, to pass the scorecard to the upcoming foursome - it has served its purpose well. For a new measure of success has sprung from challenges met and wisdom gained in the years of competition.

Mastery of the game.

Today, triumph comes in looking back upon endless links of achievement. For This Three-Wood has gracefully conquered both distance and terrain throughout the years, and along the many miles traveled. Yet, the course most to be savored..... the one to be perfected, remains that familiar green meadow nearest to home.

The Mayonnaise Jar

I am indebted to my good friend, Bob McAllister, (no mean golfer himself) who sent me the following, which I use to emphasise the importance of health not wealth for after-dinner speeches etc:

A prominent professor had some items in front of him. When the class began, he picked up a very large and empty mayonnaise jar without saying a word, and proceeded to fill it with golf balls. He then asked the students if the jar was full. They agreed that it was. The professor then picked up a box of pebbles and poured them into the jar. He shook the jar lightly. The pebbles rolled into the open areas between the golf balls. He then asked the students again if the jar was full. They agreed it was. The professor next picked up a box of sand and poured it into the jar. Of course, the sand filled up everything else. He asked once more if the jar was full. The students responded with a unanimous 'yes.' The professor then produced two cups of coffee from under the table and poured the entire contents into the jar, effectively filling the empty space between the sand. The students laughed. 'Now,' said the professor as the laughter subsided, 'I want you to recognize that this jar represents your life. The golf balls are the important things, God, your family, children, health, friends, and favourite passions, things that if everything else was lost and only they remained, your life would still be full. The pebbles are the other things that matter like your job, house, and car. The sand is everything else, the small stuff.'

'If you put the sand into the jar first,' he continued, 'there is no room for the pebbles or the golf balls. The same goes for life. If you spend all your time and energy on the small stuff, you will never have room for the things that are important to you. Take care of the golf balls first, they are the things that really matter. Set your priorities. The rest is just sand.' One of the students raised her hand and inquired what the coffee represented. The professor smiled. 'I'm glad you asked.' It just goes to show you that no matter how full your life may seem, there's always room for a couple of cups of coffee with a friend.'

My Toys for Tots partner, general good guy, sound golfer and great wit, Scott Ramey, sent me this ... enjoy!

Big Scots New Book

Many of you may not realize it, but I've been very busy planning my retirement putting my thoughts and ideas together in a book.

I believe my new book on golf gives the reader valuable playing tips and insider information I've gained through my years of lessons, struggle and experiment. I am very proud of the results, and to assist with marketing, I am asking friends and family to help me out. I hope you find this a useful tool to help you enjoy your game much more while you enjoy the great outdoors. The cost is only $19.95. Don't wait until they're all gone!

Table of Contents:
Chapter   1 - How to properly line up your fourth putt.
Chapter   2 - How to hit a nike from the rough, when you hit a titlist from the tee.
Chapter   3 - How to avoid the water when you lie 8 in a bunker.
Chapter   4 - How to get more distance off the shank.
Chapter   5 - When to give the ranger the finger.
Chapter   6 - Using your shadow on the greens to maximize earnings.
Chapter   7 - When to implement handicap 'management'.
Chapter   8 - Proper excuses for drinking beer before 9.00 a.m.
Chapter   9 - How to rationalize a 6-hour round.
Chapter 10 - When does a divot become classified as sod.
Chapter 11 - How to find that ball that everyone else saw go in the water.
Chapter 12 - Why your girlfriend doesn't care that you birdied the 5th hole.
Chapter 13 - Using curse words creatively to control ball flight.
Chapter 14 - When to let a foursome play through your twosome.
Chapter 15 - How to relax when you are hitting five off the tee.
Chapter 16 - When to suggest major swing corrections to your opponents.
Chapter 17 - God and the meaning of the birdie-to-bogey-three-putt.
Chapter 18 - When to regrip your ball retriever.
Chapter 19 - Throwing your clubs: an effective stress-reduction technique.
Chapter 20 - Can you purchase a better golf game?
Chapter 21 - Why male golfers will pay $6 a beer from the cart girl and give her a $4 tip, but will balk at $4 a beer at the 19th hole and then stiff the bartender.

Thanking you in advance for your order.

Matron, Sat Nav Sarah … and Florida fun!

There are advantages and disadvantages to involving your spouse on social golf trips. From my perspective, the main advantage is that she lets me go where I want and has no comments on the golfing side at all. The downside is that any non-golf days inevitably lead to shopping days out.

On this trip, I left the week between the first event and the Bay Hill Event pretty clear. I did not want to get golfed out, needed to buy a car as car hire here in Florida is getting so expensive and – much more importantly – I needed to buy the tiles, paint etc, that matron needed to enable her to decorate the bathrooms whilst I was tied up with five days golfing the following week. That's the type of guy I am you see, ensuring that she can do the things she enjoys whilst I am working hard on the golf course.

Buying the car was much more problematic that I'd expected – the car colour was as important as its mileage, comfortable seats as vital as engine capacity and fuel consumption, but eventually we agreed and bought a silver 4-litre Buick DeSabre. Now here's something peculiar that could only happen in the States. They have no car tax preferring instead something called a tag, but what's different is that you pay this annual fee on the birthday of the owner, nothing to do with the car, so on each birthday now, Mr Pedder, tax collector on behalf of Mr Obama will send me a tax bill instead of a birthday card. How nice of Barack.

Having bought the car, Matron needed a sat nav system as well and so I acquired a Tom Tom as she only wanted the model that she was familiar with, not the much cheaper Garmin version. I set this up and tried to put a male voice on it but again ended up with sat nav Sarah, which effectively means if I switch it on I am nagged at in stereo, Sarah and Matron both having a go at me.

Sat Navs are just not suitable for male drivers, who quite frankly know their way round better,

Matron thinks she is Nigel Mansell.

including all the short cuts and ways to avoid congested areas etc. But that doesn't stop Sarah, backed up by matron, telling me what to do. Within half an hour I had taken the North Bound Interstate instead of South, a twenty-five mile detour that was avoidable if I had ignored them both. That's my view anyway. An hour later, it sends me through the prepaid toll charges which costs me a $100 fine. So I switch her off but unfortunately, I can't do the same with Matron. She has a much better relationship with Sarah who seems to give her clear, concise instructions without any problem …

However, when on the I4 coming back from Bella Collina, a sequence of large beepings started from the dashboard, we both became concerned. Stopping the car, examining the tyres, the boot, the bonnet, the doors, the windows, all seemed in order we could not understand it, nothing was flashing on the dashboard. We drove off and it started again, we hit some congestion and it stopped but when in free traffic again, it restarted. This went on for three days, I read every manual, but it only happened when Matron drove, then it dawned on me it was Sarah. Every time Matron broke the speed limit, she immediately chorused a dad a bum bum bum…

Of course, Matron accused me of setting it up, felt it would be better to set it to stop me driving so slowly and simply turned up the radio and carried on driving at whatever speed she wished. A 4-litre car for Matron makes her feel like the I4 is Silverstone, I think.

Mount Dora and the ten seconds from glory

One weekend in Florida which just happened to be the only weekend apart from Matron's birthday that I was not golfing, I knew before we left the UK that this was going to be a fraught one as Matron would want to do something inexorably connected to shopping or spending. As the week before progressed and her decorating and tiling neared completion, mutterings from the bathrooms included a new dining table and chairs, new lamps, carpets, rugs, laminating– all at some stage or other. So I played the Mount Dora card.

Mount Dora is a quaint old-fashioned town north of Orlando about one hour from the villa, with a plethora of antique shops, curio shops, good restaurants and plenty of bars. It is one of her favourite places and a must-visit on every trip. Furthermore, because on the weekend of my birthday, she had a severe mouth infection and had been on antibiotics and steroids so we had cancelled our planned trip, I suggested celebrating my birthday now. She readily agreed but with the proviso on the way back we visited Altamonte where the furniture shops are.

So we booked into the splendidly located Lakeside Inn, as the Magnolia was full, overlooking (not surprisingly) Lake Dora. Our room had an impressive vista which took in the lake and showed off the idyllic sunsets – romantic and therapeutic even to someone like me. The place is still as it was in its halcyon days of prohibition in the 1920s and that remains its principal charm although it could do with a touch of sprucing up. It is remarkably good value at 200 dollars for the weekend, you got a room, 90 dollars in food vouchers and a free bottle of wine. I strongly recommend it!

Mount Dora has not escaped the ravages of the economic downturn and we did notice several empty shop units that previously had been well-stocked, and prosperous-looking trade outlets at which we had often acquired useless or essential bric-a-brac for the home, depending on whose view you took. Thankfully, all the local bars and restaurants seemed to be thriving. Firm favourites of ours are the Frosty Mug and the Goblins Market. A few years ago for no apparent reason, the Mug relocated to the Mexican, the Mexican to the Irish bar which in turn relocated at the original Mug Site but as an English bar. It could only happen here. Two minutes from the centre is the massive flea market and antique mall, Rennigers. Essential visiting if in town.

As you can tell, golf takes a back seat when visiting Dora, however my research for future visits, showed that within five miles, there was a bevy of Florida's finest, principally Mission Inn, Eagle Creek, Deer Island, Plantation, Mount Dora, Black Bear. Purely for research, my clubs will be joining us on my next visit.

America was in the middle of a sporting frenzy as the play-offs in ice hockey and basketball reached a thrilling conclusion. My local team, Orlando Magic (Go Magic, go go …) were into what I thought was a quarter final against last year's defending world champions, the Boston Celtics. Yes, although primarily a North American competition, a few interlopers from Canada were tolerated, only our American cousins would have the cheek to call it a World Championship.

Orlando is, I think, the Liverpool of basketball. A champion team of a few years back whilst Boston is more like Manchester United. That particular week, I caught the back end of a thrilling match in Orlando. We had been trailing throughout but took the lead 94 to 93 with a free throw (I know all the lingo), with just ten seconds of the fourth and final quarter on the clock left. Some twenty-two minutes later, I kid you not; we were left gut-wrenched as the Boston guard, one Le Bron, with 0.02 seconds left, dumped an outrageous shot in our basket.

Those last ten seconds took that long to complete, with full time-outs, twenty-second timeouts, advertisers had a field day. The phrase 'It's never over till the fat lady sings' was clearly invented for the American audience, indeed she can sing four songs before the last ten-seconds play is concluded. Fear not Magic fans, I later find out these ties are best of seven and it's only 2 to 2. Perhaps Messrs Wenger, Dalglish, Mancini *et al* need to mention this to the FA and UEFA. Over seven legs, they may have a chance of deposing the Scots Grandads' charges.

8. A Massive THANK YOU

To all my fellow social golfers I have met along this journey. There are many of you who keep in touch on facebook and our continued friendships have been a continued source of comfort and encouragement as I have proceeded along my journey.

Many of you are referred to in this journal, more are not, but rest assured you are equally as important in the end product, your camaraderie, your continued support of the social golfer ethos has seen me to the fruition of this diary. I have lived the dream and each and every one of you has touched my inner being more than you will ever know. I sincerely hope we get a chance to have another knock together again.

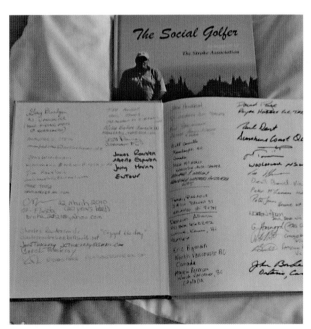

*Many of the fellow golfers I have met on my journeys, all received a copy of the first book
… hope they go out and buy this one. Ha Ha!*

As a writer of no particular renown or note, I have however had considerable pleasure from the numerous notes of thanks from my fellow social golfers who have received a copy of the original book, very often on behalf of other stroke victims.

As I write, I know for absolute certainty, a copy of the *Social Golfer* book is in Australia, New Zealand, China, Dubai, South Africa, USA, Spain, Portugal, Canada, and Argentina. A copy on every continent. And that does make me pretty proud. But without my fellow SGs, it would just be on Ebay, which again it is and yes I am reet chuffed about that too.

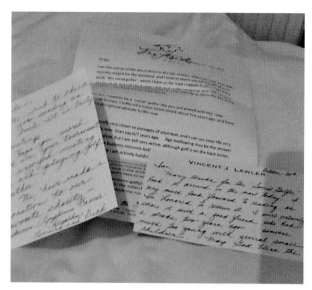

Some of my notes of thanks.

I hope this book is as well received, you never know. I have enjoyed writing it, more than my first book, because it has involved so much more than the first which was a little self-centred on my illness and recovery, but I do not ever want to get away from the aim of showing fellow victims, there is a fulfilling life out there if you still have a dream and try to live it.

Keep well, my friends, and in good health.

9. The Charitable Endeavours Continue

The biggest achievement since my stroke has been the work I have been involved with in stroke awareness, which certainly had the extra benefit of my involvement on and with the Celebrity Golf Tour. The original book and our charity golf days has raised over £30,000 for the Stroke Association and Stroke-related charities. I continue to be extremely grateful to my many colleagues and friends who continue to support my charitable endeavours. I am also indebted to the many celebrities who, in many cases, have become great friends and golfing buddies, for without them, none of this would ever have been possible. Thanks, guys, from the bottom of my heart.

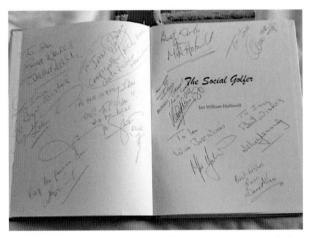

Above, below & overleaf: A selection of autographs of the stars who attended our Golf Celebrity Days.

Ultimately, it is all about raising money, but what fun we had along the way. It was great to involve the staff at the Countess of Chester Hospital at our events. Those people were pivotal to my recovery. It was also great to involve my family who had to get on with their lives with the worry and concern of my battle at the back of their minds. Looking back at this sad, difficult time now, the golf days were, I suppose, the start of a normal life again.

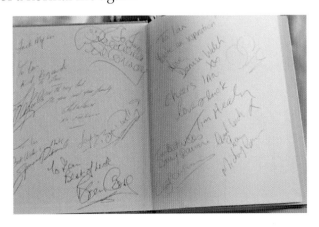

Golfing celebrity buddies, including Frank Worthington,
John Lowe and Bob Champion

The real heroes, the magnificent staff
from the Countess of Chester Hospital.

My family team (and they didn't finish last!)
son, son-in-law and brother-in-law with former Everton manager,
Gordon Lee, who put up with them.

SUSPECT A STROKE?
ACT FAST

Facial weakness

Arm & leg weakness

Speech problems

Time to call 999

What is **FAST**?

FAST requires an assessment of three specific symptoms of stroke.

Facial weakness – can the person smile? Has their mouth or eye drooped?

Arm weakness – can the person raise both arms?

Speech problems – can the person speak clearly and understand what you say?

Time to call 999

Stroke Awareness – please read

Blood clots/stroke – they now have a fourth indicator, the tongue. I will continue to forward this every time it comes around! STROKE: Remember the first three letters … STR stroke identification.

During a BBQ, a woman stumbled and took a little fall – she assured everyone that she was fine (they offered to call paramedics). She said she had just tripped over a brick because of her new shoes. They got her cleaned up and got her a new plate of food. While she appeared a bit shaken up, Jane went about enjoying herself for the rest of the evening. Jane's husband called later telling everyone that his wife had been taken to the hospital (at 6:00 pm Jane passed away). She had suffered a stroke at the BBQ. Had they known how to identify the signs of a stroke, perhaps Jane would be with us today. Some don't die. They end up in a helpless, hopeless condition instead. It only takes a minute to read this …

A neurologist says that if he can get to a stroke victim within three hours, he can totally reverse the effects of a stroke … totally. He said the trick was getting a stroke recognized, diagnosed, and then getting the patient medically cared for within three hours, which is tough.

Recognizing a stroke – thank God for the sense to remember the three steps, STR. Read and learn! Sometimes symptoms of a stroke are difficult to identify. Unfortunately, the lack of awareness spells disaster. The stroke victim may suffer severe brain damage when people nearby fail to recognize the symptoms of a stroke. Now doctors say a bystander can recognize a stroke by asking three simple questions: S – ask the individual to smile. T – ask the person to talk and speak a simple sentence coherently (e.g. 'It is sunny out today'). R – ask him or her to raise both arms. If he or she has trouble with any one of these tasks, call the emergency number immediately and describe the symptoms to the dispatcher. New sign of a stroke … stick out your tongue. Ask the person to 'stick' out his tongue, if the tongue is 'crooked', if it goes to one side or the other, that is also an indication of a stroke. A cardiologist says if everyone who gets this e-mail sends it to ten people; you can bet that at least one life will be saved. I have done my part. Will you?

Act FAST … face, arms, speech … Lisa Burke did and I am evidence of the above.

10. I Say Adieu

– with my biggest success story

Recovering from a brain tumour and a stroke ain't hard when you've got a family like mine. There is so much we still need to do with and for each other. What you see here are my greatest achievements, not my golf or my book … this is my family.

In generations to come, I hope my grandchildren, great-grandchildren etc., look at this book and read this and get a feel of where they came from. And let me tell you, Granddad Paul, Grandmas Shelley, Tanya and Emma and the Matron, Great Matriarch Karen, were and are very, very special people, be proud of your heritage. I was and am …